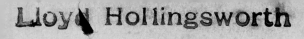

Lloyd Hollingsworth

Robert Browning.

Riverside College Classics

SELECTED POEMS OF
ROBERT BROWNING

EDITED WITH INTRODUCTION AND NOTES

BY

GEORGE HERBERT CLARKE, M.A., D.Litt.

Professor of English in Queen's University
Kingston, Canada

TOVT
BIEN OV
RIEN

HOUGHTON MIFFLIN COMPANY
BOSTON · NEW YORK · CHICAGO · DALLAS · SAN FRANCISCO
The Riverside Press Cambridge

The Riverside Press
CAMBRIDGE · MASSACHUSETTS
PRINTED IN THE U.S.A.

CONTENTS

FROM *DRAMATIC ROMANCES*

FROM *MEN AND WOMEN*

CONTENTS

INTRODUCTION

"Shakespeare," says Emerson — and he speaks for all high poets — "is the only biographer of Shakespeare; and even he can tell nothing, except to the Shakespeare in us, that is, to our most apprehensive and sympathetic hour. . . . With Shakespeare for biographer, instead of Aubrey and Rowe, we have really the information which is material; that which describes character and fortune. . . . We have his recorded convictions on those questions which knock for answer at every heart. . . ." [1]

The relief and resilience with which the great dramatic poet 'impersonally' discusses such questions seem often to make for determined reticence on the 'personal' side. In one sense Browning is right in insisting that Shakespeare did not unlock his heart even in the *Sonnets;* in another, Emerson is equally right in believing that Shakespeare has revealed there, "under masks that are no masks to the intelligent, the lore of friendship and of love. . . . What trait of his private mind has he hidden in his dramas?" [1] But Browning the poet enters directly an anticipative disclaimer in *House* and *Pambo* and *Pacchiarotto* (with its *Epilogue*), and, indirectly, in *At the "Mermaid,"* setting down his dislike of peerers into his private affairs and his disinclination to conciliate his critics by this concession and that. To be a poet does not mean to forego a gentleman's just reserve, to become a piece of public property, open to the inspection of all comers.

> Which of you did I enable
> Once to slip inside my breast,
> There to catalogue and label
> What I like least, what love best,

[1] *Shakespeare; or, The Poet.*

Hope and fear, believe and doubt of.
Seek and shun, respect — deride?
Who has right to make a rout of
Rarities he found inside? [1]

And again:

. . . whoso desires to penetrate
Deeper, must dive by the spirit-sense. [2]

And yet the man who wrote *Fra Lippo Lippi*, *Colombe's Birthday*, *Luria*, and *Why I am a Liberal* shows a warm humanity and a democratic quality of mind and spirit that seem to accord but curiously with his shyer manner. The truth is, on the one hand, that Browning was at once a sturdy member of the British middle class and a firm believer in the aristocracy of will, intelligence, and character; and, on the other hand, that he was a true poet and had, therefore, no real party but mankind. "I sympathize just as much with these," he wrote Elizabeth Barrett concerning the antagonists of Luria, "as with him." At root, of course, the democratic and aristocratic instincts do not quarrel. In *Strafford* Pym reminds King Charles of that "deeper question":

How long the Many must endure the One;

yet in *Luria* Domizia rightly dissects the pride of the sheltered Many in grudging —

. . . the station of the elected ones,
Who, greater than their kind, are truly great
Only in voluntary servitude.

In a word, then, Browning is, like Nature herself, an aristo-democrat. Like Chaucer, Shakespeare, Fielding, and Dickens, he wishes to make full provision in his work for Human Nature. "My stress," he wrote in his Preface to the 1863 version of *Sordello*, "lay on the incidents in the development of a soul: little else is worth study. I, at least, always thought so." And probably none of his works shows his thought of the intense aliveness and awareness of the artist

---

[1] *At the "Mermaid."*   [2] *House.*

quite so well as *Sordello*, *Fra Lippo Lippi*, the closing words of *The Ring and the Book* and of *The Two Poets of Croisic*, his noble essay on Shelley,[1] and that curiously illuminating review of the poet's 'way' — *How It Strikes a Contemporary.*

Robert Browning was born in a house on Southampton Street, in the parish of St. Giles, Camberwell, then a country suburb of London, on May 7, 1812. His paternal ancestry is traced remotely to a manor-owning family of northwest Dorsetshire, whose direct line seems to have vanished under Henry VII. Browning himself called Woodyates, in the parish of Pentridge, Dorsetshire, the cradle of his actual family, for his great-grandfather Thomas was owner of the Woodyates Inn. The poet's grandfather, Robert (Robert was a family name in four generations of the Brownings), was for fifty years a member of the staff of the Bank of England, eventually becoming Principal of the Bank Stock Office. He was a provincial Englishman, who read and re-read the Bible and *Tom Jones*. He married Miss Margaret Morris Tittle, a native of the West Indies, in 1778. Of the three children of these parents, Robert, the poet's father, born 1781, was the eldest. The mother died when he was seven years old, and five years later the father married a Miss Jane Smith, who bore him a considerable family. He was pensioned by the Bank in 1821, and died, at the age of eighty-four, in 1833.

Between this father and son, especially after the second marriage, there was slight sympathy. The son had inherited a little money from his mother's brother and desired a university education, but this was forbidden him. His sketching proclivities were likewise discouraged. For a time he was em-

---

[1] In the *Essay on Shelley* he insists that the subjective poet (who "is impelled to embody the thing he perceives, not so much with reference to the many below as the One above him, the supreme Intelligence which apprehends all things in their absolute truth") is to be regarded as a seer rather than as a fashioner, "and what he produces will be less a work than an effluence. That effluence cannot be easily considered in abstraction from his personality, — being indeed the very radiance and aroma of his personality, projected from it but not separated. Therefore, in our approach to the poetry, we necessarily approach the personality of the poet; in apprehending it we apprehend him, and certainly we cannot love it without loving him. Both for love's and for understanding's sake we desire to know him, and, as readers of his poetry, must be readers of his biography also."

ployed on his mother's West Indian plantation at St. Kitts,
but threw up his position there as a protest against the pre-
vailing slave system. When twenty-two he, in his turn, became a clerk in the Bank of England, consuming his life, as
the poet once wrote Miss Barrett, "after a fashion he always
detested." And again, "my father is tender-hearted to a
fault . . . chivalrous. . . . There is no service which the ugliest,
oldest, crossest woman in the world might not exact of him."
He was not only a clever draughtsman and caricaturist, but
read copiously in Latin, Greek,[1] French, Spanish, Italian
and Hebrew literatures, with a scholarly delight in critical
and antiquarian annotation. He was, too, himself, no mean
poet, handling the heroic couplet with some skill. Indeed,
Browning always maintained that both his wife and his
father were his superiors as poetic artists, — a preference,
however, more creditable to his marital and filial affection
than to his critical judgement.

The poet's father married Miss Sarah Anne Wiedemann in
1811. On her mother's side she was Scottish; on her father's,
German;[2] but she was born and bred in Scotland, and Carlyle thought her "the true type of a Scottish gentlewoman."
Her character was serene and gracious, she loved music and
poetry, and her devotion to evangelical religion was deeply
real. Originally a member of the Kirk of Scotland, she later
became a Congregationalist, as did her husband also. Her
son's love for her throughout his life was intense, and she
exercised a constant influence in guiding the social and religious tendencies of his youth.

The poet was the eldest of three children, the others being
Clara, who died young, and Sarianna, who survived him. He
was a lively, rather irrepressible boy, "unluckily precocious,"
(as he himself declared) — "verses at six years old, and draw-
ings still earlier." After a brief experience at a small school
hard by, he was given home instruction until received at the
age of eight or nine by the Misses Ready at Peckham to pre-

---

[1] See the beginning of the poem, *Development*.
[2] William Wiedemann, shipowner, was a Hamburger living in Dundee. The poet
has described him as an accomplished draughtsman and musician.

pare for entrance to the school kept there by their brother, the Rev. Thomas Ready, under whose able yet distasteful tutelage the boy remained until fourteen. During these early years he cherished a small menagerie of unusual domestic pets, including owls, geese, magpies, and a lonely eagle, together with dogs, frogs, hedgehogs, monkeys, and even snakes.[1] He made many visits while yet a boy to the neighbouring Dulwich Art Gallery, feeding his soul on great works of Rembrandt, Murillo, Giorgione, Watteau, and Poussin.

Charles Lamb recommends the turning of children into the pasture of a home library. They will feed there on the food that is convenient for them, and, like Pompilia, "will not take corruption." Browning was happily preserved from lifeless adaptations. His father's library was large and select, and the boy was wisely given the run of it, under due but not rigid supervision. While still an infant, he was lulled to sleep by bits out of Anacreon chanted by his father, who also told him again and again the tale of windy Troy. Among the books that charmed his boyhood (he read and wrote before he was five years old) were old editions of the Bible, of Milton, of Quarles's *Emblemes*, of *Robinson Crusoe*, and of Pope's *Homer*. He knew also Bernard de Mandeville's *Fable of the Bees*, Nathaniel Wanley's *Wonders of the Little World* (a great favourite), Horace Walpole's *Letters*, *The Letters of Junius* (on which his father was an authority), Voltaire and Byron. The first book he ever bought was Ossian, and before that event his first composition had been imitatively Ossianic. He was early inducted into Horace, of whose easier odes he made boyish translations and imitations. Other juvenilia included a group of short Byronic poems he called *Incondita* (seen by the hymn-writing sisters, the Misses Eliza and Sarah Flower, and afterwards, through them, by that capable and influential Unitarian minister, the Rev. William

[1] *Cf.* for understanding allusions to animal life such poems as *Saul, How They Brought the Good News from Ghent to Aix, Tray, The Flight of the Duchess, Donald, On the Cliff* (in *James Lee's Wife*), *The Eagle* (in *Ferishtah's Fancies*), *Development, White Witchcraft*, and *The Lady and the Painter.*

Johnson Fox) and a fragment modelled upon Coleridge.
The maturer Browning soon suppressed these fledgeling songs.

If Byron's hold upon the boy's imagination was magnetic,
it was, after all, momentary. Browning always felt and admired that poet's facile and rather feverish power. but his
affection for Byron had its lapses, and he can hardly have
regarded him as a spiritual friend and fellow. And he needed
much at this hesitating moment the steady, directive impetus
of a true disciplehood. The principle of the torch or mantle
in the history of art and artists has constantly to be considered. Just as Shelley derived himself largely out of Plato
and the Greek tragedians; and Keats out of Spenser, Shakespeare, and Milton (Milton, as Dryden asserts, being himself
the poetical son of Spenser); so the young Browning was
imaginatively set on fire by contact with the works of Shelley
and of Keats. Habitually a hoverer over likely book-stalls,
he found one day in his early youth, according to William
Sharp's questionable narrative, a second-hand copy of some
miscellaneous poems of Shelley appended to *The Dæmon of
the World* (the revised *Queen Mab*), described as "Mr. Shelley's Atheistical Poem: very scarce." Although he had
never before heard of Shelley, whose life had overlapped his
own by ten years, this discovery so impressed the youth that
his mother sought and found for him (with difficulty, for
'Ariel' was little known), most of Shelley's poems. C. and
J. Ollier, the publishers, persuaded her to buy Keats's poems
also. This is the substance of Sharp's too imaginative
account of the matter, but it now seems established that
the circumstances of this first contact with Shelley were
otherwise.[1] The result of the contact, however, was immedi-

[1] In a letter to Thomas J. Wise, dated March 3, 1886, Browning writes: "As for the
early editions of Shelley, they were obtained for me some time before 1830 (or even
earlier) in the *regular way*, from Hunt and Clarke, in consequence of a direction I obtained from the *Literary Gazette*."

Professor Frederick A. Pottle, of the University of New Hampshire, in his book
Shelley and Browning: A Myth and Some Facts (Chicago: The Pembroke Press), con-
tradicts, as do others, Sharp's account. He presents the evidence of a copy of
Shelley's *Poems* which once belonged to Browning, passed through the hands of
various purchasers, and was in 1923 in the possession of Mr. Charles A. Stonehill,
Jr., of Chicago. The book contains the following memorandum in Browning's
handwriting: "This book was given to me — probably as soon as published — by
my cousin J. S. [James Silverthorne]: the foolish markings and still more foolish

ate. As Sir Sidney Colvin has pointed out, "very few judges have seemed able to care equally for Keats and Shelley"; but young Browning, although inclining more to Shelley, was deeply stirred also by the Keatsian lyrics, odes, and tales. He liked to think of the two poets as inspiring the two night-ingales he heard on the night of that memorable May day when they first became his friends. In *Pauline*, where the notes of both those nightingales may at times be heard, Browning hails his first Master as "Sun-treader"; in *Memorabilia* he tersely yet movingly recalls the story of their first communion; in *Sordello* he adjures Shelley to remain aloof from that irrelevant adventure; in *Cenciaja* he offers "a rescued anecdote" to illustrate Shelley's "superb achievement" in *The Cenci;* and in his essay on Shelley he pays a wise and grateful tribute; while in *Popularity* he warmly praises "my star, God's glow-worm," Keats, and pays tribute to him in *One Word More.* The letters of Browning to Miss Barrett also make many references to both Keats and Shelley.

After the boy had spent two years in Mr. Ready's school, it was decided to carry on his education at home. It included wide reading and study in the Greek and Latin classics, in French and English literatures, and in history. To these were added some little scientific experimenting, the technique of music [1] (he composed settings for several lyrics,

scribblings show the impression made on a boy by this first specimen of Shelley's poetry." This is dated June 2, 1878, and is signed Robert Browning. Below it is the Shelleyan verse, "O World, O Life, O Time!" This pirated collection (from the *Posthumous Poems*) called *Miscellaneous Poems*, by Percy Bysshe Shelley, was published at London by William Benbow in 1826. It contains seventy-five poems, including *Arethusa, Hymn of Apollo, Hymn of Pan, Liberty, Lines to an Indian Air, Ode to Naples, Prince Athanase, Stanzas Written in Dejection near Naples, The Pine Forest, The Question, To a Skylark,* and several of the shorter songs. It does not contain *The Cloud* nor the *Ode to the West Wind,* nor does it include anything from *Queen Mab,* even in its modified form as *The Dæmon of the World.* It seems true, then, that Browning first read Shelley in this collection, possibly when he was but fourteen or fifteen, and that afterwards he applied to the *Literary Gazette* for further 'direction' as to other works by Shelley, securing these through his mother's ready efforts, with three volumes of Keats's poems, directly or indirectly, from John and Henry Hunt or the Olliers. *Queen Mab* may also have become available about the same time. The Clarke mentioned in the letter to Wise is, no doubt, as Professor Pottle thinks, the William Clark who pirated *Queen Mab.*

Writing to Dr. F. J. Furnivall (December, 1885), Browning said: "For myself, I painfully contrast my notions of Shelley the *man* and Shelley, well, even the poet, with what they were sixty years ago." See also *Poet-Lore,* vol. III, January, 1895.

[1] In Browning's poems references may be found to Bach, Brahms, Beethoven, Schumann, Vogler, Galuppi, and other musicians.

and remained always a lover of organ and piano), of singing and of dancing; together with practice in riding, boxing, and fencing. In his eighteenth year Browning studied Greek for a short time under Professor Long at University College, London.

Before the appearance of *Pauline*, which won for its writer the valuable friendship of the Rev. William Johnson Fox, and later of Dante Gabriel Rossetti, he had formed intimate and enduring associations with two young men of Camberwell — Joseph Arnould and Alfred Domett. The Domett attachment became especially strong, as poems and letters attest.[1] Domett afterwards lived in New Zealand for some thirty years, eventually becoming its Prime Minister. Browning's three Silverthorne cousins were also neighbours and companions.

When he was between eighteen and twenty the young man's choice of a career was made. He decided seriously and definitely to become a professional poet. He had thought of painting and of sculpture — arts in which he had developed some untutored skill [2] — and his father had hoped that he might incline to the law, while his mother perhaps secretly cherished the idea of the ministry for her boy. Even Shelley had once played with the same idea.[3] Browning's father quickly understood and approved, as he had indeed in part fostered, his son's choice, and resolved to help him in every way possible to succeed, through reading, travel, and social contacts. As the poet once said, "Italy was my University."

Pauline, Browning's first published work, written in blank verse in the autumn of 1832, obviously under the influence of Shelley, was brought out anonymously at his aunt Christiana Silverthorne's expense by Saunders and Otley, 1833. It presents the fragmentary confession of a young poet to his

---

[1] See the poems, *The Guardian Angel* and *Waring;* the book, *Robert Browning and Alfred Domett*, edited by Frederic G. Kenyon; and Domett's diary.
[2] See the passage in *One Word More*, Section XII.
[3] "Of the moral doctrines of Christianity I am a more decided disciple than many of its more ostentatious professors. And consider for a moment how much good a good clergyman may do." So Shelley, in a conversation with Thomas Love Peacock, reported by the latter.

beloved, and reviews his mental and spiritual changes. While it records some rather painful introspections and adolescent self-bewilderments, and while the author reluctantly included it, with an "exculpatory word" of introduction, in the edition of 1868, yet it is a sincere and useful, if somewhat diffuse and at times even mawkish, account of the young writer's thoughts and feelings, or of those of the not too alien hero, "the verse being as the mood it paints." It contains foregleams of freer and finer works, such as *Pippa Passes*, *Agamemnon*, *Pompilia*, *Prospice* and the *Epilogue to Asolando*, and it rises at times into phrases and whole passages of conspicuous worth and of lingering lyric beauty. The man Browning was much averse to showing it to Miss Barrett, calling it "ambiguous, feverish." [1] It was discerningly reviewed by Mr. Fox in his periodical, the *Monthly Repository*, and also by Allan Cunningham in the *Athenæum*. The two other notices were decidedly unfavourable.

In the winter of 1833–34 Browning visited Russia, nominally as the secretary of the Russian consul-general in England, a Mr. Benckhausen, who was going to St. Petersburg on a special mission. He was away for about three months, and seems to have been delighted with his journey and even desirous of further diplomatic experience. After contributing a few verses to Mr. Fox's magazine, he finished *Paracelsus*, begun late in 1834, the first long poem which he publicly acknowledged. It appeared in 1835, and is dedicated to Count Amédée de Ripert-Monclar, who had suggested the subject. The young count (four years the poet's senior) was an ardent French Royalist and secret agent, who spent several summers in England, and whose cultivated mind and manner strongly attracted the Browning family.

Paracelsus is a poem of more than four thousand lines in blank verse, comprising five parts. It reviews in semi-dramatic dialogue form the career of its famous hero as Würzburg student, Basle professor, physician, author, and reformer. Mystic and occultist as he was, he deserves his

---

[1] See also the letter of Robert Browning to Elizabeth Barrett, of January 12, 1846.

title of "father of modern chemistry." The poet's father paid for its publication by Effingham Wilson. Browning was so anxious to have his poetic method understood that he said in the original Preface:

> ... it is an attempt, probably more novel than happy, to reverse the method usually adopted by writers whose aim it is to set forth any phenomenon of the mind or the passions, by the operation of persons and events ... Instead of having recourse to an external machinery of incidents to create and evolve the crisis I desire to produce, I have ventured to display somewhat minutely the mood itself in its rise and progress, and have suffered the agency by which it is influenced and determined to be generally discernible in its effects alone, and subordinate throughout, if not altogether excluded: and this for a reason. I have endeavoured to write a poem, not a drama.

That is, he had determined to concern himself with a subjective history, with subjective conflict, crisis and catastrophe, and was not trying for an actable play. Despite this disclaimer, however, it is plain that *Paracelsus* is qualitatively as much a drama as are *In a Balcony* and *A Soul's Tragedy*. From the first, it was characteristic of Browning that he was far less interested in concrete action than in the springs and sources of such action,[1] and that he really anticipated the later movement toward closet or literary drama, as exemplified in writers like Maeterlinck (who feels that "the stage is a place where masterpieces die"), Tchekhov, Gorky, Hauptmann, Sudermann and Thomas Hardy.

Despite some youthful floridity, the poem is written with a deeply intelligent sympathy for the aspirations, mistakes and dejections of this tireless thirster after knowledge and power, half Faust, half Hamlet, this would-be synthesizer of traditional values and empirical tentatives with what he felt to be achievable in scientific spirit and method. The poem examines and illustrates the interrelations of

[1] *Cf.* the following passage from *Luria*, Act III, ll. 68–71.

> To the motive, the endeavour, the heart's self,
> Your quick sense looks: you crown and call aright
> The soul o' the purpose, ere 'tis shaped as act,
> Takes flesh i' the world, and clothes itself a king.

power, knowledge and love (always a favourite theme of Browning) as conditioning truth and progress. And Paracelsus the man as well as the thinker is treated with intimate understanding. If Browning's interpretation of his character may not be altogether sound historically, it is yet credible and complete, a poetic unit of real beauty and power, rising now to a Platonic quality of thought, and now (although rarely) to an almost Shakespearean mode of expression. Rather over-praised by Berdoe and underpraised by Gosse, it is, in the large, true to its interest and inspiration, and gives much more constant promise than *Pauline* of the great works to follow. Its songs show Browning's potential mastery in the purely lyric field, had he cared to range that field widely, and from among its many lovely verses may be chosen these:

. . . . to know,
Rather consists in opening out a way
Whence the imprisoned splendour may escape,
Than in effecting entry for a light
Supposed to be without.

. . . . A light
Will struggle through these thronging words at last,
As in the angry and tumultuous West
A soft star trembles through the drifting clouds.

The gulf rolls like a meadow-swell, o'erstrewn
With ravaged boughs and remnants of the shore;
And now some islet, loosened from the land,
Swims past with all its trees, sailing to ocean;
And now the air is full of uptorn canes,
Light strippings from the fan-trees, tamarisks
Unrooted, with their birds still clinging to them,
All high in the wind.

The great quarterlies let *Paracelsus* severely alone, but the *Athenæum*, while conceding its author's talent, called the poem "dreamy and obscure" and imitative of "the mysticism and vagueness of Shelley," and the other reviews and newspapers, as Browning wrote ten years later, "laughed my

Paracelsus to scorn." The great exception was the *Examiner*, for which John Forster, who afterwards became a warm friend of the poet, wrote a long and careful appreciation. Fox's review was a little late, on account of his many preoccupations. It was in Fox's sitting-room that Browning first met the great actor William Macready, with whom he was to have close relations for some seven years Browning was much impressed by Macready's interpretation of Hamlet,[1] and Macready delighted in *Paracelsus*. Late in 1835, at Macready's country home, Browning and Forster began their friendship. Through Forster he met Bulwer, Maclise, Talfourd, and Bryan Waller Procter ('Barry Cornwall'). Leigh Hunt shared a lock of Milton's hair with the rising young poet, whose health was proposed at a dinner given by Talfourd when "the Poets of England" were toasted, and was drunk by the veterans, William Wordsworth and Walter Savage Landor.[2]

So pleased was Macready with both the work and the personality of his new friend and so confident of that friend's future that he now asked Browning to write him a play for stage production. Browning at once assented, but he was concerned with *Sordello* at the moment, and not for two months after Macready's request was *Strafford*[3] actually undertaken. It was finished in March, 1837. Macready warmly approved the subject, but thought the play itself "too historical" and afterwards made some captious notes about it in his diary. Osbaldistone, however, then the manager of Covent Garden (despite, perhaps because of, his financial straits), had no doubt of its success and produced it on May 1, 1837, with Macready as Strafford, Vandenhoff as Pym, and Helen Faucit as Lady Carlisle. Several of the other parts were badly allotted, and the poet was not a little vexed at the stupidity of some of the actors and at certain difficulties

[1] *Cf.* from *Waring*:

> Some Garrick, say, out shall not he
> The heart of Hamlet's mystery pluck?

[2] *Strafford* is dedicated to Macready, *Pippa Passes* to Talfourd, *Colombe's Birthday* to Barry Cornwall, and *Luria* to Landor.

[3] His friend Forster's *Life of Strafford* was then engaging Browning's keen interest.

encountered in staging the play. The production of this thoughtful and powerful tragedy proved acceptable enough, yet ill-starred, lasting only five nights, as the sixth performance had to be cancelled owing to the sudden defection of Vandenhoff. Macready later declined *King Victor and King Charles* and *The Return of the Druses* as too static, and his acceptance of *A Blot in the 'Scutcheon* proved unfortunate for the friendship of the two men. This is not to say that *Strafford* and *A Blot in the 'Scutcheon* and other of the dramas are without much value for the theatre. Performed by a carefully selected company before a really cultured audience, they can more than justify themselves as plays, and both of those mentioned above have been revived with success. But although Browning was a great dramatic poet, he was never much at ease in constraining his art into stage-harness and never became a first-rate playwright or adapter of nervous poetic soul-discoveries in monologue to the technical limitations of the actual stage. *Strafford* was published on the day of its first performance. Although necessarily inaccurate at times in point of historical fact, it is finely true to the characters of Wentworth, its hero, and of his antagonist, Pym. The tragedy depends upon the passing of Wentworth from the Parliamentary to the Court Party, from the normal human friendship with Pym to the romantic passion for Charles I, with its assured fatal consequences, and upon the possibility of his return. It contains many noble passages and develops not a few tensely dramatic moments, especially the decision in Act II, Scene ii; the crisis in Act III, Scene iii; and the poignant final suspense in Act V, Scene ii.

Sordello was conceived and perhaps begun in 1835, but interruptions and postponements delayed its completion until five years later. The theme is much the same as that of *Pauline* — the growth of a poet's mind and spirit — but Browning has given the story of this somewhat neglected Mantuan poet an elaborate historical framework, and has diverted the interest from the Sordello-Cunizza (Palma) romance to the development in *Sordello* of a Hamlet-like criti-

cism of life, of a Paracelsus-like passion for its renovation.[1]
The poem is not merely a psychological excursion into the
inner experience of a mediæval poet, but contains an auto-
biographic revelation less strained and sentimental than in
Pauline, and yet, on occasion, as recognizably personal.

The language of *Sordello* is so closely woven and its mediæval allusiveness so considerable that it is almost inevitably
dragged into court as a witness to support the familiar
charge of obscurity against its author. Even Carlyle, Tennyson, Landor and Domett all found something to frown at
in *Sordello's* style, while the reading world for long complacently ignored the poem. Browning, for his part, lost no sleep,
no good-humour, over this, and once or twice referred to the
poem ironically as "the entirely unintelligible *Sordello.*" He
even undertook to revise it somewhat in 1855, and again in
1862. Other poems, too (*Fifine at the Fair, Aristophanes'
Apology, Mr. Sludge the Medium* and *Prince Hohenstiel-
Schwangau*), are cited as cryptic and confusing, and the fact
that such works do not quickly yield their secret has led some
casual readers — even some professional critics — to assert
that Browning's style is *characteristically* crabbed and
obscure. A cultivated Swiss friend writes me as follows:

> I must confess that I shall never be a regular admirer of his
> work. I am afraid my turn of mind is too much influenced by
> our Latin love of clearness. Obscure authors make me "climb
> along the walls," as we say in French! Of course, there are ad-
> mirable things in Browning. I have been able to speak very en-
> thusiastically and very sincerely of many poems from *Men and
> Women* or *Dramatis Personæ*, but I deplore his indifference
> towards form, his excessive self-will and his lack of self-control.
> I mean by lack of self-control not a moral defect (for he was the
> manliest of men and poets) but the incapacity to limit himself,
> to control his inspiration and reject unnecessary elements.

So general has this point of view become that it would be
idle to deny some degree of justification for it, yet it not in-
frequently occurs in the history of literature that critical dis-

[1] See Dante's *Purgatorio* and *De Vulgari Eloquentia*, and especially Verci's *Storia
Degli Eceleni* (the latter cited by Griffin and Minchin).

like of a manner occasionally employed magnifies that manner into serious, continuous, and deliberate use of mannerism. The none too smooth accomplishment of a peculiarly complicated artistic task is presented as evidence of a persistent disregard of the canons of good writing. Even capable and conscientious critics are sometimes tempted to be lazy-minded and to decry Browning's alleged obscurity with much the same traditionalism as that, for example, which has crystallized the essence of Thomas Hardy's genius into the term 'pessimism.'

Really obscure writing, however, is that which is difficult to understand on account of either slovenliness of expression or confusion of thought on the part of the author. If the subject treated is itself confessedly difficult, the language of the author may be admirably clear and yet, on account of the complications of the theme, may incur the charge of obscurity. As Swinburne, in his essay on George Chapman, has finely said of Browning:

> If there is any quality more perceptible than another in Mr. Browning's intellect, it is his decisive and incisive faculty of thought, his sureness and intensity of perception, his rapid and trenchant resolution of aim. To charge him with obscurity is about as accurate as to call Lynceus purblind, or complain of the sluggish action of the telegraphic wire. He is something too much the reverse of obscure. . . . He never thinks but at full speed ; and the rate of his thought is to another man's as the speed of a railway to that of a waggon, or the speed of a telegraph to that of a railway.

And Browning himself, in a letter to W. G. Kingsland, denied that he had ever "designedly tried to puzzle people, as some of my critics have supposed."

> On the other hand, I never pretended to offer such literature as should be a substitute for a cigar, or a game of dominoes, to an idle man. So perhaps, on the whole, I get my deserts and something over — not a crowd, but a few I value more.

After all, to pause before a poem and nibble at it tentatively is no right attitude. Mrs. Browning shows us better in her *Aurora Leigh:*

> . . . We get no good
> By being ungenerous, even to a book,
> And calculating profits, — so much help
> By so much reading. It is rather when
> We gloriously forget ourselves, and plunge
> Soul-forward, headlong, into a book's profound,
> Impassioned for its beauty and salt of truth, —
> 'Tis then we get the right good from a book.

To ask impatiently of a poet or a poem, What do you mean?
implies an accusation of failure. Although Browning sometimes answered sincere requests for more light, he was oftener
quizzical or silent. All this outcry about form, although
based on a lawful and natural desire for rightness, may
easily become wrong-headed. Æsthetically considered, not
all apparent distortions are actual distortions. The masterly
simplicities of Mozart and Haydn are neither more nor less
lawful than the intricate intellectual excursions and returns of
Brahms and the later Beethoven. Browning's style in some
measure anticipates the nervous, exploratory, directed indi-
rections of such masters as Conrad and Henry James in contemporary fiction. Life, as Comte and Hardy suggest, follows a looped orbit. Why should not life's interpreters sym-
pathetically do likewise? Browning makes it his business
thus to scent the world (to use his own phrase),[1] tracing patiently the significant flexures of life's happenings, their remote
slow shadings, the *scent* of their course, that he may revivify
the involved past, with parallel involutions of imaginative
sympathy, and may recover treasure otherwise lost to the
minds and hearts of men. He is no mere artificer in words,
no mere melodist of the moment. One may be a perfect
painter, like Andrea del Sarto, and yet paint less than greatly.
It is even possible to fail in art (or artifice), Browning tells
us in his essay on Shelley, "only to succeed in highest art."
His whole thought of art finds over-finesse distasteful and
unwholesome. He would rather think than titillate. He
would rather be compelling than fastidious. And he tells
his critics in the last six sections of *Pacchiarotto* the true

[1] See *How It Strikes a Contemporary.*

difference between his own huge and challenging task and their petty preoccupation with his faults of technique. More definite determinations of his theory of art may be found in *Old Pictures in Florence*, *Pictor Ignotus*, *Fra Lippo Lippi*, *Fifine at the Fair*, and *The Two Poets of Croisic*.

On Browning's first visit to Italy in 1838 he went to Venice, Bassano, Asolo, Possagno, Romano, Vicenza, Padua, and Verona, his imagination not only gaining in Verona new values for the Sordello story, but also, through the other contacts, storing countless impressions and experiences for his future work. *Sordello* was published by Edward Moxon in 1840, and at the end of the same year the poet's parents removed from Camberwell to Hatcham. In this new home were produced the eight parts of the series that Browning called *Bells and Pomegranates* (1841–46), including the dramas, *Pippa Passes*, *King Victor and King Charles*, *The Return of the Druses*, *A Blot in the 'Scutcheon*, *Colombe's Birthday*, *Luria*, *A Soul's Tragedy;* and some thirty of the poems designated as dramatic lyrics or dramatic romances. The poet explained the meaning of the inclusive title [1] to Miss Barrett (afterward his wife) by reminding her that

> the Rabbis make Bells and Pomegranates symbolical of Pleasure and Profit, the gay and the grave, the Poetry and the Prose, Singing and Sermonizing — such a mixture of effects as in the original hour (that is, quarter of an hour) of confidence and creation I meant the whole should have at last.

And for the benefit of the general reader he appended the following statement to the eighth number of the series:

> ... I only meant by the title to indicate an endeavour towards something like an alternation, or mixture, of music with discoursing, sound with sense, poetry with thought; which looks too ambitious, thus expressed, so the symbol was preferred. It is little to the purpose that such is actually one of the most familiar of the many Rabbinical (and Patristic) acceptations of the phrase; because I confess that, letting authority alone, I supposed the bare words, in such juxtaposition, would sufficiently convey the desired meaning.

---

[1] See Exodus XXVIII. 33, 34.

The publisher was Moxon, but the expense of the successive issues was borne by the poet's father. At Moxon's suggestion the format adopted was small and cheap, with yellow paper-covers. "I amuse myself by fancying," wrote Browning, "that the cheap mode in which they appear, will for once help me to a sort of Pit-audience again."

The first number was *Pippa Passes*, a work of which Miss Barrett was especially fond, telling its creator that she could find it in her heart to covet the authorship of it more than any other of his works, and writing to her friend Thomas Westwood: "*Pippa Passes* I lean to, or kneel to, with the deepest reverence." It is described by Sharp as "a lyrical masque, with interspersed dramatic episodes, and subsidiary interludes in prose." Perhaps it would be more accurate to call it a cross-episodical idyll-drama. Certainly, it is markedly panoramic and episodical, although rather less so than some contemporary plays of merit.[1] Its diurnal movement is a favourite one with Browning, as in *Colombe's Birthday*, *The Return of the Druses*, and *Luria*. Although the scene is laid in Asolo, not a word of the poem was written there. "The idea," said Browning, "struck me when walking in an English wood, and I made use of the Italian memories." The English wood is Dulwich Wood, where, during a long walk, says Mrs. Orr,

> ... the image flashed upon him of someone walking thus alone through life; one apparently too obscure to leave a trace of his or her passage, yet exercising a lasting though unconscious influence at every step of it; and the image shaped itself into the little silk-winder of Asolo, Felippa, or Pippa.

"It is this motive," according to Arthur Symons, "that makes unity in variety, linking together a sequence of otherwise independent scenes." But unity is also achieved by placing all the scenes in or about Asolo, introducing dramatic cross-references, and complicating the fourth episode with the revelation of Pippa's identity and the grave danger that threatens her life-happiness.

[1] *Pippa Passes* was presented in New York in November, 1906, by Henry Miller, Mrs. Sarah Cowell Lemoyne taking the rôle of Monsignor.

Like all of Browning's dramas, *Pippa Passes* illustrates and justifies the self-effecting, self-redeeming power of the love-idea; of a love, in these instances, including yet transcending the lesser loves which here severally lose themselves in a sense of what may be called the 'Godness' of things —

> The feeling that there's God, he reigns and rules
> Out of this low world.

Of these lesser loves the Ottima-Sebald scene powerfully depicts the worst, through finely discriminated hintings at character, the fatal inevitableness of its dénouement, and its tragic storm-picture of the pain and penalty of passion. Much to be admired also are the simple homelikeness of Pippa's message-songs; the swift, nervous humour and vigour of the prose dialogues; and the sheer poetry of the opening chant of sunrise, the friendly confidences of Pippa with her martagon lily, and the romantic joy of Luigi's review and renunciation of life.

King Victor and King Charles followed early in 1842. Although its historical framework is more accurate than that of *Strafford*, it is a much less successful attempt to reveal character through the play of politics, the dynamic of history. The devotion of Charles Emanuel to his higher duty to the State as against his lower duty to his father provides some opportunity for dramatic conflict, and the character of Polyxena, wife of Charles, belongs to the gallery of Browning's great, fine-grained women.

The third part of *Bells and Pomegranates* appeared in December of the same year, and comprised fourteen titles in the *Dramatic Lyrics*. Part Four, published in January, 1843, consisted of the tragedy called *The Return of the Druses*. These Druses are a very ancient people, who still dwell in the Hauran and on the southern slopes of the Lebanon country. They sprang from the Fatimites, who made a schism in Mohammedanism after its founder's death. They consider their own Khalif Hâkim (who lived about 996 to 1021) to be the last of ten great incarnations of the Deity, all really one, and of Hâkim's power to return they are assured. Browning makes no pretence here of historical accuracy, yet *The Return of the Druses* is a warm, vivid, vigorous play. It is well constructed, save for the too long asides; the author's imagination glows with the strange glamour of his subject, and he does indeed here 're-people the old solitudes.' Although the remote theme requires the nervous research of a modern mind like Browning's, he gives its treatment at times an echoing Shakespearean quality. There is a Stephano-Trinculo note in the Introduction; a Hamlet note in Djabal, especially in the second and third acts; a Desdemona note in Anael's haunting death-cry; and a Lear and Cordelia note in the touching appeal of Khalil in Act Five.

The domestic tragedy, *A Blot in the 'Scutcheon*, came next in the series, and was also published in 1843. It had been accepted by Macready two years earlier, but for various reasons he had delayed in producing it. When it was at last played, on February 11, 1843, at Drury Lane, Macready, largely through his own uncertainty and petulance, was not permitted by Browning to resume the part of Thorold he had studied and abandoned, but was superseded by Samuel Phelps. Although the play ran for a few nights, and had, on the whole, a good reception, the friendship of the actor and the poet ceased for some twenty years.[1]

Critical opinions concerning *A Blot in the 'Scutcheon* have clashed through many years. Fault has been found with the character, behaviour, and the extreme youth of Mildred; with the lack of necessity for the intrigue; and with what William Sharp regards as the anti-climax. No doubt, Browning has made here some doubtful concessions to stage conventions and has admitted a touch of melodrama at times (the work was completed in five days), yet in the beauty

---

[1] Accounts of the misunderstanding may be found in Gosse: *Personalia*, pp. 59–69; Mrs. Orr: *Life and Letters of Robert Browning*, pp. 109–18; Griffin and Minchin: *Life of Robert Browning*, pp. 114–19; Kenyon: *Robert Browning and Alfred Domett*, pp. 59–67; and Browning's letter to Frank Hill, editor of the *London Daily News*, written December 15, 1884, and quoted by Mrs. Orr (pp. 110–14).

The play was revived by Phelps in 1848, by Lawrence Barrett in America in 1885, and by Mrs. Lemoyne's company in 1905.

of its style and the social intimacy of its double motive, the play pulses with power. This double motive embraces the brother's love of honour, the sister's love of purity; and the course of their interrelation and of its inevitable end in tragic doom is traced with close understanding and not often faltering skill. Too little attention has been paid to the living poetry of the *Blot*, for here Browning's language mounts high in freedom and flexibility; and too much attention has been concentrated on mere stage points and probabilities, with little regard for the poet's obvious right to expect of his reader "that willing suspension of disbelief which constitutes poetic faith."

Colombe's Birthday, a politico-romantic comedy, appeared the next year, 1844. It was first presented at The Haymarket Theatre on April 25, 1853, with Helen Faucit as Colombe and Barry Sullivan as Valence, ran for a fortnight, and was afterwards performed in other English cities, and in Boston, U.S.A.[1] There is no dire note in the play. In place of tragic suffering, there is unease; in place of tragic struggle, there is half-resigned longing merely; in place of tragic fate, there is a cautious, monitory, almost good-natured operation of Nemesis, which seems not only to justify the hero and heroine, but to encourage the dramatic antagonist as well. It is a very simple, straightforward comedy, observing all three unities and following Browning's favourite time-scheme. Its criticisms of political craft and mere material success and its movingly eloquent love-passages are especially noteworthy. Browning's own politically liberal yet poetically impartial sympathies come out finely here, as in the other historical or semi-historical plays.

Another event of 1844 was the poet's second voyage to Italy. This time he explored Naples and the scenes of lovely Sorrento, many of which reappear in *The Englishman in Italy*. Thereafter he saw Rome in the company of a Signor Scotti, visiting old churches and Shelley's grave. Probably also at this time he went to Leghorn for a talk with Shel-

[1] It was revived in 1885 for the London Browning Society.

ley's and Byron's nomadic friend, Edward John Trelawny. Among his other English friends he now numbered Carlyle, Henry Chorley, Harriet Martineau, Fanny Haworth, and John Kenyon, to whom Browning was to owe the introduction to his friend of friends, Kenyon's second cousin, Miss Barrett, herself a recognized poet and an ardent student of literature, but an apparently confirmed invalid.

Elizabeth Barrett Barrett was six years Browning's senior, having been born March 6, 1806, at Coxhoe Hall, a few miles below Durham. She was the eldest of the eleven children (three girls and eight boys) of Edward Moulton Barrett and his wife Mary, whose maiden name was Graham-Clarke and who died when Elizabeth was twenty-two. The girl spent her first twenty years, for the most part, at Hope End, Herefordshire, near Malvern, scribbling verses early, steeping herself in her favourite poetry (especially that of Pope, Byron, and Coleridge), and studying Greek for Homer's sake and Latin for Greek's sake. Her first publicly announced volume of verse — *An Essay on Mind, and other Poems* — was printed in 1826. The didactic title-poem she refers to as "written when I was seventeen or eighteen, and long repented of." Of fragile health from the first, she sustained an injury to the spine and suffered from a weakness in the lungs while still young, and was under medical care for many years. In 1832 her father took the family to Sidmouth, Devonshire, and the next year she published her translation of the *Prometheus Bound* of Æschylus, together with some individual poems.

On the removal to London in 1835, the family first lived at 74, Gloucester Place, Portland Square; and afterward at 50, Wimpole Street, where she and Browning first met. She read Greek with Hugh Stuart Boyd, the blind scholar, and through the encouragement of R. H. Horne began in 1836 to contribute poems and articles to the periodicals. She now made the acquaintance of Wordsworth, Landor, Harriet Martineau, Mary Russell Mitford, and her kinsman Kenyon, the two last-named becoming her constant friends. In 1838 she published *The Seraphim, and other Poems.* The same year her poor health obliged her to go to Torquay, where she lived for three years, during which time, to her intense distress, her much loved brother Edward was drowned. In 1841, when she was again at home in Wimpole Street, Kenyon proposed that he should bring the poet Browning to see her, but she demurred. We find her writing to Boyd the next year that "Mr. Browning is said to be learned in Greek, especially in the dramatists." On April 28, 1843, she tells Cornelius Mathews. then editor of *Graham's Magazine*, that although she has never seen nor even corresponded with Browning, she is "very sensitive to the thousand and one stripes with which the assembly of critics doth expound its vocation over him. . . . The truth is . . . it is easier to find a more faultless writer than a poet of equal genius." Kenyon had shown Browning his cousin's poem *The Dead Pan*, and the approving letter he received from Browning Kenyon sent to Miss Barrett, who begged to retain it. In a letter to Thomas Westwood, September 2, 1843, she remarks: "Tennyson is a great poet, I think, and Browning, the author of *Paracelsus*, has to my mind very noble capabilities." On the last day of the year she mentions to Westwood that "Robert Browning is meditating a new poem, and an excursion on the Continent." She refers to Browning's absence abroad in a letter to Mathews dated November 14, 1844; and on January 11, 1845, in a letter to Mrs. James Martin, thus exults: "And I had a letter from Browning the poet last night, which threw me into ecstasies — Browning, the author of *Paracelsus*, and king of the mystics." This letter contains Browning's praise of Miss Barrett's two-volume edition of *Poems* of the summer of 1844 (the reading of which his Italian journey had prevented until the following December), and his acknowledgement of the tribute paid him in the forty-first stanza of *Lady Geraldine's Courtship:*

Or from Browning some "Pomegranate," which, if cut deep
    down the middle,
Shows a heart within blood-tinctured, of a veined humanity.

The history of the courtship and married life of these kindred souls is one in which both 'lived their minstrelsy.' Letter followed letter in quick succession, and Miss Barrett was persuaded to receive Browning as a visitor when spring should come. The promise was redeemed on the 20th of the following May. Love of this frail, gifted, lonely woman was immediate and unalterable for Browning. Exactly five months after that memorable visit his wife wrote to her friend Mrs. James Martin a long letter from the Collegio Ferdinando at Pisa,[1] where she and Browning had settled for a time, reviewing the whole case and circumstance, and humbly remarking that "the only wonder is how such a man, whom any woman could have loved, should have loved *me;* but men of genius, you know, are apt to love with their imagination." Although Browning had supposed that she would never be able to stand (for she spent nearly all her hours in the one room, visited by affectionate brothers and sisters, by a too stern and self-centred father, and by a very few cherished friends, yet seldom free from a great loneliness of the spirit), he at once resolved to devote himself to the care of her, and opened his heart accordingly in the first letter following his visit. The invalid, however, repressed the woman, and, for her lover's own sake, forbade any renewal of the subject, although she was deeply moved and heartened that so great a man could feel such need of her. She considered such denials her plain duty, and even wondered whether Browning's forthright offer might not be "a bare impulse — a generous man of quick sympathies taking up a sudden interest with both hands." While Browning respected her reluctance to discuss even the possibility of marriage, it was difficult to discourage so patient, so considerate, and so determined a lover. As the Pisa letter goes on to say:

. . . in the meantime the letters and the visits rained down more and more, and in every one there was something which was too slight to analyse and notice, but too decided not to be

[1] See *The Letters of Elizabeth Barrett Browning*, edited by Frederic G. Kenyon, vol I, pp. 286–97.

understood; so that at last, when the 'proposed respect' of the
silence gave way, it was rather less dangerous. So then I
showed him how he was throwing into the ashes his best affec-
tions — how the common gifts of youth and cheerfulness were
behind me — how I had not strength, even of *heart*, for the
ordinary duties of life — everything I told him and showed
him. 'Look at this — and this — and this,' throwing down
all my disadvantages. To which he did not answer by a
single compliment, but simply that he had not then to choose,
and that I might be right or he might be right, he was not there
to decide; but that he loved me and should to his last hour. He
said that the freshness of youth had passed with him also, and
that he had studied the world out of books and seen many
women, yet had never loved one until he had seen me. That he
knew himself, and knew that, if ever so repulsed, he should
love me to his last hour — it should be first and last. At the
same time, he would not tease me, he would wait twenty years
if I pleased, and then, if life lasted so long for both of us, then
when it was ending perhaps, I might understand him and feel
that I might have trusted him. . . . He preferred, he said, of
free and deliberate choice, to be allowed to sit only an hour a
day by my side, to the fulfilment of the brightest dream which
should exclude me, in any possible world.

Such an avowal was not to be resisted. Despite the unhappy necessity of concealing the position from her father,
(whose opposition, should he be informed, his daughter,
though she had always loved him, forecast as certain and
unrelenting); [1] despite her apparently chronic invalidism;
despite many fears and scruples, Miss Barrett at length
promised that if she did not suffer the expected physical
relapse during the ensuing winter, she would, did Browning
still so desire, become his wife, but that he must meantime
consider himself "absolutely free." Browning as friend and
lover gladly accepted these conditions, and when, after a re-
markably mild winter, the spring and summer of 1846 found
her health and spirits both better than she had thought possible (she was able to drive to the parks and to walk a little),
Browning as suitor secured her definite consent to an early

[1] He would not even countenance her departure for Italy that winter (1845-46)
for her health's sake, although her physician had strongly advised it.

marriage. It took place on the morning of September 12, 1846, at Saint Marylebone Church, none of the family but the two sisters, Henrietta and Arabel, being aware of the engagement and not even they knowing of the actual arrangements, lest their father's anger should be visited on them. Miss Barrett's maid, however, accompanied her mistress to the church and witnessed the ceremony. James Silverthorne, Browning's cousin, was also a witness. A week later (during which time Browning scrupulously remained away from Wimpole Street rather than ask for his wife by her former name), on September 19th, the bride quietly left her home for the last time with Wilson and Flush (her maid and her dog), joined her husband, and proceeded with him to Havre and Paris. Her father never forgave her nor received her again, even after hearing of the birth of her child; returned all her letters unopened, with a rude and abrupt answer to her husband, who had also written; and austerely remarked to John Kenyon, who sought to reconcile him to the event: "I have no objection to the young man, but my daughter should have been thinking of another world."

In Paris the Brownings encountered a surprised but delighted friend, Mrs. Anna Brownell Jameson, the author of *Characteristics of Women*, of *Winter Studies and Summer Rambles* (the record of her long visit to Canada), and of *The House of Titian*. She was travelling with a young niece, Geraldine Bate. Mrs. Jameson did much for their comfort during their week's stay in town, and carefully ministered to Mrs. Browning as all four travelled together to Pisa. The long journey was accomplished partly by rail to Orleans, partly by river steamers, again by a sea-going vessel from Marseilles to Leghorn, and thence by rail again for the few miles to Pisa. Here, after a little, Mrs. Browning's health seemed to Mrs. Jameson 'transformed,' and she was able to spend golden hours in the air and sunshine of the country she soon came to love so deeply, watching the ways of the life about her, and tracing the memoried footsteps of

> ... poor, proud Byron, sad as grave
> And salt as life; forlornly brave
> And quivering with the dart he drave,

and of

> ... Shelley in his white ideal,
> All statue-blind.

After six weeks Mrs. Jameson and her niece bade the married pair farewell, and man and wife came to be even further assured of the lasting worth and sufficiency of their union. One morning early in 1847 Mrs. Browning disclosed to her husband a long cherished secret of her art and her love — the existence in manuscript of the sonnet-sequence she had composed before the marriage, afterward known in its completed form by the title chosen by Browning, *Sonnets from the Portuguese*. Other poems of Mrs. Browning's that touch her early love-experience are to be found in the little group, *Life and Love*, *A Denial*, *Proof and Disproof*, *Inclusions*, and *Insufficiency*. While she is, of course, the inspiration of Browning's finest love poetry, the six poems that refer to her most personally are *My Star*, *By the Fireside*, *One Word More*, *Prospice*, the dedicatory verses — *O Lyric Love* — concluding the Prologue to *The Ring and the Book*, and the song-preface to *The Two Poets of Croisic*.

This rare partnership — itself a poem — prospered for fifteen years, until Mrs. Browning's death in 1861. With the exception of short visits to Paris and England, the pair lived in Italy during the entire period. After a trial of Florence in the spring of 1847, they established there a permanent home in Casa Guidi, on the Via Maggio and the Via Mazetta, and facing the Pitti Palace. Here they were sought out from time to time by not a few admirers — the American sculptors, Hiram Powers and William Wetmore Story; the young American journalist, George William Curtis; Miss Mary Boyle, who became a close friend; the always valued Mrs. Jameson; Father Prout; Miss Isa Blagden and Miss Frances Power Cobbe, who shared a villa at Bellosguardo; the New England transcendentalist, Margaret Fuller, Countess Ossoli; and other pilgrims anxious to make or to renew ties of friendship. Mrs. Browning's lively interest in contemporary Italian politics and in the effort for Italian freedom and unification finds earnest expression in *Casa Guidi Windows* (1851) and *Poems before Congress* (1860), while Browning's earlier *Italian in England* (1845) sufficiently reveals his own feeling. In 1848 the two visited Fano, Ancona, Ravenna, Forli, and other towns. On March 9, 1849, to their great happiness, a son was born to them, whom they christened Robert Wiedemann Barrett, but who was afterwards known familiarly as 'Penini' or 'Pen.' Not long afterward their joy was clouded by the death of Browning's mother. The succeeding summer was spent on the heights of Bagni Caldi, and the next year they visited Venice, Lucerne, and England, seeing much of Browning's father and sister, of Mrs. Browning's family (save her father), of the Procters and Mrs. Jameson, and something also of Forster, Ruskin, Kingsley, and Patmore. On the return journey Carlyle accompanied them as far as Paris, where they met George Sand, and, in the later winter, Joseph Milsand, who became Browning's close friend. Tennyson (with whom Browning was on excellent terms) had greeted them in Paris as they went northward.

The seventh number of *Bells and Pomegranates* (1845) contained a score of dramatic lyrics and romances; and the eighth and last (1846) included *Luria* and *A Soul's Tragedy*. *Luria* is among the noblest of Browning's works, and illustrates the fact that his dramatic writing became increasingly subjective. It was never offered to the theatre, being composed, as Browning declared, "for a purely imaginary stage — very simple and straightforward." Its great truth, as of all Browning's dramas, is the inalienable power of a truly unselfish love (and to Browning there is no other) to fortify and redeem the lover, be the object what it may. The whole play is developed out of a sentence or two in Sapio Amminato's *History of Florence*. It is interesting to notice that Maeterlinck has frankly borrowed the framework and parts of the plot of *Luria* for his *Monna Vanna*. *A Soul's Tragedy* differs from Browning's other plays in three respects, particularly: it is his only two-act play; it uses verse throughout the first act, prose throughout the second; and it is peculiarly a person-play, the tragedy of a single character (even more so than *Luria*). Chiappino is the building; the others, so to speak, the scaffolding. Browning himself calls it, in a letter to Domett, "a wise metaphysical play (about a great mind and soul turning to ill)." It, too, is frankly a closet drama. The First Bystander, to be sure, is better informed (for purposes of economy) than dramatic propriety would warrant, and Luitolfo's long aside in the second act is stagey and unfortunate. Yet these are sun-spots, for *A Soul's Tragedy* has a sun's warmth in point of its humanity and the clearness of the images it projects of justice and injustice, love and selfishness, heroism and temporizing, and even of life and death.

The year 1850 marked the appearance of *Christmas-Eve and Easter-Day*, which, of all Browning's poems on religious hunger and experience, save the Pope's monologue, is the most critically searching. Other poems that deal with such problems and aspirations are *Paracelsus, Saul, Caliban upon Setebos, A Death in the Desert, The Boy and the Angel, Cleon, An Epistle Containing the Strange Medical Experience of Karshish, Rabbi Ben Ezra, La Saisiaz,* and *Reverie.* Browning cared much more about the uses of faith than its grounds, frequently as he explored the latter. Although declining labels, he made a manly and useful effort to reconcile the genius of Christianity with the philosophy of evolution. He believed intensely in the reality and immortality of the human soul, and in the existence of a governing and loving God. In *La Saisiaz* especially he records and rejoices in these beliefs as sufficient for any superstructure that the sincere thought of this man or that may need or conceive. He has his sharp word at times for mere professionalism in religion or elsewhere, but his own faith is vigorous and persistent. Life is to him a great moment of experience in the nature and use of love as the most powerful human agent of a divine idealism. Life is a probation-time for the learning of love, and for realizing power and growth through love. The religion of poets is little concerned with credal compromises, but much with wonder and awe and love, in the contemplation of the mystery of life and the universe; and with faith in the worth of life and the universe. Browning has this faith in ample measure. In *La Saisiaz* he tells us that God and the soul are the only facts for him.

> Prove them facts? that they o'erpass my power of proving, proves them such.

Paracelsus feels that "Man is not Man as yet." Cleon questions: "Why stay we on the earth unless to grow?" "Life," broods Pope Innocent —

> Life is probation and the earth no goal
> But starting-point of man.[1]

But since love, as Browning interprets it (and he is strongly influenced here by Plato) is that impulse or energy in man which makes him long to partake in and to possess the beautiful and the good, it becomes to him the true motive-power of life and of the growth of the soul's character. It is indeed

> ... the only good in the world.[2]

> There is no good of life but love — but love!
> What else looks good, is some shade flung from love;
> Love gilds it, gives it worth.[3]

For it is incompatible

> With falsehood — purifies, assimilates
> All other passions to itself.[4]

The love of one is a means to the love of many, and again to the love of all (as with Pompilia), and finally to the true love of God. Scores of Browning's poems are devoted to this favourite theme, in its various phases. Most of the love-

---

[1] *The Ring and the Book*, Book x, ll. 1435-36. [2] *The Flight of the Duchess*, l. 615.
[3] *In a Balcony*, ll. 374-76. [4] *Colombe's Birthday*, Act v, ll. 306-07.

monologues can be classified as falling under one or another
of the three heads — Failure to Come Together, Failure after Coming Together, Understanding; and in each of these
again the theme is treated on the man's side, on the woman's
side, or on behalf of both. It may readily be seen, then,
what stirring human reading we have in these many illustra-
tive poems. And Browning's cosmopolitanism seems to be
one of sex as of country, for no other English poet — not
even Shakespeare himself — seems to have come so close in
interpretative sympathy to the nature of women as has
Browning in Colombe, Constance, Ottima, Phene, Pippa,
Polyxena, Anael, Balaustion, Pompilia, and the whole
splendid gallery. Yet a man's purely romantic love need
not be directed toward a woman only. *Strafford* deals with
the love of its hero for an unworthy king, *Luria* with a Moor's
love for the city of Florence, and both discover virtue
powerfully active in and through love. As Plato makes
Pausanias say in the *Symposium*, it does not matter greatly
whether the object of a true love prove itself worthy or unworthy, so long as it is the occasion of the functioning of the
love-instinct.

> She has lost me; I have gained her.[1]

To Browning, therefore, love, as he recognizes and unfolds
its spiritual meanings, is intimately associated with the essence of a pure religion, and is the beginning and the movement and the end of life. Who loves, lives; and who lives,
loves.

Before returning to Florence in November, 1852, the
Brownings paid another visit to England, seeing Landor,
Kingsley, Mazzini (in exile), D. G. Rossetti, Ruskin, and
Tennyson. The essay on Shelley belongs to this year. The
two volumes of *Men and Women* followed in 1855, containing
among their fifty members many of the most important of
Browning's shorter poems. Meantime Mrs. Browning was
writing *Aurora Leigh*. The two now travelled through the

[1] *Cristina.*

"holy ground" of Assisi to Rome, whither the Storys had preceded them. Besides these friends, they were glad to meet in Rome the young American sculptor, Hatty Hosmer; and, among the British visitors, the actress, Fanny Kemble, and her sister, Adelaide Sartoris; Sir Frederick Leighton, J. G. Lockhart, and others. "I certainly have met with many admirable natures in my life," the poet once wrote to Miss Blagden. They were back in Florence by May, 1854, and a year later, after the serious illness of Mrs. Browning, sought London again, where *One Word More*, the last of the *Men and Women* poems, was written. Here also they were once more in touch with the Procters, with Ruskin, and with Forster and Carlyle; and here they met the American Ambassador and man of letters, James Russell Lowell. One evening there came to the Brownings' house on Dorset Street both D. G. and W. M. Rossetti, and Tennyson besides. Tennyson gave Browning a copy of *Maud* and read the poem in his reverberating way. Browning, in turn, read *Fra Lippo Lippi*, and there was much rare conversation. A 'vision of poets' indeed! A quiet winter was spent in Paris, and the succeeding summer in London, followed by a visit to the Isle of Wight, where John Kenyon (to whom *Aurora Leigh* is dedicated) was trying to ward off death. In the ensuing December he died, leaving the Brownings eleven thousand pounds; and about four months later Mr. Barrett passed away, unreconciled to the last.

Trying weather in Florence, the loss of her cousin and her father, and the too engrossing care of her child all affected Mrs. Browning's now lowered vitality. Several changes of scene and air were tried, until Havre proved propitious, and eight weeks were spent there. Leaving Paris again, the poet pair crossed the Alps, reached Genoa and made a rough voyage to Leghorn, but stayed at home a brief time only. For Mrs. Browning's sake — dear as Florence was to her — the next two Florentine winters were avoided in favour of Rome. In 1858 they were visited by Nathaniel Hawthorne, who described Mrs. Browning as "a pale, small person, scarcely embodied at all." In 1859 the effect on Mrs. Browning's health of the Latin-Austrian political excitements and disappointments of the time proved trying and even serious, as the months passed, and she had also to endure the shock of her sister Henrietta's death. Henrietta had married (she also suffering the paternal anger) a Mr. Surtees Cook, and her death left three small children motherless. Landor meantime had quarrelled with his family at Florence, and Browning and the Storys secured lodgings for him at Siena (in which lovely hill-town all these friends foregathered), and afterwards saw him safely domiciled in Florence. One more happy stay in Siena at the Villa Alberti was to be theirs, but towards its end Mrs. Browning became so unwell that she was with difficulty brought back, as she desired, to Florence — all of it peculiarly her home — and to Casa Guidi — the heart of her home. There, held in her husband's arms, she died in the early morning of June 29, 1861. She rests in the beautiful Protestant Cemetery at Florence, where the poets Clough and Landor were afterwards buried, and her chaste, simple tomb bears only this legend: "E. B. B. Ob. 1861."

Browning's sorrow was profound and persistent, but so were his faith and his remembrance. He himself could hardly express his grief, nor did he attempt it, save in a very few intimate letters to close friends. "I shall go away," he told Story, "break up everything, go to England, and live and work and write." And to Miss Haworth, after giving her a simple but moving account of his wife's last hours, he wrote:

> I shall leave Italy altogether for years — go to London for a few days' talk with Arabel — then go to my father and begin to try leisurely what will be the best for Peni — but no more "housekeeping" for me, even with my family. I shall grow, still, I hope — but my root is taken and remains.

On August 1st, then, Florence lost Browning forever. Miss Isa Blagden, who had long been a devoted friend of

Mrs. Browning, as of Browning himself, accompanied the bereaved father and son to Paris. Thence, with the boy and with his own father and sister, the poet went on to the French coast town of St. Enogat, where change and rest renewed his strength. In October he proceeded to London, secured a tutor for Pen, saw his wife's *Last Poems* through the press (he took a frank pride in the popular success of her work, and insisted always that the truer genius and achievement were hers), and settled at length at 19, Warwick Crescent (the most permanent of his residences), near Arabel Barrett. Her, and also the Procters, he saw frequently. He wrote busily in the mornings, and published *Dramatis Personæ*, containing eighteen poems, in 1864. During Pen's holidays father and son more than once went to French coast towns, or to the rugged Basque country — to Sainte Marie, Pornic, Croisic (with which three places several of the poems of *Dramatis Personæ* are associated), Saint-Jean-de-Luz, and Cambo.

Only a year before his wife's death Browning had found, among "odds and ends of ravage" displayed for sale on a stall of the Piazza San Lorenzo in Florence, a square old yellow vellum-covered volume, whose contents, "part print, part manuscript," concerned an important murder case tried in Rome in 1698. This book (now in the library of Balliol College) became the source of Browning's epic masterpiece, *The Ring and the Book*, which was published in four monthly parts of three books each during the winter of 1868–69. The title refers to the source-book and to the image of a ring worn by his wife and carried by Browning on his watch-chain after her death. As the soft gold could not be rounded into

> The rondure brave, the lilied loveliness,

save by admixture with gold's alloy, so, though by reversal, the crude, hard fact of the Book's record cannot be made to yield pure truth save by admixture with the softening alloy of fancy; for truth, being spiritually born, is spiritually perceived, and the very hardness of fact makes it alien to inter-

pretative truth until mingled with the leavening, controlling
power of the imagination. Fancy and fact combine, then,
to round out this epical ring of truth, which becomes "just
one fact the more."

The Book contains a number of documents concerning the
trial for murder of the chief criminal, Count Guido Franceschini, and his four retainers. Fourteen of these documents
are official records setting forth the pleadings and the tes-
timony. The others are letters and pamphlets. All of them
were probably collected by one Cencini, a friend of Guido's
advocate. Another source is an account published not long
after the execution of the five assassins, which Browning
secured in London in 1864. A third account, unknown to
the poet, is a pamphlet found in January, 1900, in the Royal
Casanatense Library at Rome.[1] Apart from the Prologue
and the Epilogue (and even in the latter, in part) Browning
employs his characteristic method of dramatic monologue in
presenting ten times the story of the whole cruel and sorrowful affair, as seen from the respective points of view of public
opinion (*Half-Rome, The Other Half-Rome* and *Tertium Quid*);
of the chief actors in the tragedy (*Count Guido Franceschini;*
the Saint-George-like hero, the priest, *Giuseppe Caponsacchi;*
and the delicate dying girl, the chief victim, *Pompilia*), of
the two professional lawyers, who represent, the one the husband (*Dominus Hyacinthus de Archangelis*), the other, the
wife (*Johannes-Baptista Bottinius*); of the *Pope* (a composite
portrait of Innocent XI and Innocent XII), who reviews and
finally adjudicates the case; and of the condemned *Guido*
as he awaits execution. All must speak freely and be heard
patiently, Browning seems to say, because the essence of
truth is spiritual and eternal and universal, while language
is human and mutable and partial; because, although Art
cannot be content to formulate expressions of fact merely, it
can and does evoke spirit from spirit, flashing out truth in
the process — essential truth, as Mrs. Browning calls it in

[1] Translations of this appear in Charles W. Hodell's *The Old Yellow Book, Source
of Browning's Ring and the Book,* and in W. H. Griffin and H. C. Minchin's *Life of
Robert Browning* (Appendix B).

her *Aurora Leigh*, not "relative, comparative, and temporal truths"; because, as the poet declares in his Epilogue,

> . . . Art remains the one way possible
> Of speaking truth, to mouths like mine at least.
>
> . . . .
>
> But Art, — wherein man nowise speaks to men,
> Only to mankind, — Art may tell a truth
> Obliquely, do the thing shall breed the thought,
> Nor wrong the thought, missing the mediate word.
> So may you paint your picture, twice show truth,
> Beyond mere imagery on the wall, —
> So, note by note, bring music from your mind,
> Deeper than ever e'en Beethoven dived, —
> So write a book shall mean beyond the facts,
> Suffice the eye and save the soul beside.

In these lines are found Browning's apology for his ample epic, in which he seeks to get at the eternal significance (that is, the truth) of the grim story with which he deals. If it were the final legal or conventionally moral pronouncement that he had hoped to disengage, his task might have deserved Carlyle's bit of badinage: "What a wonderful fellow you are, Browning; you have written a whole series of 'books' about what could be summed up in a newspaper paragraph!" But though Browning is here patiently tracing the maze of facts, he does so only that he may at length strike through to the 'true truth,' as the French call it, back of human shadows and semblances. What that true truth is, all who read this monumental poem (which Browning himself regarded as the wide gateway to his work at large) may come to feel; and each reader may make it his own possession according to the degree of imaginative sympathy with which he recreates this seventeenth-century scene that the poet has caused to "step on the stage again."

The Ring and the Book is the great modern epic. It is penetrated with a nervous, nimble delight in soul-discovery; with an imaginative subtlety and power that now light up an obscured or unsuspected situation, now revivify a dramatic personal characteristic, or now inspire an eloquent lyric cry of hope, or faith, or despair. The many changing tones and rhythms, the intricate but firm patternings, and the felicitous imagery combine with the psychological insight, with the dramatic ascent toward the story of the central figure, Pompilia, and with the descent toward final suspense and catastrophe, to make great poetry. In proportion to the exceptional length of the epic, its technical weaknesses are few, and there is no real ground for the doctrine of improvement by elimination, preached so discontentedly by Sharp and Brooke and Hugh Walker. On the contrary, the work is as sound architecturally as inspirationally. Its very existence preaches the gospel of literature, and long, loyal, loving readings of it must result in quickening both æsthetic joy and personal loving-kindness.

Two sorrows that came to Browning before the completion of his masterpiece were the deaths of his father in June, 1866, and of Arabel Barrett two years later. His sister Sarianna, after the former event, took charge of the poet's home and shared his life. In 1867 the University of Oxford made him a Master of Arts, and Balliol College gave him an honorary fellowship. The composition of his vast epic tired his imagination for a time, and he travelled with the Storys to Scotland, and walked and talked with Milsand (who is described in *Red Cotton Night-Cap Country*) at Saint-Aubyn in France. *Balaustion's Adventure* and *Prince Hohenstiel-Schwangau* both belong to the year 1871. The first is an appreciation of Browning's admired Euripides and a flexible reproduction of his *Alcestis;* the second a monologue in which Louis Napoleon III — always the political hero of Mrs. Browning's devotion, but not always nor altogether of Browning's — reveals some of the shadings of his strange character.

The succeeding year (1872) marks the publication of *Fifine at the Fair* and the renewal of the old intimacy with the poet's lifelong friend, Alfred Domett (1811–87), who had just then returned from the long sojourn in New Zealand begun in 1842. There he had filled various public offices,

including, as we have seen, that of prime minister. He
himself was no mean poet, his chief work being the epic
Ranolf and Amohia, published during the year of his return.
Browning's own *Fifine* has Pornic for its background, and
true and specious forms of love for its theme. The intellectual Don Juan type of man who speaks with his wife
Elvira of the gypsy Fifine and of the symbol-values of the
one as against those of the other, proves himself a "sadly
mixed nature" — a student, not a saint, of love. A long
narrative poem, *Red Cotton Night-Cap Country*, which is associated with Saint-Aubyn and is based on the tragic history of one Antoine Mellerio, a Parisian jeweller, followed
in 1873. During the next year Browning was busy with
Aristophanes' Apology, including *The Last Adventure of Balaustion* (1875). Here, in a poem "crowded with culture,"
he considers afresh the virtues of Euripides as seer and dra-
matist, and compares that poet's intentions and methods
with those of Aristophanes. In the same year he published *The Inn Album*. Like *Red Cotton Night-Cap Country*,
it unfolds a tale corresponding, in the main, to actual history. Browning somewhat redeems the sordidness of the
details through the skilled and subtle handling, yet the at-
mosphere remains rather murkier than need be.

During the summers of the years between 1874 and 1877
Browning and his sister greatly prized the holiday companion-
ship of Miss Anne Egerton Smith, a musical and finely cultivated woman, in whose memory *La Saisiaz* was written. She
passed away at the chalet whose name the poem takes, below
the Salève, near Geneva, September 14, 1877. The previous
year witnessed the appearance of a group of poems including *Pacchiarotto, and How He Wrought in Distemper*, a work
of rapid movement and grotesque manner, in which the poet
has his say — good-natured on the whole, yet forthright —
about some of his would-be critics. This is the most direct
and determined expression of Browning's honest disgust not
merely at the inability of certain lazy and captious minds to
understand his poetic programme, but at their unwillingness

even to try to do so, and at the littleness of spirit exhibited in the arbitrary and traditionalistic tone of their attacks. Elsewhere in the same volume, especially in *House, Shop, At the "Mermaid"* and *Epilogue* the poet more mildly reveals something of his aims. *La Saisiaz* itself is among the greatest of his later poems. It is touched with a deep and true emotion, and represents with serene dignity his ripest religious faith. In October, 1877, his translation of the *Agamemnon* of Æschylus was published. It was a task suggested by Carlyle, and is a very careful and useful rendering, in which, however, Browning the scholar has hardly allowed scope enough to Browning the poet.

The long absence from Italy (graven, as he said, on his heart) was in no sense due to alienation. In 1878, the year of the publication of *La Saisiaz* and of *The Two Poets of Croisic,* and almost annually thereafter, the poet spent his autumns in Venice. Beautiful Asolo, too, in the Veneto, so happily associated with his first visit to Italy, with *Pippa Passes* and with other poems, attracted him in 1878 and again in 1889. In 1879–80 the two series of *Dramatic Idyls* appeared, including *Pheidippides, Ivàn Ivànovitch, Muléykeh,* and *Clive.* In 1881, through the efforts of Dr. F. J. Furnivall and Miss Emily H. Hickey, the Browning Society was formed in London — a movement so successful that in due time the example was followed in Boston and in some smaller communities. While Browning was benevolently neutral in his attitude toward such undertakings, he valued the long delayed recognition that the London organization both represented and encouraged, as he became more and more aware of the impersonal and genuine interest in his work shown in the proceedings of that society. To be sure, there have been a few rather fashionable and faddish groups who have perhaps retarded rather than advanced the poet's influence by professing to see the poems as tortuous puzzles challenging solutions which only the intellectually elect could supply. But no reproach of this kind can be visited upon the useful and meritorious work of the serious-minded group whom Browning himself called 'disinterested' and 'well-intentioned.'

> When all is done, I cannot but be very grateful for the institution of the Society; for to what else but the eight years' persistent calling attention of my works can one attribute the present demand for them?

In the same year Carlyle passed away, and a few years later Browning lost his spiritual intimate, Milsand (1886), and his familiar friend, Alfred Domett (1887).

In 1879 Cambridge bestowed upon the poet the honorary degree of LL.D.; in 1882 Oxford gave him the D.C.L. degree; and two years later Edinburgh also honoured him with the LL.D. *Jocoseria* (1883) is a small collection of ten poems. *Ferishtah's Fancies* (1884), as Mrs. Orr says,

> grew out of a fable by Pilpay, which Mr. Browning read when a boy. He put this into verse; and it then occurred to him to make the poem the beginning of a series, in which the Dervish, who is first introduced as a learner, should reappear in the character of a teacher. Ferishtah's fancies are the familiar illustrations by which his teachings are enforced.

In 1885 Barrett Browning, or 'Pen,' whose professional painting was now attracting favourable attention, spent the autumn with his father in Venice; in 1887 he married Miss Fannie Coddington, an American lady, and soon afterward settled in Venice, buying the Rezzonico Palace for a home. In 1887 also *Parleyings with Certain People of Importance in their Day*, dedicated to the memory of Milsand, was published.

Browning's last year was a peculiarly happy one. It marked the completion of the work of general revision, the appearance of *Asolando*, long walks in loved places, and long talks with cherished friends. It marked also the poet's final and perhaps happiest visit to Asolo, as the guest of a valued American friend, Mrs. Katherine C. (Arthur) Bronson, who had entertained the Brownings — brother and sister — at her home in Venice, and who now wished to wel-

SELECTIONS FROM BROWNING

• •

"EYES CALM BESIDE THEE"

Eyes calm beside thee (Lady, couldst thou know!)
  May turn away thick with fast-gathering tears:
I glance not where all gaze: thrilling and low
    Their passionate praises reach thee — my cheek wears
      Alone no wonder when thou passest by;   5
      Thy tremulous lids, bent and suffused, reply
To the irrepressible homage which doth glow
  On every lip but mine: if in thine ears
Their accents linger — and thou dost recall
    Me as I stood, still, guarded, very pale,   10
  Beside each votarist whose lighted brow
Wore worship like an aureole, "O'er them all
    My beauty," thou wilt murmur, "did prevail
Save that one only": — Lady, could'st thou know!

HELEN'S TOWER

Who hears of Helen's Tower, may dream perchance
  How the Greek Beauty from the Scæan Gate
  Gazed on old friends unanimous in hate,
Death-doom'd because of her fair countenance.
Hearts would leap otherwise, at thy advance,   5
  Lady, to whom this Tower is consecrate!
  Like hers, thy face once made all eyes elate,
Yet, unlike hers, was bless'd by every glance.

The Tower of Hate is outworn, far and strange:
  A transitory shame of long ago,   10
    It dies into the sand from which it sprang;

But thine, Love's rock-built Tower, shall fear no change:
  God's self laid stable earth's foundation so,
    When all the morning-stars together sang.

GOLDONI

GOLDONI — good, gay, sunniest of souls —
  Glassing half Venice in that verse of thine —
  What though it just reflect the shade and shine
Of common life, nor render, as it rolls,
Grandeur and gloom? Sufficient for thy shoals   5
  Was Carnival; Parini's depths enshrine
  Secrets unsuited to that opaline
Surface of things which laughs along thy scrolls.

There throng the people: how they come and go,
  Lisp the soft language, flaunt the bright garb — see — 10
On Piazza, Calle, under Portico
  And over Bridge! Dear king of Comedy,
Be honoured! Thou that didst love Venice so,
  Venice, and we who love her, all love thee!

RAWDON BROWN

"Tutti ga i so gusti, e mi go i mii."
(*Venetian saying.*)

SIGHED Rawdon Brown: "Yes, I'm departing, Toni!
  I needs must, just this once before I die,
  Revisit England: *Anglus* Brown am I,
Although my heart's Venetian.   Yes, old crony —
Venice and London — London's 'Death the bony'   5
  Compared with Life — that's Venice! What a sky,
  A sea, this morning! One last look! Good-bye,
Cà Pesaro! No, lion — I'm a cony
To weep! I'm dazzled; 'tis that sun I view
  Rippling the . . . the . . . *Cospetto*, Toni! Down   10
    With carpet-bag, and off with valise-straps!
Bella Venezia, non ti lascio più!"

Nor did Brown ever leave her: well, perhaps
Browning, next week, may find himself quite Brown!

THE NAMES

(TO SHAKESPEARE)

SHAKESPEARE! — to such name's sounding what succeeds
   Fitly as silence?   Falter forth the spell, —
   Act follows word, the speaker knows full well,
Nor tampers with its magic more than needs.
Two names there are: That which the Hebrew reads   5
   With his soul only: if from lips it fell,
   Echo, back thundered by earth, heaven and hell,
Would own "Thou did'st create us!"   Naught impedes
We voice the other name, man's most of might,
   Awesomely, lovingly: let awe and love   10
Mutely await their working, leave to sight
   All of the issue as — below — above —
   Shakespeare's creation rises: one remove,
Though dread — this finite from that infinite.

WHY I AM A LIBERAL

"WHY?"   Because all I haply can and do,
   All that I am now, all I hope to be —
   Whence comes it save from fortune setting free
Body and soul the purpose to pursue,
God traced for both?   If fetters, not a few,   5
   Of prejudice, convention, fall from me,
   These shall I bid men — each in his degree
Also God-guided — bear, and gaily, too?

But little do or can the best of us:
   That little is achieved through Liberty.   10
Who, then, dares hold — emancipated thus —
   His fellow shall continue bound?   Not I
Who live, love, labour freely, nor discuss
   A brother's right to freedom.   That is "Why."

CAVALIER TUNES

I. MARCHING ALONG

KENTISH Sir Byng stood for his King,
Bidding the crop-headed Parliament swing:
And, pressing a troop unable to stoop
And see the rogues flourish and honest folk droop,
Marched them along, fifty-score strong,   5
Great-hearted gentlemen, singing this song.

God for King Charles!   Pym and such carles
To the Devil that prompts 'em their treasonous parles!
Cavaliers, up!   Lips from the cup,
Hands from the pasty, nor bite take nor sup   10
Till you're —
    CHORUS. — Marching along, fifty-score strong,
                Great-hearted gentlemen, singing this song.

Hampden to hell, and his obsequies' knell.
Serve Hazelrig, Fiennes, and young Harry as well!   15
England, good cheer!   Rupert is near!
Kentish and loyalists, keep we not here,
    CHO. — Marching along, fifty-score strong,
                Great-hearted gentlemen, singing this song?

Then, God for King Charles!   Pym and his snarls   20
To the Devil that pricks on such pestilent carles!
Hold by the right, you double your might;
So, onward to Nottingham, fresh for the fight,
    CHO. — March we along, fifty-score strong,
                Great-hearted gentlemen, singing this song!   25

II. GIVE A ROUSE

King Charles, and who'll do him right now?
King Charles, and who's ripe for fight now?
Give a rouse: here's, in hell's despite now,
King Charles!

Who gave me the goods that went since? 5
Who raised me the house that sank once?
Who helped me to gold I spent since?
Who found me in wine you drank once?
    Cho. — King Charles, and who'll do him right now?
        King Charles, and who's ripe for fight now? 10
        Give a rouse: here's, in hell's despite now,
        King Charles!

To whom used my boy George quaff else,
By the old fool's side that begot him?
For whom did he cheer and laugh else, 15
While Noll's damned troopers shot him?
    Cho. — King Charles, and who'll do him right now?
        King Charles, and who's ripe for fight now?
        Give a rouse: here's, in hell's despite now,
        King Charles! 20

III. BOOT AND SADDLE

Boot, saddle, to horse, and away!
Rescue my castle before the hot day
Brightens to blue from its silvery grey,
    Cho. — Boot, saddle, to horse, and away!

Ride past the suburbs, asleep as you'd say; 5
Many's the friend there, will listen and pray
"God's luck to gallants that strike up the lay —
    Cho. — "Boot, saddle, to horse, and away!"

Forty miles off, like a roebuck at bay,
Flouts Castle Brancepeth the Roundheads' array: 10
Who laughs, "Good fellows ere this, by my fay,
    Cho. — "Boot, saddle, to horse, and away!"

Who? My wife Gertrude; that, honest and gay,
Laughs when you talk of surrendering, "Nay!
I've better counsellors; what counsel they? 15
    Cho. — "Boot, saddle, to horse, and away!"

THE LOST LEADER

JUST for a handful of silver he left us,
  Just for a riband to stick in his coat —
Found the one gift of which fortune bereft us,
  Lost all the others she lets us devote;
They, with the gold to give, doled him out silver,   5
  So much was theirs who so little allowed:
How all our copper had gone for his service!
  Rags — were they purple, his heart had been proud!
We that had loved him so, followed him, honoured him,
  Lived in his mild and magnificent eye,   10
Learned his great language, caught his clear accents,
  Made him our pattern to live and to die!
Shakespeare was of us, Milton was for us,
  Burns, Shelley, were with us, — they watch from their
    graves!
He alone breaks from the van and the freemen,   15
  — He alone sinks to the rear and the slaves!

We shall march prospering, — not through his presence;
  Songs may inspirit us, — not from his lyre;
Deeds will be done, — while he boasts his quiescence,
  Still bidding crouch whom the rest bade aspire: 20
Blot out his name, then, record one lost soul more,
  One task more declined, one more footpath untrod,
One more devils'-triumph and sorrow for angels,
  One wrong more to man, one more insult to God!
Life's night begins: let him never come back to us!   25
  There would be doubt, hesitation and pain,
Forced praise on our part — the glimmer of twilight,
  Never glad confident morning again!
Best fight on well, for we taught him — strike gallantly,
  Menace our heart ere we master his own;   30
Then let him receive the new knowledge and wait us,
  Pardoned in heaven, the first by the throne!

"HOW THEY BROUGHT THE GOOD NEWS
FROM GHENT TO AIX"

[16—]

I SPRANG to the stirrup, and Joris, and he;
I galloped, Dirck galloped, we galloped all three;
"Good speed!" cried the watch, as the gatebolts undrew;
"Speed!" echoed the wall to us galloping through;
Behind shut the postern, the lights sank to rest,   5
And into the midnight we galloped abreast.

Not a word to each other; we kept the great pace
Neck by neck, stride by stride, never changing our place;
I turned in my saddle and made its girths tight,
Then shortened each stirrup, and set the pique right,   10
Rebuckled the cheek-strap, chained slacker the bit,
Nor galloped less steadily Roland a whit.

'Twas moonset at starting; but while we drew near
Lokeren, the cocks crew and twilight dawned clear;
At Boom, a great yellow star came out to see;   15
At Düffeld, 'twas morning as plain as could be;
And from Mecheln church-steeple we heard the half-chime,
So, Joris broke silence with, "Yet there is time!"

At Aershot, up leaped of a sudden the sun,
And against him the cattle stood black every one, ·   20
To stare through the mist at us galloping past
And I saw my stout galloper Roland at last,
With resolute shoulders, each butting away
The haze, as some bluff river headland its spray:

And his low head and crest, just one sharp ear bent back 25
For my voice, and the other pricked out on his track;
And one eye's black intelligence, — ever that glance
O'er its white edge at me, his own master, askance!
And the thick heavy spume-flakes which aye and anon
His fierce lips shook upwards in galloping on.   30

By Hasselt, Dirck groaned; and cried Joris, "Stay spur!
Your Roos galloped bravely, the fault's not in her,
We'll remember at Aix" — for one heard the quick wheeze
Of her chest, saw the stretched neck and staggering knees,
And sunk tail, and horrible heave of the flank,   35
As down on her haunches she shuddered and sank.

So, we were left galloping, Joris and I,
Past Looz and past Tongres, no cloud in the sky;
The broad sun above laughed a pitiless laugh,
'Neath our feet broke the brittle bright stubble like chaff;
Till over by Dalhem a dome-spire sprang white,   41
And "Gallop," gasped Joris, "for Aix is in sight!"

"How they'll greet us!" — and all in a moment his roan
Rolled neck and croup over, lay dead as a stone;
And there was my Roland to bear the whole weight   45
Of the news which alone could save Aix from her fate,
With his nostrils like pits full of blood to the brim,
And with circles of red for his eye-sockets' rim.

Then I cast loose my buffcoat, each holster let fall,
Shook off both my jack-boots, let go belt and all,   50
Stood up in the stirrup, leaned, patted his ear,
Called my Roland his pet-name, my horse without peer;
Clapped my hands, laughed and sang, any noise, bad or good,
Till at length into Aix Roland galloped and stood.

And all I remember is — friends flocking round   55
As I sat with his head 'twixt my knees on the ground;
And no voice but was praising this Roland of mine,
As I poured down his throat our last measure of wine,
Which (the burgesses voted by common consent)
Was no more than his due who brought good news from
      Ghent.   60

THROUGH THE METIDJA TO ABD–EL–KADR

As I ride, as I ride,
With a full heart for my guide,
So its tide rocks my side,
As I ride, as I ride,
That, as I were double-eyed,   5
He, in whom our Tribes confide,
Is descried, ways untried,
As I ride, as I ride.

As I ride, as I ride
To our Chief and his Allied,   10
Who dares chide my heart's pride
As I ride, as I ride?
Or are witnesses denied —
Through the desert waste and wide
Do I glide unespied   15
As I ride, as I ride?

As I ride, as I ride,
When an inner voice has cried,
The sands slide, nor abide
(As I ride, as I ride)   20
O'er each visioned homicide
That came vaunting (has he lied?)
To reside — where he died,
As I ride, as I ride.

As I ride, as I ride,   25
Ne'er has spur my swift horse plied,
Yet his hide, streaked and pied,
As I ride, as I ride,
Shows where sweat has sprung and dried,
— Zebra-footed, ostrich-thighed —   30
How has vied stride with stride
As I ride, as I ride!

As I ride, as I ride,
Could I loose what Fate has tied,
Ere I pried, she should hide   35
(As I ride, as I ride)
All that's meant me — satisfied
When the Prophet and the Bride
Stop veins I'd have subside
As I ride, as I ride!   40

SOLILOQUY OF THE SPANISH CLOISTER

Gr-r-r — there go, my heart's abhorrence!
    Water your damned flower-pots, do!
If hate killed men, Brother Lawrence,
    God's blood, would not mine kill you!
What? your myrtle-bush wants trimming?   5
    Oh, that rose has prior claims —
Needs its leaden vase filled brimming?
    Hell dry you up with its flames!

At the meal we sit together:
    Salve tibi! I must hear   10
Wise talk of the kind of weather,
    Sort of season, time of year:
Not a plenteous cork-crop: scarcely
    Dare we hope oak-galls, I doubt:
What's the Latin name for "parsley"?   15
    What's the Greek name for Swine's Snout?

Whew! We'll have our platter burnished,
    Laid with care on our own shelf!
With a fire-new spoon we're furnished,
    And a goblet for ourself,   20
Rinsed like something sacrificial
    Ere 'tis fit to touch our chaps —
Marked with L. for our initial!
    (He-he! There his lily snaps!)

Saint, forsooth!   While brown Dolores   25
   Squats outside the Convent bank
With Sanchicha, telling stories,
   Steeping tresses in the tank,
Blue-black, lustrous, thick like horsehairs
   — Can't I see his dead eye glow,   30
Bright as 'twere a Barbary corsair's?
   (That is, if he'd let it show!)

When he finishes refection,
   Knife and fork he never lays
Cross-wise, to my recollection,   35
   As do I, in Jesu's praise.
I the Trinity illustrate,
   Drinking watered orange-pulp —
In three sips the Arian frustrate;
   While he drains his at one gulp.   40

Oh, those melons!   If he's able
   We're to have a feast! so nice!
One goes to the Abbot's table,
   All of us get each a slice.
How go on your flowers?   None double?   45
   Not one fruit-sort can you spy?
Strange! — And I, too, at such trouble,
   Keep them close-nipped on the sly!

There's a great text in Galatians,
   Once you trip on it, entails   50
Twenty-nine distinct damnations,
   One sure, if another fails:
If I trip him just a-dying,
   Sure of heaven as sure can be,
Spin him round and send him flying   55
   Off to hell, a Manichee?

Or, my scrofulous French novel
   On grey paper with blunt type!

Simply glance at it, you grovel
    Hand and foot in Belial's gripe: 60
If I double down its pages
    At the woeful sixteenth print,
When he gathers his greengages,
    Ope a sieve and slip it in't?

Or, there's Satan! — one might venture   65
    Pledge one's soul to him, yet leave
Such a flaw in the indenture
    As he'd miss till, past retrieve,
Blasted lay that rose-acacia
    We're so proud of! *Hy, Zy, Hine* . . .   70
'St, there's Vespers! *Plena gratiâ,*
    Ave, Virgo! Gr-r-r — you swine!

THE LABORATORY

ANCIEN RÉGIME

Now that I, tying thy glass mask tightly,
May gaze through these faint smokes curling whitely,
As thou pliest thy trade in this devil's-smithy —
Which is the poison to poison her, prithee?

He is with her, and they know that I know   5
Where they are, what they do: they believe my tears flow
While they laugh, laugh at me, at me fled to the drear
Empty church, to pray God in, for them! — I am here.

Grind away, moisten and mash up thy paste,
Pound at thy powder, — I am not in haste!   10
Better sit thus, and observe thy strange things,
Than go where men wait me and dance at the King's.

That in the mortar — you call it a gum?
Ah, the brave tree whence such gold oozings come!

And yonder soft phial, the exquisite blue,   15
Sure to taste sweetly, — is that poison too?

Had I but all of them, thee and thy treasures,
What a wild crowd of invisible pleasures!
To carry pure death in an earring, a casket,
A signet, a fan-mount, a filigree basket!   20

Soon, at the King's, a mere lozenge to give,
And Pauline should have just thirty minutes to live!
But to light a pastile, and Elise, with her head
And her breast and her arms and her hands, should drop
       dead!

Quick — is it finished?   The colour's too grim!   25
Why not soft like the phial's, enticing and dim?
Let it brighten her drink, let her turn it and stir,
And try it and taste, ere she fix and prefer!

What a drop!   She's not little, no minion like me!
That's why she ensnared him: this never will free   30
The soul from those masculine eyes, — say, "no!"
To that pulse's magnificent come-and-go.

For only last night, as they whispered, I brought
My own eyes to bear on her so, that I thought
Could I keep them one half minute fixed, she would fall   35
Shrivelled; she fell not; yet this does it all!

Not that I bid you spare her the pain;
Let death be felt and the proof remain:
Brand, burn up, bite into its grace —
He is sure to remember her dying face!   40

Is it done?   Take my mask off!   Nay, be not morose;
It kills her, and this prevents seeing it close:
The delicate droplet, my whole fortune's fee!
If it hurts her, beside, can it ever hurt me?

Now, take all my jewels, gorge gold to your fill,   45
You may kiss me, old man, on my mouth if you will!
But brush this dust off me, lest horror it brings
Ere I know it — next moment I dance at the King's!

CRISTINA

SHE should never have looked at me
    If she meant I should not love her!
There are plenty . . . men, you call such,
    I suppose . . . she may discover
All her soul to, if she pleases,   5
    And yet leave much as she found them:
But I'm not so, and she knew it
    When she fixed me, glancing round them.

What? To fix me thus meant nothing?
    But I can't tell (there's my weakness)   10
What her look said! — no vile cant, sure,
    About "need to strew the bleakness
Of some lone shore with its pearl-seed
    That the sea feels" — no "strange yearning
That such souls have, most to lavish   15
    Where there's chance of least returning."

Oh, we're sunk enough here, God knows!
    But not quite so sunk that moments,
Sure though seldom, are denied us,
    When the spirit's true endowments   20
Stand out plainly from its false ones,
    And apprise it if pursuing
Or the right way or the wrong way,
    To its triumph or undoing.

There are flashes struck from midnights,   25
    There are fire-flames noondays kindle,
Whereby piled-up honours perish,
    Whereby swollen ambitions dwindle,

While just this or that poor impulse,
    Which for once had play unstifled,   30
Seems the sole work of a lifetime,
    That away the rest have trifled.

Doubt you if, in some such moment,
    As she fixed me, she felt clearly,
Ages past the soul existed,   35
    Here an age 'tis resting merely,
And hence fleets again for ages,
    While the true end, sole and single,
It stops here for is, this love-way,
    With some other soul to mingle?   40

Else it loses what it lived for,
    And eternally must lose it;
Better ends may be in prospect,
    Deeper blisses (if you choose it),
But this life's end and this love-bliss   45
    Have been lost here.   Doubt you whether
This she felt as, looking at me,
    Mine and her souls rushed together?

Oh, observe! Of course, next moment,
    The world's honours, in derision,   50
Trampled out the light for ever:
    Never fear but there's provision
Of the devil's to quench knowledge
    Lest we walk the earth in rapture!
— Making those who catch God's secret   55
    Just so much more prize their capture!

Such am I: the secret's mine now!
    She has lost me, I have gained her;
Her soul's mine: and thus, grown perfect,
    I shall pass my life's remainder.   60

Life will just hold out the proving
  Both our powers, alone and blended:
And then, come the next life quickly!
  This world's use will have been ended.

MEETING AT NIGHT

THE grey sea and the long black land;
And the yellow half-moon large and low;
And the startled little waves that leap
In fiery ringlets from their sleep,
As I gain the cove with pushing prow,   5
And quench its speed i' the slushy sand.

Then a mile of warm sea-scented beach;
Three fields to cross till a farm appears;
A tap at the pane, the quick sharp scratch
And blue spurt of a lighted match,   10
And a voice less loud, through its joys and fears,
Than the two hearts beating each to each!

PARTING AT MORNING

ROUND the cape of a sudden came the sea,
And the sun looked over the mountain's rim:
And straight was a path of gold for him,
And the need of a world of men for me.

A WOMAN'S LAST WORD

LET's contend no more, Love,
  Strive nor weep:
All be as before, Love,
  — Only sleep!

What so wild as words are?   5
  I and thou

In debate, as birds are,
  Hawk on bough!

See the creature stalking
  While we speak!   10
Hush and hide the talking,
  Cheek on cheek!

What so false as truth is,
  False to thee?
Where the serpent's tooth is   15
  Shun the tree —

Where the apple reddens
  Never pry —
Lest we lose our Edens,
  Eve and I.   20

Be a god and hold me
  With a charm!
Be a man and fold me
  With thine arm!

Teach me, only teach, Love!   25
  As I ought
I will speak thy speech, Love,
  Think thy thought —

Meet, if thou require it,
  Both demands,   30
Laying flesh and spirit
  In thy hands.

That shall be to-morrow,
  Not to-night:
I must bury sorrow   35
  Out of sight:

— Must a little weep, Love,
    (Foolish me!)
And so fall asleep, Love,
    Loved by thee.   40

EVELYN HOPE

BEAUTIFUL Evelyn Hope is dead!
    Sit and watch by her side an hour.
That is her book-shelf, this her bed;
    She plucked that piece of geranium-flower,
Beginning to die too, in the glass;   5
    Little has yet been changed, I think:
The shutters are shut, no light may pass
    Save two long rays through the hinge's chink.

Sixteen years old when she died!
    Perhaps she had scarcely heard my name;   10
It was not her time to love; beside,
    Her life had many a hope and aim,
Duties enough and little cares,
    And now was quiet, now astir,
Till God's hand beckoned unawares, —   15
    And the sweet white brow is all of her.

Is it too late then, Evelyn Hope?
    What, your soul was pure and true,
The good stars met in your horoscope,
    Made you of spirit, fire and dew —   20
And, just because I was thrice as old
    And our paths in the world diverged so wide,
Each was naught to each, must I be told?
    We were fellow mortals, naught beside?

No, indeed! for God above   25
    Is great to grant, as mighty to make,

And creates the love to reward the love:
 I claim you still, for my own love's sake!
Delayed it may be for more lives yet,
 Through worlds I shall traverse, not a few: 30
Much is to learn, much to forget
 Ere the time be come for taking you.

But the time will come, — at last it will,
 When, Evelyn Hope, what meant (I shall say)
In the lower earth, in the years long still,   35
 That body and soul so pure and gay?
Why your hair was amber, I shall divine,
 And your mouth of your own geranium's red —
And what you would do with me, in fine,
 In the new life come in the old one's stead.   40

I have lived (I shall say) so much since then,
 Given up myself so many times,
Gained me the gains of various men,
 Ransacked the ages, spoiled the climes;
Yet one thing, one, in my soul's full scope,   45
 Either I missed or itself missed me:
And I want and find you, Evelyn Hope!
 What is the issue? let us see!

I loved you, Evelyn, all the while!
 My heart seemed full as it could hold;   50
There was place and to spare for the frank young smile,
 And the red young mouth, and the hair's young gold.
So, hush, — I will give you this leaf to keep:
 See, I shut it inside the sweet cold hand!
There, that is our secret: go to sleep!   55
 You will wake, and remember, and understand.

LOVE AMONG THE RUINS

WHERE the quiet-coloured end of evening smiles
      Miles and miles
On the solitary pastures where our sheep
      Half-asleep
Tinkle homeward through the twilight, stray or stop 5
      As they crop —
Was the site once of a city great and gay,
      (So they say)
Of our country's very capital, its prince
      Ages since   10
Held his court in, gathered councils, wielding far
      Peace or war.

Now, — the country does not even boast a tree,
      As you see,
To distinguish slopes of verdure, certain rills   15
      From the hills
Intersect and give a name to, (else they run
      Into one),
Where the domed and daring palace shot its spires
      Up like fires   20
O'er the hundred-gated circuit of a wall
      Bounding all,
Made of marble, men might march on nor be pressed,
      Twelve abreast.

And such plenty and perfection, see, of grass   25
      Never was!
Such a carpet as, this summer-time, o'erspreads
      And embeds
Every vestige of the city, guessed alone,
      Stock or stone —   30
Where a multitude of men breathed joy and woe
      Long ago;

Lust of glory pricked their hearts up, dread of shame
        Struck them tame;
And that glory and that shame alike, the gold   35
        Bought and sold.

Now, — the single little turret that remains
        On the plains,
By the caper overrooted, by the gourd
        Overscored,   40
While the patching houseleek's head of blossom winks
        Through the chinks —
Marks the basement whence a tower in ancient time
        Sprang sublime,
And a burning ring, all round, the chariots traced   45
        As they raced,
And the monarch and his minions and his dames
        Viewed the games.

And I know, while thus the quiet-coloured eve
        Smiles to leave   50
To their folding, all our many-tinkling fleece
        In such peace,
And the slopes and rills in undistinguished grey
        Melt away —
That a girl with eager eyes and yellow hair   55
        Waits me there
In the turret whence the charioteers caught soul
        For the goal,
When the king looked, where she looks now, breathless,
        dumb
        Till I come.   60

But he looked upon the city, every side,
        Far and wide.
All the mountains topped with temples, all the glades'
        Colonnades,

All the causeys, bridges, aqueducts — and then,   65
    All the men!
When I do come, she will speak not, she will stand,
    Either hand
On my shoulder, give her eyes the first embrace
    Of my face,   70
Ere we rush, ere we extinguish sight and speech
    Each on each.

In one year they sent a million fighters forth
    South and North,
And they built their gods a brazen pillar high   75
    As the sky,
Yet reserved a thousand chariots in full force —
    Gold, of course.
Oh heart! oh blood that freezes, blood that burns!
    Earth's returns   80
For whole centuries of folly, noise and sin!
    Shut them in,
With their triumphs and their glories and the rest!
    Love is best.

UP AT A VILLA — DOWN IN THE CITY

(AS DISTINGUISHED BY AN ITALIAN PERSON OF QUALITY)

HAD I but plenty of money, money enough and to spare,
The house for me, no doubt, were a house in the city-square;
Ah, such a life, such a life, as one leads at the window there!

Something to see, by Bacchus, something to hear, at least!
There, the whole day long, one's life is a perfect feast;   5
While up at a villa one lives, I maintain it, no more than a
    beast.

Well now, look at our villa! stuck like the horn of a bull
Just on a mountain-edge as bare as the creature's skull,

Save a mere shag of a bush with hardly a leaf to pull!
— I scratch my own, sometimes, to see if the hair's turned
    wool.   10

But the city, oh, the city — the square with the houses!
    Why?
They are stone-faced, white as a curd, there's something to
    take the eye!
Houses in four straight lines, not a single front awry;
You watch who crosses and gossips, who saunters, who hur-
    ries by;
Green blinds, as a matter of course, to draw when the sun
    gets high;   15
And the shops with fanciful signs which are painted properly.

What of a villa?   Though winter be over in March by rights,
'Tis May perhaps ere the snow shall have withered well off
    the heights:
You've the brown ploughed land before, where the oxen
    steam and wheeze,
And the hills over-smoked behind by the faint grey olive-
    trees.   20

Is it better in May, I ask you?   You've summer all at once;
In a day he leaps complete with a few strong April suns.
'Mid the sharp short emerald wheat, scarce risen three
    fingers well,
The wild tulip, at end of its tube, blows out its great red
    bell
Like a thin clear bubble of blood, for the children to pick and
    sell.   25

Is it ever hot in the square?   There's a fountain to spout
    and splash!
In the shade it sings and springs; in the shine such foambows
    flash
On the horses with curling fish-tails, that prance and paddle
    and pash

Round the lady atop in her conch — fifty gazers do not
    abash,
Though all that she wears is some weeds round her waist in
    a sort of sash.   30

All the year long at the villa, nothing to see though you
    linger,
Except yon cypress that points like death's lean lifted fore-
    finger.
Some think fireflies pretty, when they mix i' the corn and
    mingle,
Or thrid the stinking hemp till the stalks of it seem a-tingle.
Late August or early September, the stunning cicala is shrill,
And the bees keep their tiresome whine round the resinous
    firs on the hill.   36
Enough of the seasons — I spare you the months of the fever
    and chill.

Ere you open your eyes in the city, the blessed church-bells
    begin:
No sooner the bells leave off than the diligence rattles in:
You get the pick of the news, and it costs you never a pin.
By-and-by there's the travelling doctor gives pills, lets blood,
    draws teeth;   41
Or the Pulcinello-trumpet breaks up the market beneath.
At the post-office such a scene-picture — the new play,
    piping hot!
And a notice how, only this morning, three liberal thieves
    were shot.
Above it, behold the Archbishop's most fatherly of rebukes,
And beneath, with his crown and his lion, some little new
    law of the Duke's!   46
Or a sonnet with flowery marge, to the Reverend Don So-
    and-so
Who is Dante, Boccaccio, Petrarca, Saint Jerome, and Cicero,
"And moreover," (the sonnet goes rhyming,) "the skirts of
    Saint Paul has reached.

Having preached us those six Lent-lectures more unctuous
    than ever he preached." 50
Noon strikes, — here sweeps the procession! our Lady borne
    smiling and smart
With a pink gauze gown all spangles, and seven swords stuck
    in her heart!
Bang-whang-whang goes the drum, *tootle-te-tootle* the fife;
No keeping one's haunches still: it's the greatest pleasure in
    life.

But bless you, it's dear — it's dear! fowls, wine, at double
    the rate. 55
They have clapped a new tax upon salt, and what oil pays
    passing the gate
It's a horror to think of. And so, the villa for me, not the city!
Beggars can scarcely be choosers: but still — ah, the pity,
    the pity!
Look, two and two go the priests, then the monks with cowls
    and sandals,
And the penitents dressed in white shirts, a-holding the
    yellow candles; 60
One, he carries a flag up straight, and another a cross with
    handles,
And the Duke's guard brings up the rear, for the better
    prevention of scandals:
Bang-whang-whang goes the drum, *tootle-te-tootle* the fife.
Oh, a day in the city-square, there is no such pleasure in
    life!

A TOCCATA OF GALUPPI'S

Oh, Galuppi, Baldassare, this is very sad to find!
I can hardly misconceive you; it would prove me deaf and
    blind;
But although I take your meaning, 'tis with such a heavy
    mind!

Here you come with your old music, and here's all the good
it brings.
What, they lived once thus at Venice where the merchants
were the kings, 5
Where Saint Mark's is, where the Doges used to wed the sea
with rings?

Ay, because the sea's the street there; and 'tis arched by . . .
what you call
. . . Shylock's bridge with houses on it, where they kept the
carnival:
I was never out of England — it's as if I saw it all.

Did young people take their pleasure when the sea was warm
in May? 10
Balls and masks begun at midnight, burning ever to mid-day,
When they made up fresh adventures for the morrow, do
you say?

Was a lady such a lady, cheeks so round and lips so red, —
On her neck the small face buoyant, like a bell-flower on its
bed,
O'er the breast's superb abundance where a man might base
his head? 15

Well, and it was graceful of them — they'd break talk off
and afford
— She, to bite her mask's black velvet — he, to finger on
his sword,
While you sat and played Toccatas, stately at the clavichord?

What? Those lesser thirds so plaintive, sixths diminished,
sigh on sigh,
Told them something? Those suspensions, those solutions
— "Must we die?" 20
Those commiserating sevenths — "Life might last! we can
but try!"

"Were you happy?" — "Yes." — "And are you still as
    happy?" — "Yes.   And you?"
— "Then, more kisses!" — "Did *I* stop them, when a million
    seemed so few?"
Hark, the dominant's persistence till it must be answered to!

So, an octave struck the answer. Oh, they praised you, I
    dare say!   25
"Brave Galuppi! that was music! good alike at grave and
    gay!
I can always leave off talking when I hear a master play!"

Then they left you for their pleasure: till in due time, one by
    one,
Some with lives that came to nothing, some with deeds as
    well undone,
Death stepped tacitly and took them where they never see
    the sun.   30

But when I sit down to reason, think to take my stand nor
    swerve,
While I triumph o'er a secret wrung from nature's close
    reserve,
In you come with your cold music till I creep through every
    nerve.

Yes, you, like a ghostly cricket, creaking where a house was
    burned:
"Dust and ashes, dead and done with, Venice spent what
    Venice earned.   35
The soul, doubtless, is immortal — where a soul can be dis-
    cerned.

"Yours, for instance: you know physics, something of geology,
Mathematics are your pastime; souls shall rise in their
    degree;
Butterflies may dread extinction, — you'll not die, it cannot
    be!

"As for Venice and her people, merely born to bloom and
    drop,   40
Here on earth they bore their fruitage, mirth and folly **were**
    the crop:
What of soul was left, I wonder, when the kissing had **to**
    stop?

"Dust and ashes!"   So you creak it, and I want the heart to
    scold.
Dear dead women, with such hair, too — what's become **of**
    all the gold
Used to hang and brush their bosoms? I feel chilly and
    grown old.   45

OLD PICTURES IN FLORENCE

The morn when first it thunders in March,
    The eel in the pond gives a leap, they say:
As I leaned and looked over the aloed arch
    Of the villa-gate this warm March day,
No flash snapped, no dumb thunder rolled   5
    In the valley beneath where, white and wide
And washed by the morning water-gold,
    Florence lay out on the mountain-side.

River and bridge and street and square
    Lay mine, as much at my beck and call,   10
Through the live translucent bath of air,
    As the sights in a magic crystal ball.
And of all I saw and of all I praised,
    The most to praise and the best to see
Was the startling bell-tower Giotto raised: 15
    But why did it more than startle me?

Giotto, how, with that soul of yours,
    Could you play me false who loved you so?

Some slights if a certain heart endures
    Yet it feels, I would have your fellows know! 20
I' faith, I perceive not why I should care
    To break a silence that suits them best,
But the thing grows somewhat hard to bear
    When I find a Giotto join the rest.

On the arch where olives overhead   25
    Print the blue sky with twig and leaf,
(That sharp-curled leaf which they never shed)
    'Twixt the aloes, I used to lean in chief,
And mark through the winter afternoons,
    By a gift God grants me now and then,   30
In the mild decline of those suns like moons,
    Who walked in Florence, besides her men.

They might chirp and chaffer, come and go
    For pleasure or profit, her men alive —
My business was hardly with them, I trow,   35
    But with empty cells of the human hive;
— With the chapter-room, the cloister-porch,
    The church's apsis, aisle or nave,
Its crypt, one fingers along with a torch,
    Its face set full for the sun to shave.   40

Wherever a fresco peels and drops,
    Wherever an outline weakens and wanes
Till the latest life in the painting stops,
    Stands One whom each fainter pulse-tick pains:
One, wishful each scrap should clutch the brick, 45
    Each tinge not wholly escape the plaster,
— A lion who dies of an ass's kick,
    The wronged great soul of an ancient Master.

For oh, this world and the wrong it does!
    They are safe in heaven with their backs to it, 50

The Michaels and Rafaels, you hum and buzz
   Round the works of, you of the little wit!
Do their eyes contract to the earth's old scope,
   Now that they see God face to face,
And have all attained to be poets, I hope?   **55**
   'Tis their holiday now, in any case.

Much they reck of your praise and you!
   But the wronged great souls — can they be quit
Of a world where their work is all to do,
   Where you style them, you of the little wit,   **60**
Old Master This and Early the Other,
   Not dreaming that Old and New are fellows:
A younger succeeds to an elder brother,
   Da Vincis derive in good time from Dellos.

And here where your praise might yield returns,   **65**
   And a handsome word or two give help,
Here, after your kind, the mastiff girns
   And the puppy pack of poodles yelp.
What, not a word for Stefano there,
   Of brow once prominent and starry,   **70**
Called Nature's Ape, and the world's despair
   For his peerless painting?   (See Vasari.)

There stands the Master.   Study, my friends,
   What a man's work comes to!   So he plans it,
Performs it, perfects it, makes amends   **75**
   For the toiling and moiling, and then, *sic transit!*
Happier the thrifty blind-folk labour,
   With upturned eye while the hand is busy,
Not sidling a glance at the coin of their neighbour!
   'Tis looking downward that makes one dizzy.   **80**

"If you knew their work you would deal your dole."
   May I take upon me to instruct you?

When Greek Art ran and reached the goal,
 Thus much had the world to boast *in fructu* —
The Truth of Man, as by God first spoken,   85
 Which the actual generations garble,
Was re-uttered, and Soul (which Limbs betoken)
 And Limbs (Soul informs) made new in marble.

So you saw yourself as you wished you were,
 As you might have been, as you cannot be;   90
Earth here, rebuked by Olympus there:
 And grew content in your poor degree
With your little power, by those statues' godhead,
 And your little scope, by their eyes' full sway,
And your little grace, by their grace embodied,   95
 And your little date, by their forms that stay.

You would fain be kinglier, say, than I am?
 Even so, you will not sit like Theseus.
You would prove a model? The Son of Priam
 Has yet the advantage in arms' and knees' use. 100
You're wroth — can you slay your snake like Apollo?
 You're grieved — still Niobe's the grander!
You live — there's the Racers' frieze to follow:
 You die — there's the dying Alexander. .

So, testing your weakness by their strength,   105
 Your meagre charms by their rounded beauty,
Measured by Art in your breadth and length,
 You learned — to submit is a mortal's duty.
— When I say "you" 'tis the common soul,
 The collective, I mean: the race of Man   110
That receives life in parts to live in a whole,
 And grow here according to God's clear plan.

Growth came when, looking your last on them all,
 You turned your eyes inwardly one fine day

And cried with a start — What if we so small   **115**
    Be greater and grander the while than they?
Are they perfect of lineament, perfect of stature?
    In both, of such lower types are we
Precisely because of our wider nature;
    For time, theirs — ours, for eternity.   **120**

To-day's brief passion limits their range;
    It seethes with the morrow for us and more.
They are perfect — how else? they shall never change:
    We are faulty — why not? we have time in store.
The Artificer's hand is not arrested   **125**
    With us; we are rough-hewn, nowise polished:
They stand for our copy, and, once invested
    With all they can teach, we shall see them abolished.

'Tis a lifelong toil till our lump be leaven —
    The better!   What's come to perfection perishes.   **130**
Things learned on earth, we shall practise in heaven:
    Works done least rapidly, Art most cherishes.
Thyself shalt afford the example, Giotto!
    Thy one work, not to decrease or diminish,
Done at a stroke, was just (was it not?) "O!"   **135**
    Thy great Campanile is still to finish.

Is it true that we are now, and shall be hereafter,
    But what and where depend on life's minute?
Hails heavenly cheer or infernal laughter
    Our first step out of the gulf or in it?   **140**
Shall Man, such step within his endeavour,
    Man's face, have no more play and action
Than joy which is crystallized for ever,
    Or grief, an eternal petrifaction?

On which I conclude, that the early painters,   **145**
    To cries of "Greek Art and what more wish you?" —

Replied, "To become now self-acquainters,
    And paint man man, whatever the issue!
Make new hopes shine through the flesh they fray,
    New fears aggrandize the rags and tatters: 150
To bring the invisible full into play!
    Let the visible go to the dogs — what matters?"

Give these, I exhort you, their guerdon and glory
    For daring so much, before they well did it.
The first of the new, in our race's story,   155
    Beats the last of the old; 'tis no idle quiddit.
The worthies began a revolution,
    Which if on earth you intend to acknowledge,
Why, honour them now! (ends my allocution)
    Nor confer your degree when the folk leave college.   160

There's a fancy some lean to and others hate —
    That, when this life is ended, begins
New work for the soul in another state,
    Where it strives and gets weary, loses and wins:
Where the strong and the weak, this world's congeries,   165
    Repeat in large what they practised in small,
Through life after life in unlimited series;
    Only the scale's to be changed, that's all.

Yet I hardly know.   When a soul has seen
    By the means of Evil that Good is best,   170
And, through earth and its noise, what is heaven's serene —
    When our faith in the same has stood the test —
Why, the child grown man, you burn the rod,
    The uses of labour are surely done;
There remaineth a rest for the people of God: 175
    And I have had troubles enough, for one.

But at any rate I have loved the season
    Of Art's spring-birth so dim and dewy;

My sculptor is Nicolo the Pisan,
  My painter — who but Cimabue?   180
Nor ever was man of them all indeed,
  From these to Ghiberti and Ghirlandajo,
Could say that he missed my critic-meed.
  So, now to my special grievance — heigh-ho!

Their ghosts still stand, as I said before,   185
  Watching each fresco flaked and rasped,
Blocked up, knocked out, or whitewashed o'er:
  — No getting again what the church has grasped!
The works on the wall must take their chance;
  "Works never conceded to England's thick clime!"   190
(I hope they prefer their inheritance
  Of a bucketful of Italian quick-lime.)

When they go at length, with such a shaking
  Of heads o'er the old delusion, sadly
Each master his way through the black streets taking,   195
  Where many a lost work breathes though badly —
Why don't they bethink them of who has merited?
  Why not reveal, while their pictures dree
Such doom, how a captive might be out-ferreted?
  Why is it they never remember me?   200

Not that I expect the great Bigordi,
  Nor Sandro to hear me, chivalric, bellicose,
Nor the wronged Lippino; and not a word I
  Say of a scrap of Frà Angelico's:
But are you too fine, Taddeo Gaddi,   205
  To grant me a taste of your intonaco,
Some Jerome that seeks the heaven with a sad eye?
  Not a churlish saint, Lorenzo Monaco?

Could not the ghost with the close red cap,
  My Pollajolo, the twice a craftsman,   210

Save me a sample, give me the hap
    Of a muscular Christ that shows the draughtsman?
No Virgin by him the somewhat petty,
    Of finical touch and tempera crumbly —
Could not Alesso Baldovinetti   215
    Contribute so much, I ask him humbly?

Margheritone of Arezzo,
    With the grave-clothes garb and swaddling barret,
(Why purse up mouth and beak in a pet so,
    You bald old saturnine poll-clawed parrot?)   220
Not a poor glimmering Crucifixion,
    Where in the foreground kneels the donor?
If such remain, as is my conviction,
    The hoarding it does you but little honour.

They pass; for them the panels may thrill,   225
    The tempera grow alive and tinglish;
Their pictures are left to the mercies still
    Of dealers and stealers, Jews and the English,
Who, seeing mere money's worth in their prize,
    Will sell it to somebody calm as Zeno   230
At naked High Art, and in ecstasies
    Before some clay-cold vile Carlino!

No matter for these! But Giotto, you,
    Have you allowed, as the town-tongues babble it —
Oh, never! it shall not be counted true —   235
    That a certain precious little tablet
Which Buonarroti eyed like a lover —
    Was buried so long in oblivion's womb
And, left for another than I to discover,
    Turns up at last! and to whom? — to whom?   240

I, that have haunted the dim San Spirito,
    (Or was it rather the Ognissanti?)

Patient on altar-step planting a weary toe!
  Nay, I shall have it yet! *Detur amanti!*
My Koh-i-noor — or (if that's a platitude)   245
  Jewel of Giamschid, the Persian Sofi's eye;
So, in anticipative gratitude,
  What if I take up my hope and prophesy?

When the hour grows ripe, and a certain dotard
  Is pitched, no parcel that needs invoicing,   250
To the worse side of the Mont Saint Gothard,
  We shall begin by way of rejoicing;
None of that shooting the sky (blank cartridge),
  Nor a civic guard, all plumes and lacquer,
Hunting Radetzky's soul like a partridge   255
  Over Morello with squib and cracker.

This time we'll shoot better game and bag 'em hot —
  No mere display at the stone of Dante,
But a kind of sober Witanagemot
  (Ex: "Casa Guidi," *quod videas ante*)   260
Shall ponder, once Freedom restored to Florence,
  How Art may return that departed with her.
Go, hated house, go each trace of the Loraine's,
  And bring us the days of Orgagna hither!

How we shall prologuize, how we shall perorate,   265
  Utter fit things upon art and history,
Feel truth at blood-heat and falsehood at zero rate,
  Make of the want of the age no mystery;
Contrast the fructuous and sterile eras,
  Show — monarchy ever its uncouth cub licks   270
Out of the bear's shape into Chimæra's.
  While Pure Art's birth is still the republic's.

Then one shall propose in a speech (curt Tuscan,
  Expurgate and sober, with scarcely an "*issimo*,")

To end now our half-told tale of Cambuscan,   275
    And turn the bell-tower's *alt* to *altissimo:*
And fine as the beak of a young beccaccia
    The Campanile, the Duomo's fit ally,
Shall soar up in gold full fifty braccia,
    Completing Florence, as Florence Italy.   280

Shall I be alive that morning the scaffold
    Is broken away, and the long-pent fire,
Like the golden hope of the world, unbaffled
    Springs from its sleep, and up goes the spire
While "God and the People" plain for its motto,   285
    Thence the new tricolour flaps at the sky?
At least to foresee that glory of Giotto
    And Florence together, the first am I!

"DE GUSTIBUS —"

Your ghost will walk, you lover of trees,
    (If our loves remain)
    In an English lane,
By a cornfield-side a-flutter with poppies.
Hark, those two in the hazel coppice —   5
A boy and a girl, if the good fates please,
    Making love, say —
    The happier they!
Draw yourself up from the light of the moon,
And let them pass, as they will too soon,   10
    With the beanflowers' boon,
    And the blackbird's tune,
    And May, and June!

What I love best in all the world
Is a castle, precipice-encurled,   15
In a gash of the wind-grieved Apennine.
Or look for me, old fellow of mine,
    (If I get my head from out the mouth

O' the grave, and loose my spirit's bands,
And come again to the land of lands) —   20
In a seaside house to the farther South,
Where the baked cicala dies of drouth,
And one sharp tree — 'tis a cypress — stands,
By the many hundred years red-rusted,
Rough iron-spiked, ripe fruit-o'ercrusted,   25
My sentinel to guard the sands
To the water's edge.   For, what expands
Before the house, but the great opaque
Blue breadth of sea without a break?
While, in the house, for ever crumbles   30
Some fragment of the frescoed walls,
From blisters where a scorpion sprawls.
A girl bare-footed brings, and tumbles
Down on the pavement, green-flesh melons,
And says there's news to-day — the king   35
Was shot at, touched in the liver-wing,
Goes with his Bourbon arm in a sling:
— She hopes they have not caught the felons.
Italy, my Italy!
Queen Mary's saying serves for me —   40
          (When fortune's malice
          Lost her, Calais) —
Open my heart and you will see
Graved inside of it, "Italy."
Such lovers old are I and she: 45
So it always was, so shall ever be!

HOME–THOUGHTS, FROM ABROAD

OH, to be in England
Now that April's there,
And whoever wakes in England
Sees, some morning, unaware,
That the lowest boughs and the brushwood sheaf   5
Round the elm-tree bole are in tiny leaf,

While the chaffinch sings on the orchard bough
In England — now!

And after April, when May follows,
And the whitethroat builds, and all the swallows!   10
Hark, where my blossomed pear-tree in the hedge
Leans to the field and scatters on the clover
Blossoms and dewdrops — at the bent spray's edge —
That's the wise thrush; he sings each song twice over,
Lest you should think he never could recapture   15
The first fine careless rapture!
And though the fields look rough with hoary dew,
All will be gay when noontide wakes anew
The buttercups, the little children's dower
— Far brighter than this gaudy melon-flower!   20

HOME–THOUGHTS, FROM THE SEA

Nobly, nobly Cape Saint Vincent to the Northwest died
      away;
Sunset ran, one glorious blood-red, reeking into Cadiz Bay;
Bluish 'mid the burning water, full in face Trafalgar lay;
In the dimmest Northeast distance dawned Gibraltar grand
      and gray;
"Here and here did England help me: how can I help Eng-
      gland?" — say,   5
Whoso turns as I, this evening, turn to God to praise and
      pray,
While Jove's planet rises yonder, silent over Africa.

SAUL

I

Said Abner, "At last thou art come! Ere I tell, ere thou
      speak,
Kiss my cheek, wish me well!" Then I wished it, and did
      kiss his cheek.

And he: "Since the King, O my friend, for thy countenance
    sent,
Neither drunken nor eaten have we; nor, until from his tent
Thou return with the joyful assurance the King liveth yet, 5
Shall our lip with the honey be bright, with the water be wet.
For out of the black mid-tent's silence, a space of three days,
Not a sound hath escaped to thy servants, of prayer nor of
    praise,
To betoken that Saul and the Spirit have ended their strife,
And that, faint in his triumph, the monarch sinks back upon
    life.   10

II

"Yet now my heart leaps, O beloved!   God's child with his
    dew
On thy gracious gold hair, and those lilies still living and
    blue
Just broken to twine round thy harp-strings, as if no wild
    heat
Were now raging to torture the desert!"

III

                   Then I, as was meet,   14
Knelt down to the God of my fathers, and rose on my feet.
And ran o'er the sand burnt to powder.   The tent was un-
    looped;
I pulled up the spear that obstructed, and under I stooped;
Hands and knees on the slippery grass-patch, all withered
    and gone,
That extends to the second enclosure, I groped my way on
Till I felt where the foldskirts fly open.   Then once more I
    prayed,   20
And opened the foldskirts and entered, and was not afraid
But spoke, "Here is David, thy servant!"   And no voice
    replied.
At the first I saw nought but the blackness: but soon I
    descried

A something more black than the blackness — the vast, the upright   24
Main prop which sustains the pavilion: and slow into sight
Grew a figure against it, gigantic and blackest of all.
Then a sunbeam, that burst through the tent-roof, showed Saul.

IV

He stood as erect as that tent-prop, both arms stretched out wide
On the great cross-support in the centre, that goes to each side;
He relaxed not a muscle, but hung there as, caught in his pangs   30
And waiting his change, the king-serpent all heavily hangs,
Far away from his kind, in the pine, till deliverance come
With the spring-time — so agonized Saul, drear and stark, blind and dumb.

V

Then I tuned my harp — took off the lilies we twine round its chords
Lest they snap 'neath the stress of the noontide — those sunbeams like swords!   35
And I first played the tune all our sheep know, as, one after one,
So docile they come to the pen-door till folding be done.
They are white and untorn by the bushes, for lo, they have fed
Where the long grasses stifle the water within the stream's bed;
And now one after one seeks its lodging, as star follows star
Into eve and the blue far above us, — so blue and so far!   41

VI

— Then the tune for which quails on the corniand will each leave his mate
To fly after the player; then, what makes the crickets elate

Till for boldness they fight one another; and then, what has
    weight   44
To set the quick jerboa a-musing outside his sand house —
There are none such as he for a wonder, half bird and half
    mouse!
God made all the creatures and gave them our love and our
    fear,
To give sign, we and they are his children, one family here.

VII

Then I played the help-tune of our reapers, their wine-song,
    when hand
Grasps at hand, eye lights eye in good friendship, and great
    hearts expand   50
And grow one in the sense of this world's life. — And then
    the last song
When the dead man is praised on his journey — "Bear,
    bear him along,
With his few faults shut up like dead flowerets! Are balm
    seeds not here
To console us? The land has none left such as he on the bier.
Oh, would we might keep thee, my brother!" — And then,
    the glad chaunt   55
Of the marriage — first go the young maidens, next, she
    whom we vaunt
As the beauty, the pride of our dwelling.— And then, the
    great march
Wherein man runs to man to assist him and buttress an arch
Nought can break; who shall harm them, our friends? —
    Then, the chorus intoned
As the Levites go up to the altar in glory enthroned.   60
But I stopped here: for here in the darkness Saul groaned.

VIII

And I paused, held my breath in such silence, and listened
    apart;
And the tent shook, for mighty Saul shuddered: and sparkles
    'gan dart

From the jewels that woke in his turban, at once with a
   start,   64
All its lordly male-sapphires, and rubies courageous at heart.
So the head: but the body still moved not, still hung there
   erect.
And I bent once again to my playing, pursued it unchecked.
As I sang: —

IX

   "Oh, our manhood's prime vigour! No spirit feels
   waste,   68
Not a muscle is stopped in its playing nor sinew unbraced.
Oh, the wild joys of living! the leaping from rock up to rock,
The strong rending of boughs from the fir-tree, the cool silver
   shock
Of the plunge in a pool's living water, the hunt of the bear,
And the sultriness showing the lion is couched in his lair.
And the meal, the rich dates yellowed over with gold dust
   divine,
And the locust-flesh steeped in the pitcher, the full draught
   of wine,   75
And the sleep in the dried river-channel where bulrushes
   tell
That the water was wont to go warbling so softly and well.
How good is man's life, the mere living! how fit to employ
All the heart and the soul and the senses for ever in joy!
Hast thou loved the white locks of thy father, whose sword
   thou didst guard   80
When he trusted thee forth with the armies, for glorious
   reward?
Didst thou see the thin hands of thy mother, held up as men
   sung
The low song of the nearly-departed, and hear her faint
   tongue
Joining in while it could to the witness, 'Let one more attest,
I have lived, seen God's hand through a life-time, and all was
   for best'?   85

Then they sung through their tears in strong triumph, not
    much, but the rest.
And thy brothers, the help and the contest, the working
    whence grew
Such result as, from seething grape-bundles, the spirit
    strained true:
And the friends of thy boyhood — that boyhood of wonder
    and hope,
Present promise and wealth of the future beyond the eye's
    scope —   90
Till lo, thou art grown to a monarch; a people is thine;
And all gifts, which the world offers singly, on one head
    combine!
On one head, all the beauty and strength, love and rage
    (like the throe
That, a-work in the rock, helps its labour and lets the gold go)
High ambition and deeds which surpass it, fame crowning
    them — all   95
Brought to blaze on the head of one creature — King Saul!"

x

And lo, with that leap of my spirit — heart, hand, harp and
    voice,
Each lifting Saul's name out of sorrow, each bidding re-
    joice
Saul's fame in the light it was made for — as when, dare I
    say,
The Lord's army, in rapture of service, strains through its
    array,   100
And upsoareth the cherubim-chariot —"Saul!" cried I, and
    stopped,
And waited the thing that should follow. Then Saul, who
    hung propped
By the tent's cross-support in the centre, was struck by his
    name.
Have ye seen when Spring's arrowy summons goes right to
    the aim,

And some mountain, the last to withstand her, that held (he alone,   105
While the vale laughed in freedom and flowers) on a broad bust of stone
A year's snow bound about for a breastplate, — leaves grasp of the sheet?
Fold on fold all at once it crowds thunderously down to his feet,
And there fronts you, stark, black, but alive yet, your mountain of old,   109
With his rents, the successive bequeathings of ages untold —
Yea, each harm got in fighting your battles, each furrow and scar
Of his head thrust 'twixt you and the tempest — all hail, there they are!
— Now again to be softened with verdure, again hold the nest
Of the dove, tempt the goat and its young to the green on his crest
For their food in the ardours of summer. One long shudder thrilled   115
All the tent till the very air tingled, then sank and was stilled
At the King's self left standing before me, released and aware.
What was gone, what remained?   All to traverse, 'twixt hope and despair;
Death was past, life not come: so he waited. Awhile his right hand
Held the brow, helped the eyes left too vacant forthwith to remand   120
To their place what new objects should enter: 'twas Saul as before.
I looked up and dared gaze at those eyes, nor was hurt any more
Than by slow pallid sunsets in autumn, ye watch from the shore,
At their sad level gaze o'er the ocean — a sun's slow decline
Over hills which, resolved in stern silence, o'erlap and entwine   125

Base with base to knit strength more intensely: so, arm
    folded arm
O'er the chest whose slow heavings subsided.

XI

                    What spell or what charm,
(For, awhile there was trouble within me) what next should
    I urge
To sustain him where song had restored him? — Song filled
    to the verge
His cup with the wine of this life, pressing all that it yields
Of mere fruitage, the strength and the beauty: beyond, on
    what fields,   131
Glean a vintage more potent and perfect to brighten the eye
And bring blood to the lip, and commend them the cup they
    put by?
He saith, "It is good"; still he drinks not: he lets me praise
    life,
Gives assent, yet would die for his own part.

XII

                    Then fancies grew rife
Which had come long ago on the pasture, when round me
    the sheep   136
Fed in silence — above, the one eagle wheeled slow as in
    sleep;
And I lay in my hollow and mused on the world that might
    lie
'Neath his ken, though I saw but the strip 'twixt the hill and
    the sky:
And I laughed — "Since my days are ordained to be passed
    with my flocks,   140
Let me people at least, with my fancies, the plains and the
    rocks,
Dream the life I am never to mix with, and image the show
Of mankind as they live in those fashions I hardly shall know!

Schemes of life, its best rules and right uses, the courage that
 gains,

And the prudence that keeps what men strive for." And
 now these old trains   145

Of vague thought came again; I grew surer; so, once more
 the string

Of my harp made response to my spirit, as thus —

XIII

       "Yea, my King,"

I began — "thou dost well in rejecting mere comforts that
 spring

From the mere mortal life held in common by man and by
 brute:

In our flesh grows the branch of this life, in our soul it bears
 fruit.   150

Thou hast marked the slow rise of the tree — how its stem
 trembled first

Till it passed the kid's lip, the stag's antler; then safely
 outburst

The fan-branches all round; and thou mindest when these
 too, in turn,

Broke a-bloom and the palm-tree seemed perfect: yet more
 was to learn,

E'en the good that comes in with the palm-fruit.   Our dates
 shall we slight,   155

When their juice brings a cure for all sorrow? or care for the
 plight

Of the palm's self whose slow growth produced them?   Not
 so! stem and branch

Shall decay, nor be known in their place, while the palm-
 wine shall staunch

Every wound of man's spirit in winter.   I pour thee such
 wine.   159

Leave the flesh to the fate it was fit for! the spirit be thine!

By the spirit, when age shall o'ercome thee, thou still shalt
 enjoy

More indeed, than at first when inconscious, the life of a
    boy.

Crush that life, and behold its wine running! Each deed
    thou hast done

Dies, revives, goes to work in the world; until e'en as the sun

Looking down on the earth, though clouds spoil him, though
    tempests efface,   165

Can find nothing his own deed produced not, must every-
    where trace

The results of his past summer-prime — so, each ray of thy
    will,

Every flash of thy passion and prowess, long over, shall
    thrill

Thy whole people, the countless, with ardour, till they, too,
    give forth

A like cheer to their sons, who, in turn, fill the South and
    the North   170

With the radiance thy deed was the germ of. Carouse in
    the past!

But the license of age has its limit; thou diest at last:

As the lion when age dims his eyeball, the rose at her height,

So with man — so his power and his beauty for ever take
    flight.

No! Again a long draught of my soul-wine! Look forth
    o'er the years!   175

Thou hast done now with eyes for the actual; begin with
    the seer's!

Is Saul dead? In the depth of the vale make his tomb —
    bid arise

A grey mountain of marble heaped four-square, till, built
    to the skies,

Let it mark where the great First King slumbers: whose
    fame would ye know?   179

Up above see the rock's naked face. where the record shall go

In great characters cut by the scribe — Such was Saul, so
    he did;

With the sages directing the work, by the populace chid —

F⁓ not half, they'll affirm, is comprised there! Which
    fault to amend,

In the grove with his kind grows the cedar, whereon they
    shall spend   184

(See, in tablets 'tis level before them) their praise, and record

With the gold of the graver, Saul's story — the statesman's
    great word

Side by side with the poet's sweet comment. The river's
    a-wave

With smooth paper-reeds grazing each other when prophet-
    winds rave:

So the pen gives unborn generations their due and their part

In thy being! Then, first of the mighty, thank God that
    thou art!"   190

XIV

And behold while I sang . . . but O Thou who didst grant me
    that day,

And before it not seldom hast granted thy help to essay,

Carry on and complete an adventure — my shield and my
    sword

In that act where my soul was thy servant, thy word was
    my word —   194

Still be with me, who then at the summit of human endeavour

And scaling the highest, man's thought could, gazed hope-
    less as ever

On the new stretch of heaven above me — till, mighty to
    save,

Just one lift of thy hand cleared that distance — God's
    throne from man's grave!

Let me tell out my tale to its ending — my voice to my
    heart

Which can scarce dare believe in what marvels last night I
    took part,   200

As this morning I gather the fragments, alone with my
    sheep,

And still fear lest the terrible glory evanish like sleep!

For I wake in the grey dewy covert, while Hebron up-
    heaves
The dawn struggling with night on his shoulder, and Kidron
    retrieves
Slow the damage of yesterday's sunshine.

XV

I say then — my song
While I sang thus, assuring the monarch, and ever more
    strong   206
Made a proffer of good to console him — he slowly re-
    sumed
His old motions and habitudes kingly. The right hand
    replumed
His black locks to their wonted composure, adjusted the
    swathes
Of his turban, and see — the huge sweat that his counte-
    nance bathes   210
He wipes off with the robe; and he girds now his loins as of
    yore,
And feels slow for the armlets of price, with the clasp set
    before.
He is Saul, ye remember in glory — ere error had bent
The broad brow from the daily communion; and still,
    though much spent
Be the life and the bearing that front you, the same, God
    did choose,   215
To receive what a man may waste, desecrate, never quite
    lose.
So sank he along by the tent-prop till, stayed by the pile
Of his armour and war-cloak and garments, he leaned
    there awhile,
And sat out my singing — one arm round the tent-prop, to
    raise
His bent head, and the other hung slack — till I touched on
    the praise   220
I foresaw from all men in all time, to the man patient there;

And thus ended, the harp falling forward.   Then first I was
    'ware

That he sat, as I say, with my head just above his vast knees

Which were thrust out on each side around me, like oak-roots
    which please   224

To encircle a lamb when it slumbers.   I looked up to know

If the best I could do had brought solace: he spoke not, but
    slow

Lifted up the hand slack at his side, till he laid it with care

Soft and grave, but in mild settled will, on my brow: through
    my hair

The large fingers were pushed, and he bent back my head,
    with kind power —   229

All my face back, intent to peruse it, as men do a flower.

Thus held he me there with his great eyes that scrutinized
    mine —

And oh, all my heart how it loved him! but where was the
    sign?

I yearned — "Could I help thee, my father, inventing a bliss,

I would add, to that life of the past, both the future and this;

I would give thee new life altogether, as good, ages hence,

As this moment — had love but the warrant, love's heart to
    dispense!"   236

XVI

Then the truth came upon me.   No harp more — no song
    more! outbroke —

XVII

"I have gone the whole round of creation: I saw, and I spoke:

I, a work of God's hand for that purpose, received in my
    brain

And pronounced on the rest of his handwork — returned him
    again   240

His creation's approval or censure: I spoke as I saw:

I report, as a man may of God's work — all's love, yet all's
    law

Now I lay down the judgeship he lent me. Each faculty
    tasked
To perceive him, has gained an abyss, where a dewdrop was
    asked.
Have I knowledge? confounded it shrivels at Wisdom laid
    bare.   245
Have I forethought? how purblind, how blank, to the Infi-
    nite Care!
Do I task any faculty highest, to image success?
I but open my eyes — and perfection, no more and no less,
In the kind I imagined, full-fronts me, and God is seen God
In the star, in the stone, in the flesh, in the soul and the
    clod.   250
And thus looking within and around me, I ever renew
(With that stoop of the soul which in bending upraises it too)
The submission of man's nothing-perfect to God's all-com-
    plete,
As by each new obeisance in spirit, I climb to his feet.
Yet with all this abounding experience, this deity known, 255
I shall dare to discover some province, some gift of my own.
There's a faculty pleasant to exercise, hard to hoodwink,
I am fain to keep still in abeyance (I laugh as I think),
Lest, insisting to claim and parade in it, wot ye, I worst
E'en the Giver in one gift. — Behold, I could love if I
    durst!   260
But I sink the pretension as fearing a man may o'ertake
God's own speed in the one way of love: I abstain for love's
    sake.
— What, my soul? see thus far and no farther? when doors
    great and small,
Nine-and-ninety, flew ope at our touch, should the hun-
    dredth appall?
In the least things have faith, yet distrust in the greatest of
    all?   265
Do I find love so full in my nature, God's ultimate gift,
That I doubt his own love can compete with it? Here, the
    parts shift?

Here, the creature surpass the Creator — the end, what
    Began?
Would I fain in my impotent yearning do all for this man,
And dare doubt he alone shall not help him, who yet alone
    can?   270
Would it ever have entered my mind, the bare will, much less
    power,
To bestow on this Saul what I sang of, the marvellous dower
Of the life he was gifted and filled with? to make such a soul,
Such a body, and then such an earth for insphering the whole?
And doth it not enter my mind (as my warm tears attest) 275
These good things being given, to go on, and give one more,
    the best?
Ay, to save and redeem and restore him, maintain at the
    height
This perfection — succeed with life's day-spring, death's
    minute of night?
Interpose at the difficult minute, snatch Saul the mistake,
Saul the failure, the ruin he seems now — and bid him
    awake   280
From the dream, the probation, the prelude, to find himself
    set
Clear and safe in new light and new life — a new harmony
    yet
To be run, and continued, and ended — who knows? — or
    endure!
The man taught enough, by life's dream, of the rest to make
    sure;
By the pain-throb, triumphantly winning intensified bliss,
And the next world's reward and repose, by the struggles in
    this.   286

XVIII

"I believe it! 'Tis thou, God, that givest, 'tis I who receive:
In the first is the last, in thy will is my power to believe.
All's one gift: thou canst grant it moreover, as prompt to
    my prayer

As I breathe out this breath, as I open these arms to the
        air.   290
From thy will stream the worlds, life and nature, thy dread
        Sabaoth:
I will? — the mere atoms despise me!   Why am I not loth
To look that, even that in the face too?   Why is it I dare
Think but lightly of such impuissance?   What stops my
        despair?
This; — 'tis not what man Does which exalts him, but what
        man Would do!   295
See the King — I would help him but cannot, the wishes fall
        through.
Could I wrestle to raise him from sorrow, grow poor to enrich,
To fill up his life, starve my own out, I would — knowing
        which,
I know that my service is perfect.   Oh, speak through me
        now!
Would I suffer for him that I love?   So would'st thou — so
        wilt thou!   300
So shall crown thee the topmost, ineffablest, uttermost
        crown —
And thy love fill infinitude wholly, nor leave up nor down
One spot for the creature to stand in!   It is by no breath,
Turn of eye, wave of hand, that salvation joins issue with
        death!
As thy Love is discovered almighty, almighty be proved 305
Thy power, that exists with and for it, of being Beloved!
He who did most, shall bear most; the strongest shall stand
        the most weak.
'Tis the weakness in strength, that I cry for! my flesh, that I
        seek
In the Godhead! I seek and I find it.   O Saul, it shall be
A Face like my face that receives thee; a Man like to me, 310
Thou shalt love and be loved by, for ever: a Hand like this
        hand
Shall throw open the gates of new life to thee!   See the
        Christ stand!"

XIX

I know not too well how I found my way home in the night.

There were witnesses, cohorts about me, to left and to right,

Angels, powers, the unuttered, unseen, the alive, the aware:

I repressed, I got through them as hardly, as strugglingly
    there,   316

As a runner beset by the populace famished for news —

Life or death. The whole earth was awakened, hell loosed
    with her crews;

And the stars of night beat with emotion, and tingled and shot

Out in fire the strong pain of pent knowledge: but I fainted
    not,   320

For the Hand still impelled me at once and supported,
    suppressed

All the tumult, and quenched it with quiet, and holy behest,

Till the rapture was shut in itself, and the earth sank to rest.

Anon at the dawn, all that trouble had withered from
    earth —   324

Not so much, but I saw it die out in the day's tender birth;

In the gathered intensity brought to the grey of the hills;

In the shuddering forests' held breath; in the sudden wind-
    thrills;

In the startled wild beasts that bore off, each with eye sidling
    still

Though averted with wonder and dread; in the birds stiff
    and chill

That rose heavily, as I approached them, made stupid with
    awe: 330

E'en the serpent that slid away silent — he felt the new law.

The same stared in the white humid faces upturned by the
    flowers;

The same worked in the heart of the cedar and moved the
    vine-bowers:

And the little brooks witnessing murmured, persistent and
    low,

With their obstinate, all but hushed voices — "E'en so, it is
    so!"   335

MY STAR

ALL that I know
   Of a certain star
Is, it can throw
   (Like the angled spar)
Now a dart of red,   5
   Now a dart of blue;
Till my friends have said
   They would fain see, too,
My star that dartles the red and the blue!
Then it stops like a bird; like a flower, hangs furled: 10
   They must solace themselves with the Saturn above it.
What matter to me if their star is a world?
   Mine has opened its soul to me; therefore I love it.

BY THE FIRESIDE

How well I know what I mean to do
   When the long dark autumn evenings come;
And where, my soul, is thy pleasant hue?
   With the music of all thy voices, dumb
In life's November too!   5

I shall be found by the fire, suppose.
   O'er a great wise book as beseemeth age,
While the shutters flap as the cross-wind blows,
   And I turn the page, and I turn the page,
Not verse now, only prose!   10

Till the young ones whisper, finger on lip,
   "There he is at it, deep in Greek:
Now then, or never, out we slip
   To cut from the hazels by the creek
A mainmast for our ship!"   15

I shall be at it indeed, my friends!
  Greek puts already on either side
Such a branch-work forth as soon extends
  To a vista opening far and wide,
And I pass out where it ends.   20

The outside-frame, like your hazel-trees —
  But the inside-archway widens fast,
And a rarer sort succeeds to these,
  And we slope to Italy at last
And youth, by green degrees.   25

I follow wherever I am led,
  Knowing so well the leader's hand:
Oh woman-country, wooed not wed,
  Loved all the more by earth's male-lands,
Laid to their hearts instead!   30

Look at the ruined chapel again
  Half-way up in the Alpine gorge!
Is that a tower, I point you plain,
  Or is it a mill, or an iron forge
Breaks solitude in vain?   35

A turn, and we stand in the heart of things;
  The woods are round us, heaped and dim;
From slab to slab how it slips and springs,
  The thread of water single and slim,
Through the ravage some torrent brings!   40

Does it feed the little lake below?
  That speck of white just on its marge
Is Pella; see, in the evening-glow.
  How sharp the silver spear-heads charge
When Alp meets heaven in snow!   45

On our other side is the straight-up rock;
   And a path is kept 'twixt the gorge and it
By boulder-stones where lichens mock
   The marks on a moth, and small ferns fit
Their teeth to the polished block.   50

Oh the sense of the yellow mountain-flowers,
   And thorny balls, each three in one,
The chestnuts throw on our path in showers!
   For the drop of the woodland fruit's begun,
These early November hours,   55

That crimson the creeper's leaf across
   Like a splash of blood, intense, abrupt,
O'er a shield else gold from rim to boss,
   And lay it for show on the fairy-cupped
Elf-needled mat of moss,   60

By the rose-flesh mushrooms, undivulged
   Last evening — nay, in to-day's first dew
Yon sudden coral nipple bulged,
   Where a freaked fawn-coloured flaky crew
Of toad-stools peep indulged.   65

And yonder, at foot of the fronting ridge
   That takes the turn to a range beyond,
Is the chapel reached by the one-arched bridge
   Where the water is stopped in a stagnant pond
Danced over by the midge.   70

The chapel and bridge are of stone alike,
   Blackish-grey and mostly wet;
Cut hemp-stalks steep in the narrow dike.
   See here again, how the lichens fret
And the roots of the ivy strike!   75

Poor little place, where its one priest comes
    On a festa-day, if he comes at all,
To the dozen folk from their scattered homes,
    Gathered within that precinct small
By the dozen ways one roams —   80

To drop from the charcoal-burners' huts,
    Or climb from the hemp-dressers' low shed,
Leave the grange where the woodman stores his nuts,
    Or the wattled cote where the fowlers spread
Their gear on the rock's bare juts.   85

It has some pretension too, this front,
    With its bit of fresco half-moon-wise
Set over the porch, Art's early wont:
    'Tis John in the Desert, I surmise,
But has borne the weather's brunt —   90

Not from the fault of the builder, though,
    For a pent-house properly projects
Where three carved beams make a certain show,
    Dating — good thought of our architect's —
'Five, six, nine, he lets you know.   95

And all day long a bird sings there,
    And a stray sheep drinks at the pond at times;
The place is silent and aware;
    It has had its scenes, its joys and crimes,
But that is its own affair.   100

My perfect wife, my Leonor,
    Oh heart, my own, oh eyes, mine too,
Whom else could I dare look backward for,
    With whom beside should I dare pursue
The path grey heads abhor?   105

For it leads to a crag's sheer edge with them;
   Youth, flowery all the way, there stops —
Not they; age threatens and they contemn,
   Till they reach the gulf wherein youth drops,
One inch from life's safe hem!   110

With me, youth led . . . I will speak now.
   No longer watch you as you sit
Reading by fire-light, that great brow
   And the spirit-small hand propping it,
Mutely, my heart knows how —   115

When, if I think but deep enough,
   You are wont to answer, prompt as rhyme;
And you, too, find without rebuff
   Response your soul seeks many a time
Piercing its fine flesh-stuff.   120

My own, confirm me! If I tread
   This path back, is it not in pride
To think how little I dreamed it led
   To an age so blest that, by its side,
Youth seems the waste instead?   125

My own, see where the years conduct!
   At first, 'twas something our two souls
Should mix as mists do; each is sucked
   In each now: on, the new stream rolls,
Whatever rocks obstruct.   130

Think, when our one soul understands
   The great Word which makes all things new
When earth breaks up and heaven expands,
   How will the change strike me and you
In the house not made with hands?   135

Oh, I must feel your brain prompt mine,
  Your heart anticipate my heart,
You must be just before, in fine,
  See and make me see, for your part,
New depths of the divine!   140

But who could have expected this
  When we two drew together first
Just for the obvious human bliss,
  To satisfy life's daily thirst
With a thing men seldom miss?   145

Come back with me to the first of all,
  Let us lean and love it over again,
Let us now forget and now recall,
  Break the rosary in a pearly rain
And gather what we let fall!   150

What did I say? — that a small bird sings
  All day long, save when a brown pair
Of hawks from the wood float with wide wings
  Strained to a bell: 'gainst noon-day glare
You count the streaks and rings.   155

But at afternoon or almost eve
  'Tis better; then the silence grows
To that degree, you half believe
  It must get rid of what it knows,
Its bosom does so heave.   160

Hither we walked then, side by side,
  Arm in arm and cheek to cheek,
And still I questioned or replied,
  While my heart, convulsed to really speak,
Lay choking in its pride.   165

Silent the crumbling bridge we cross,
  And pity and praise the chapel sweet,
And care about the fresco's loss,
  And wish for our souls a like retreat,
And wonder at the moss.   170

Stoop and kneel on the settle under,
  Look through the window's grated square:
Nothing to see! For fear of plunder,
  The cross is down and the altar bare,
As if thieves don't fear thunder.   175

We stoop and look in through the grate,
  See the little porch and rustic door,
Read duly the dead builder's date;
  Then cross the bridge that we crossed before,
Take the path again — but wait!   180

Oh, moment, one and infinite!
  The water slips o'er stock and stone;
The West is tender, hardly bright:
  How grey at once is the evening grown —
One star, its chrysolite!   185

We two stood there with never a third,
  But each by each, as each knew well:
The sights we saw and the sounds we heard,
  The lights and the shades made up a spell
Till the trouble grew and stirred.   190

Oh, the little more, and how much it is!
  And the little less, and what worlds away!
How a sound shall quicken content to bliss,
  Or a breath suspend the blood's best play,
And life be a proof of this!   195

Had she willed it, still had stood the screen
　　So slight, so sure, 'twixt my love and her:
I could fix her face with a guard between,
　　And find her soul as when friends confer,
Friends — lovers that might have been.　　　200

For my heart had a touch of the woodland-time,
　　Wanting to sleep now over its best.
Shake the whole tree in the summer-prime,
　　But bring to the last leaf no such test!
"Hold the last fast!" runs the rhyme.　　　205

For a chance to make your little much,
　　To gain a lover and lose a friend,
Venture the tree and a myriad such,
　　When nothing you mar but the year can mend:
But a last leaf — fear to touch!　　　210

Yet should it unfasten itself and fall
　　Eddying down till it find your face
At some slight wind — best chance of all!
　　Be your heart henceforth its dwelling-place
You trembled to forestall!　　　215

Worth how well, those dark grey eyes,
　　That hair so dark and dear, how worth
That a man should strive and agonize,
　　And taste a veriest hell on earth
For the hope of such a prize!　　　220

You might have turned and tried a man,
　　Set him a space to weary and wear,
And prove which suited more your plan,
　　His best of hope or his worst despair,
Yet end as he began.　　　225

But you spared me this, like the heart you are,
    And filled my empty heart at a word.
If two lives join, there is oft a scar,
    They are one and one, with a shadowy third;
One near one is too far.   230

A moment after, and hands unseen
    Were hanging the night around us fast;
But we knew that a bar was broken between
    Life and life: we were mixed at last
In spite of the mortal screen.   235

The forests had done it; there they stood;
    We caught for a moment the powers at play:
They had mingled us so, for once and good,
    Their work was done — we might go or stay,
They relapsed to their ancient mood.   240

How the world is made for each of us!
    How all we perceive and know in it
Tends to some moment's product thus,
    When a soul declares itself — to wit,
By its fruit, the thing it does!   245

Be hate that fruit or love that fruit,
    It forwards the general deed of man,
And each of the Many helps to recruit
    The life of the race by a general plan;
Each living his own, to boot.   250

I am named and known by that moment's feat;
    There took my station and degree;
So grew my own small life complete,
    As Nature obtained her best of me —
One born to love you, sweet!   9 5

And to watch you sink by the fireside now
    Back again, as you mutely sit
Musing by firelight, that great brow
    And the spirit-small hand propping it,
Yonder, my heart knows how!   260

So, earth has gained by one man the more,
    And the gain of earth must be heaven's gain too;
And the whole is well worth thinking o'er
    When autumn comes: which I mean to do
One day, as I said before.   265

ANY WIFE TO ANY HUSBAND

My love, this is the bitterest, that thou —
Who art all truth, and who dost love me now
    As thine eyes say, as thy voice breaks to say —
Shouldst love so truly, and couldst love me still
A whole long life through, had but love its will,   5
    Would death that leads me from thee brook delay.

I have but to be by thee, and thy hand
Will never let mine go, nor heart withstand
    The beating of my heart to reach its place.
When shall I look for thee and feel thee gone?   10
When cry for the old comfort and find none?
    Never, I know!   Thy soul is in thy face.

Oh, I should fade — 'tis willed so!   Might I save,
Gladly I would, whatever beauty gave
    Joy to thy sense, for that was precious too.   15
It is not to be granted.   But the soul
Whence the love comes, all ravage leaves that whole;
    Vainly the flesh fades; soul makes all things new.

It would not be because my eye grew dim
Thou couldst not find the love there, thanks to Him   20

Who never is dishonoured in the spark
He gave us from his fire of fires, and bade
Remember whence it sprang, nor be afraid
　　While that burns on, though all the rest grow dark.

So, how thou wouldst be perfect, white and clean　25
Outside as inside, soul and soul's demesne
　　Alike, this body given to show it by!
Oh, three-parts through the worst of life's abyss,
What plaudits from the next world after this,
　　Couldst thou repeat a stroke and gain the sky!　30

And is it not the bitterer to think
That disengage our hands and thou wilt sink
　　Although thy love was love in very deed?
I know that nature!　Pass a festive day,
Thou dost not throw its relic-flower away　35
　　Nor bid its music's loitering echo speed.

Thou let'st the stranger's glove lie where it fell;
If old things remain old things all is well,
　　For thou art grateful as becomes man best:
And hadst thou only heard me play one tune,　40
Or viewed me from a window, not so soon
　　With thee would such things fade as with the rest.

I seem to see!　We meet and part; 'tis brief;
The book I opened keeps a folded leaf,
　　The very chair I sat on, breaks the rank;　45
That is a portrait of me on the wall —
Three lines, my face comes at so slight a call:
And for all this, one little hour to thank!

But now, because the hour through years was fixed,
Because our inmost beings met and mixed,　50
　　Because thou once hast loved me — wilt thou dare
Say to thy soul and Who may list beside,

"Therefore she is immortally my bride;
  Chance cannot change my love, nor time impair.

"So, what if in the dusk of life that's left,   55
I, a tired traveller of my sun bereft,
  Look from my path when, mimicking the same,
The firefly glimpses past me, come and gone?
— Where was it till the sunset?   Where anon
  It will be at the sunrise!   What's to blame?"   60

Is it so helpful to thee?   Canst thou take
The mimic up, nor, for the true thing's sake,
  Put gently by such efforts at a beam?
Is the remainder of the way so long,
Thou need'st the little solace, thou the strong?   65
  Watch out thy watch, let weak ones doze and dream!

— Ah, but the fresher faces!   "Is it true,"
Thou'lt ask, "some eyes are beautiful and new?
  Some hair — how can one choose but grasp such wealth?
And if a man would press his lips to lips   70
Fresh as the wilding hedge-rose-cup there slips
  The dewdrop out of, must it be by stealth?

"It cannot change the love still kept for Her,
More than if such a picture I prefer
  Passing a day with, to a room's bare side: 75
The painted form takes nothing she possessed,
Yet, while the Titian's Venus lies at rest,
  A man looks.   Once more, what is there to chide?"

So must I see, from where I sit and watch,
My own self sell myself, my hand attach   80
  Its warrant to the very thefts from me —
Thy singleness of soul that made me proud,
Thy purity of heart I loved aloud,
  Thy man's-truth I was bold to bid God see!

Love so, then, if thou wilt!   Give all thou canst   85
Away to the new faces — disentranced,
   (Say it and think it) obdurate no more:
Re-issue looks and words from the old mint,
Pass them afresh, no matter whose the print,
   Image and superscription once they bore!   90

Re-coin thyself and give it them to spend, —
It all comes to the same thing at the end,
   Since mine thou wast, mine art and mine shalt be,
Faithful or faithless, sealing up the sum
Or lavish of my treasure, thou must come   95
   Back to the heart's place here I keep for thee!

Only, why should it be with stain at all?
Why must I, 'twixt the leaves of coronal,
   Put any kiss of pardon on thy brow?
Why need the other women know so much,   100
And talk together, "Such the look and such
   The smile he used to love with, then as now!"

Might I die last and show thee!   Should I find
Such hardship in the few years left behind,
   If free to take and light my lamp, and go   105
Into thy tomb, and shut the door and sit,
Seeing thy face on those four sides of it
   The better that they are so blank, I know!

Why, time was what I wanted, to turn o'er
Within my mind each look, get more and more   110
   By heart each word, too much to learn at first:
And join thee all the fitter for the pause
'Neath the low doorway's lintel. That were cause
   For lingering, though thou calledst, if I durst!

And yet thou art the nobler of us two: 115
What dare I dream of, that thou canst not do,

Outstripping my ten small steps with one stride?
I'll say then, here's a trial and a task —
Is it to bear? — if easy, I'll not ask:
    Though love fail, I can trust on in thy pride.   120

Pride? — when those eyes forestall the life behind
The death I have to go through! — when I find,
    Now that I want thy help most, all of thee!
What did I fear? Thy love shall hold me fast
Until the little minute's sleep is past   125
    And I wake saved. — And yet it will not be!

TWO IN THE CAMPAGNA

I wonder do you feel to-day
    As I have felt since, hand in hand,
We sat down on the grass, to stray
    In spirit better through the land,
This morn of Rome and May?   5

For me, I touched a thought, I know,
    Has tantalized me many times,
(Like turns of thread the spiders throw
    Mocking across our path) for rhymes
To catch at and let go.   10

Help me to hold it! First it left
    The yellowing fennel, run to seed
There, branching from the brickwork's cleft,
    Some old tomb's ruin: yonder weed
Took up the floating weft,   15

Where one small orange cup amassed
    Five beetles — blind and green they grope
Among the honey-meal: and last,
    Everywhere on the grassy slope
I traced it.   Hold it fast!   20

The champaign with its endless fleece
    Of feathery grasses everywhere!
Silence and passion, joy and peace,
    An everlasting wash of air —
Rome's ghost since her decease.   **25**

Such life here, through such lengths of hours,
    Such miracles performed in play,
Such primal naked forms of flowers,
    Such letting Nature have her way
While Heaven looks from its towers!   **30**

How say you? Let us, O my dove,
    Let us be unashamed of soul,
As earth lies bare to Heaven above!
    How is it under our control
To love or not to love?   **35**

I would that you were all to me,
    You that are just so much, no more.
Nor yours nor mine, nor slave nor free!
    Where does the fault lie? What the core
O' the wound, since wound must be?   **40**

I would I could adopt your will,
    See with your eyes, and set my heart
Beating by yours, and drink my fill
    At your soul's springs — your part my part
In life, for good and ill.   **45**

No. I yearn upward, touch you close,
    Then stand away. I kiss your cheek,
Catch your soul's warmth — I pluck the rose
    And love it more than tongue can speak —
Then the good minute goes.   **50**

Already how am I so far
    Out of that minute?   Must I go
Still like the thistle-ball, no bar,
    Onward, whenever light winds blow,
Fixed by no friendly star?   **55**

Just when I seemed about to learn!
    Where is the thread now?   Off again!
The old trick!   Only I discern —
    Infinite passion, and the pain
Of finite hearts that yearn.   **60**

MISCONCEPTIONS

THIS is a spray the Bird clung to,
    Making it blossom with pleasure,
Ere the high tree-top she sprung to,
    Fit for her nest and her treasure.
    Oh, what a hope beyond measure   **5**
Was the poor spray's, which the flying feet hung to —
So to be singled out, built in, and sung to!

This is a heart the Queen leant on,
    Thrilled in a minute erratic,
Ere the true bosom she bent on,   **10**
    Meet for love's regal dalmatic.
    Oh, what a fancy ecstatic
Was the poor heart's, ere the wanderer went on —
Love to be saved for it, proffered to, spent on!

A SERENADE AT THE VILLA

THAT was I, you heard last night,
    When there rose no moon at all,
Nor, to pierce the strained and tight
    Tent of heaven, a planet small:
Life was dead and so was light.   **5**

Not a twinkle from the fly,
   Not a glimmer from the worm;
When the crickets stopped their cry.
   When the owls forbore a term,
You heard music; that was I.   10

Earth turned in her sleep with pain,
   Sultrily suspired for proof:
In at heaven and out again,
   Lightning! — where it broke the roof,
Bloodlike, some few drops of rain.   15

What they could my words expressed,
   O my love, my all, my one!
Singing helped the verses best,
   And when singing's best was done,
To my lute I left the rest.   20

So wore night; the East was grey,
   White the broad-faced hemlock-flowers:
There would be another day;
   Ere its first of heavy hours
Found me, I had passed away.   25

What became of all the hopes,
   Words and song and lute as well?
Say, this struck you — "When life gropes
   Feebly for the path where fell
Light last on the evening slopes,   30

"One friend in that path shall be,
   To secure my step from wrong;
One to count night day for me,
   Patient through the watches long,
Serving most with none to see."   35

ONE WAY OF LOVE

Never say — as something bodes —
    "So, the worst has yet a worse!
When life halts 'neath double loads,
    Better the taskmaster's curse
Than such music on the roads!   40

"When no moon succeeds the sun,
    Nor can pierce the midnight's tent
Any star, the smallest one,
    While some drops, where lightning rent,
Show the final storm begun —   45

"When the firefly hides its spot,
    When the garden-voices fail
In the darkness thick and hot —
    Shall another voice avail,
That shape be where these are not?   50

"Has some plague a longer lease,
    Proffering its help uncouth?
Can't one even die in peace?
    As one shuts one's eyes on youth,
Is that face the last one sees?"   55

Oh, how dark your villa was,
    Windows fast and obdurate!
How the garden grudged me grass
    Where I stood — the iron gate
Ground its teeth to let me pass!   60

ONE WAY OF LOVE

ALL June I bound the rose in sheaves.
Now, rose by rose, I strip the leaves
And strew them where Pauline may pass.
She will not turn aside?   Alas!

Let them lie.   Suppose they die?   5
The chance was they might take her eye.

How many a month I strove to suit
These stubborn fingers to the lute!
To-day I venture all I know.
She will not hear my music?   So!   10
Break the string; fold music's wing:
Suppose Pauline had bade me sing!

My whole life long I learned to love.
This hour my utmost art I prove
And speak my passion — heaven or hell?   15
She will not give me heaven?   'Tis well!
Lose who may — I still can say,
Those who win heaven, blest are they!

ANOTHER WAY OF LOVE

JUNE was not over
   Though past the full,
And the best of her roses
   Had yet to blow,
    When a man I know   5
(But shall not discover,
   Since ears are dull,
   And time discloses)
Turned him and said with a man's true air,
Half sighing a smile in a yawn, as 'twere, —   10
"If I tire of your June, will she greatly care?"

Well, dear, indoors with you!
   True! serene deadness
Tries a man's temper.
   What's in the blossom   15
   June wears on her bosom?

Can it clear scores with you?
   Sweetness and redness,
   Eadem semper!
Go, let me care for it greatly or slightly!   20
If June mend her bower now, your hand left unsightly
By plucking the roses, — my June will do rightly.

And after, for pastime,
   If June be refulgent
With flowers in completeness,   25
   All petals, no prickles,
   Delicious as trickles
Of wine poured at mass-time —
   And choose One indulgent
   To redness and sweetness: 30
Or if, with experience of man and of spider,
June use my June-lightning, the strong insect-ridder,
And stop the fresh film-work — why, June will consider.

A PRETTY WOMAN

THAT fawn-skin-dappled hair of hers,
   And the blue eye
   Dear and dewy,
And that infantine fresh air of hers!

To think men cannot take you, Sweet,   5
   And enfold you,
   Ay, and hold you,
And so keep you what they make you, Sweet!

You like us for a glance, you know —
   For a word's sake   10
   Or a sword's sake,
All's the same, whate'er the chance, you know.

And in turn we make you ours, we say —
    You and youth too,
    Eyes and mouth too,   15
All the face composed of flowers, we say.

All's our own, to make the most of, Sweet —
    Sing and say for,
    Watch and pray for,
Keep a secret or go boast of, Sweet!   20

But for loving, why, you would not, Sweet,
    Though we prayed you,
    Paid you, brayed you
In a mortar — for you could not, Sweet!

So, we leave the sweet face fondly there: 25
    Be its beauty
    Its sole duty!
Let all hope of grace beyond, lie there!

And while the face lies quiet there,
    Who shall wonder   30
    That I ponder
A conclusion?   I will try it there.

As — why must one, for the love foregone,
    Scout mere liking?
    Thunder-striking   35
Earth — the heaven, we looked above for, gone!

Why, with beauty, needs there money be,
    Love with liking?
    Crush the fly-king
In his gauze, because no honey-bee?   40

May not liking be so simple-sweet,
    If love grew there
    'Twould undo there
All that breaks the cheek to dimples sweet?

Is the creature too imperfect, say?   45
    Would you mend it
    And so end it?
Since not all addition perfects aye!

Or is it of its kind, perhaps,
    Just perfection —   50
    Whence, rejection
Of a grace not to its mind, perhaps?

Shall we burn up, tread that face at once
    Into tinder,
    And so hinder   55
Sparks from kindling all the place at once?

Or else kiss away one's soul on her?
    Your love-fancies!
    — A sick man sees
Truer, when his hot eyes roll on her!   60

Thus the craftsman thinks to grace the rose —
    Plucks a mould-flower
    For his gold flower,
Uses fine things that efface the rose:

Rosy rubies make its cup more rose,   65
    Precious metals
    Ape the petals —
Last, some old king locks it up, morose!

Then how grace a rose?   I know a way!
    Leave it, rather.   70
    Must you gather?
Smell, kiss, wear it — at last, throw away!

RESPECTABILITY

DEAR, had the world in its caprice
 Deigned to proclaim "I know you both,
 Have recognized your plighted troth,
Am sponsor for you: live in peace!" —
How many precious months and years   5
 Of youth had passed, that speed so fast,
 Before we found it out at last,
The world, and what it fears!

How much of priceless life were spent
 With men that every virtue decks,   10
 And women models of their sex,
Society's true ornament, —
Ere we dared wander, nights like this,
 Through wind and rain, and watch the Seine,
 And feel the Boulevart break again   15
To warmth and light and bliss!

I know! the world proscribes not love;
 Allows my finger to caress
 Your lips, contour and downiness,
Provided it supply a glove.   20
The world's good word! — the Institute!
 Guizot receives Montalembert!
 Eh?   Down the court three lampions flare:
Put forward your best foot!

IN THREE DAYS

So, I shall see her in three days
And just one night, but nights are short,
Then two long hours, and that is morn.
See how I come, unchanged, unworn!
Feel, where my life broke off from thine,   5

How fresh the splinters keep and fine —
Only a touch and we combine!

Too long, this time of year, the days!
But nights, at least the nights are short.
As night shows where her one moon is,   10
A hand's-breadth of pure light and bliss,
So life's night gives my lady birth
And my eyes hold her!   What is worth
The rest of heaven, the rest of earth?

O loaded curls, release your store   15
Of warmth and scent, as once before
The tingling hair did, lights and darks
Outbreaking into fairy sparks,
When under curl and curl I pried
After the warmth and scent inside,   20
Through lights and darks how manifold —
The dark inspired, the light controlled!
As early Art embrowns the gold.

What great fear, should one say, "Three days
That change the world might change as well   25
Your fortune; and if joy delays,
Be happy that no worse befell!"
What small fear, if another says,
"Three days and one short night beside
May throw no shadow on your ways;   30
But years must teem with change untried,
With chance not easily defied,
With an end somewhere undescried."
No fear! — or if a fear be born
This minute, it dies out in scorn.   35
Fear?   I shall see her in three days
And one night, now the nights are short,
Then just two hours, and that is morn.

IN A YEAR

NEVER any more,
  While I live,
Need I hope to see his face
  As before.
Once his love grown chill,   5
  Mine may strive:
Bitterly we re-embrace,
  Single still.

Was it something said,
  Something done,   10
Vexed him?   Was it touch of hand,
  Turn of head?
Strange! that very way
  Love begun:
I as little understand   15
  Love's decay.

When I sewed or drew,
  I recall
How he looked as if I sung,
  — Sweetly too.   20
If I spoke a word,
  First of all
Up his cheek the colour sprung,
  Then he heard.

Sitting by my side,   25
  At my feet,
So he breathed but air I breathed,
  Satisfied!
I, too, at love's brim
  Touched the sweet: 30
I would die if death bequeathed
  Sweet to him.

"Speak, I love thee best!"
   He exclaimed:
"Let thy love my own foretell!"   35
   I confessed:
"Clasp my heart on thine
   Now unblamed,
Since upon thy soul as well
   Hangeth mine!"   40

Was it wrong to own,
   Being truth?
Why should all the giving prove
   His alone?
I had wealth and ease,   45
   Beauty, youth:
Since my lover gave me love,
   I gave these.

That was all I meant
   — To be just,   50
And the passion I had raised,
   To content.
Since he chose to change
   Gold for dust,
If I gave him what he praised   55
   Was it strange?

Would he loved me yet,
   On and on,
While I found some way undreamed
   — Paid my debt!   60
Gave more life and more,
   Till, all gone,
He should smile "She never seemed
   Mine before.

"What, she felt the while,   65
   Must I think?

Love's so different with us men!"
  He should smile:
"Dying for my sake —
  White and pink!   70
Can't we touch these bubbles then
  But they break?"

Dear, the pang is brief,
  Do thy part,
Have thy pleasure!   How perplexed   75
  Grows belief!
Well, this cold clay clod
  Was man's heart:
Crumble it, and what comes next?
  Is it God?   80

WOMEN AND ROSES

I

I DREAM of a red-rose tree.
And which of its roses three
Is the dearest rose to me?

II

Round and round, like a dance of snow
In a dazzling drift, as its guardians, go   5
Floating the women faded for ages,
Sculptured in stone, on the poet's pages.
Then follow women fresh and gay,
Living and loving and loved to-day,
Last, in the rear, flee the multitude of maidens, 10
Beauties yet unborn.   And all, to one cadence,
They circle their rose on my rose tree.

III

Dear rose, thy term is reached,
Thy leaf hangs loose and bleached:
Bees pass it unimpeached.   15

IV

Stay, then, stoop, since I cannot climb,
You, great shapes of the antique time!
How shall I fix you, fire you, freeze you,
Break my heart at your feet to please you?
Oh, to possess and be possessed!   20
Hearts that beat 'neath each pallid breast!
Once but of love, the poesy, the passion,
Drink but once and die! — In vain, the same fashion,
They circle their rose on my rose tree.

V

Dear rose, thy joy's undimmed,   25
Thy cup is ruby-rimmed,
Thy cup's heart nectar-brimmed.

VI

Deep, as drops from a statue's plinth
The bee sucked in by the hyacinth,
So will I bury me while burning,   30
Quench like him at a plunge my yearning,
Eyes in your eyes, lips on your lips!
Fold me fast where the cincture slips,
Prison all my soul in eternities of pleasure,
Girdle me for once!   But no — the old measure,   35
They circle their rose on my rose tree.

VII

Dear rose without a thorn,
Thy bud's the babe unborn:
First streak of a new morn.

VIII

Wings, lend wings for the cold, the clear!   40
What is far conquers what is near.

Roses will bloom nor want beholders,
Sprung from the dust where our flesh moulders,
What shall arrive with the cycle's change?
A novel grace and a beauty strange.   45
I will make an Eve, be the artist that began her,
Shaped her to his mind! — Alas! in like manner
They circle their rose on my rose tree.

BEFORE

Let them fight it out, friend! things have gone too far.
God must judge the couple: leave them as they are
— Whichever one's the guiltless, to his glory,
And whichever one the guilt's with, to my story!

Why, you would not bid men, sunk in such a slough,   5
Strike no arm out further, stick and stink as now,
Leaving right and wrong to settle the embroilment,
Heaven with snaky hell, in torture and entoilment?

Who's the culprit of them?   How must he conceive
God — the queen he caps to, laughing in his sleeve,   10
"'Tis but decent to profess oneself beneath her:
Still, one must not be too much in earnest, either!"

Better sin the whole sin, sure that God observes;
Then go live his life out!   Life will try his nerves,
When the sky, which noticed all, makes no disclosure,   15
And the earth keeps up her terrible composure.

Let him pace at pleasure, past the walls of rose,
Pluck their fruits when grape-trees graze him as he goes!
For he 'gins to guess the purpose of the garden,
With the sly mute thing, beside there, for a warden.   20

What's the leopard-dog-thing, constant at his side,
A leer and lie in every eye of its obsequious hide?

When will come an end to all the mock obeisance,
And the price appear that pays for the misfeasance?

So much for the culprit.   Who's the martyred man?   25
Let him bear one stroke more, for be sure he can!
He that strove thus evil's lump with good to leaven,
Let him give his blood at last and get his heaven!

All or nothing, stake it!   Trusts he God or no?
Thus far and no farther? farther? be it so!   30
Now, enough of your chicane of prudent pauses,
Sage provisos, sub-intents and saving-clauses!

Ah, "forgive" you bid him?   While God's champion lives,
Wrong shall be resisted: dead, why, he forgives.
But you must not end my friend ere you begin him;   35
Evil stands not crowned on earth, while breath is in him.

Once more — Will the wronger, at this last of all,
Dare to say, "I did wrong," rising in his fall?
No? — Let go, then!   Both the fighters to their places!
While I count three, step you back as many paces!   40

AFTER

TAKE the cloak from his face, and at first
    Let the corpse do its worst!

How he lies in his rights of a man!
    Death has done all death can.
And, absorbed in the new life he leads,   5
    He recks not, he heeds
Nor his wrong nor my vengeance; both strike
    On his senses alike,
And are lost in the solemn and strange
    Surprise of the change.   10

Ha, what avails death to erase
   His offence, my disgrace?
I would we were boys as of old
   In the field, by the fold:
His outrage, God's patience, man's scorn   15
   Were so easily borne!

I stand here now, he lies in his place:
   Cover the face!

THE GUARDIAN-ANGEL

A PICTURE AT FANO

DEAR and great Angel, wouldst thou only leave
   That child, when thou hast done with him, for me!
Let me sit all the day here, that when eve
   Shall find performed thy special ministry,
And time come for departure, thou, suspending   5
Thy flight, may'st see another child for tending,
   Another still, to quiet and retrieve.

Then I shall feel thee step one step, no more,
   From where thou standest now, to where I gaze,
— And suddenly my head is covered o'er   10
   With those wings, white above the child who prays
Now on that tomb — and I shall feel thee guarding
Me, out of all the world; for me, discarding
   Yon heaven thy home, that waits and opes its door

I would not look up thither past thy head   15
   Because the door opes, like that child, I know,
For I should have thy gracious face instead,
   Thou bird of God!   And wilt thou bend me low
Like him, and lay, like his, my hands together,
And lift them up to pray, and gently tether   20
   Me, as thy lamb there, with thy garment's spread?

If this was ever granted, I would rest
  My head beneath thine, while thy healing hands
Close-covered both my eyes beside thy breast,
  Pressing the brain, which too much thought expands,
Back to its proper size again, and smoothing   26
Distortion down till every nerve had soothing,
  And all lay quiet, happy and suppressed.

How soon all worldly wrong would be repaired!
  I think how I should view the earth and skies   30
And sea, when once again my brow was bared
  After thy healing, with such different eyes.
O world, as God has made it! All is beauty:
And knowing this, is love, and love is duty.
  What further may be sought for or declared?   35

Guercino drew this angel I saw teach
  (Alfred, dear friend!) — that little child to pray,
Holding the little hands up, each to each
  Pressed gently, — with his own head turned away
Over the earth where so much lay before him   40
Of work to do, though heaven was opening o'er him,
  And he was left at Fano by the beach.

We were at Fano, and three times we went
  To sit and see him in his chapel there,
And drink his beauty to our soul's content   45
  — My angel with me too: and since I care
For dear Guercino's fame (to which in power
And glory comes this picture for a dower,
  Fraught with a pathos so magnificent) —

And since he did not work thus earnestly   50
  At all times, and has else endured some wrong —
I took one thought his picture struck from me,
  And spread it out, translating it to song.

My love is here.   Where are you, dear old friend?
How rolls the Wairoa at your world's far end?   **55**
   This is Ancona, yonder is the sea.

MEMORABILIA

   Aʜ, did you once see Shelley plain,
     And did he stop and speak to you,
   And did you speak to him again?
     How strange it seems and new!

   But you were living before that,   **5**
     And also you are living after;
   And the memory I started at —
     My starting moves your laughter!

   I crossed a moor, with a name of its own
     And a certain use in the world no doubt,   **10**
   Yet a hand's-breadth of it shines alone
     'Mid the blank miles round about:

   For there I picked up on the heather,
     And there I put inside my breast
   A moulted feather, an eagle-feather!   **15**
     Well, I forget the rest.

POPULARITY

   Sᴛᴀɴᴅ still, true poet that you are!
     I know you; let me try and draw you.
   Some night you'll fail us: when afar
     You rise, remember one man saw you,
   Knew you, and named a star!   **5**

   My star, God's glow-worm!   Why extend
     That loving hand of his which leads you,
   Yet locks you safe from end to end
     Of this dark world, unless he needs you,
   Just saves your light to spend?   **10**

His clenched hand shall unclose at last,
  I know. and let out all the beauty:
My poet holds the future fast,
  Accepts the coming ages' duty,
Their present for this past.   15

That day, the earth's feast-master's brow
  Shall clear, to God the chalice raising:
"Others give best at first, but thou
  Forever set'st our table praising,
Keep'st the good wine till now!"   20

Meantime, I'll draw you as you stand.
  With few or none to watch and wonder:
I'll say — a fisher, on the sand
  By Tyre the old, with ocean-plunder,
A netful, brought to land.   25

Who has not heard how Tyrian shells
  Enclosed the blue, that dye of dyes
Whereof one drop worked miracles,
  And coloured like Astarte's eyes
Raw silk the merchant sells?   30

And each bystander of them all
  Could criticise, and quote tradition
How depths of blue sublimed some pall
  — To get which pricked a king's ambition;
Worth sceptre, crown and ball.   35

Yet there's the dye, in that rough mesh,
  The sea has only just o'er-whispered!
Live whelks, each lip's beard dripping fresh,
  As if they still the water's lisp heard
Through foam the rock-weeds thresh.   40

*simple
poem
on surface*

Enough to furnish Solomon
   Such hangings for his cedar-house,
That, when gold-robed he took the throne
   In that abyss of blue, the Spouse
Might swear his presence shone   45

Most like the centre-spike of gold
   Which burns deep in the bluebell's womb,
What time, with ardours manifold,
   The bee goes singing to her groom,
Drunken and overbold.   50

Mere conchs! not fit for warp or woof!
   Till cunning come to pound and squeeze
And clarify — refine to proof
   The liquor filtered by degrees,
While the world stands aloof.   55

And there's the extract, flasked and fine,
   And priced and salable at last!
And Hobbs, Nobbs, Stokes and Nokes combine
   To paint the future from the past,
Put blue into their line.   60

Hobbs hints blue — straight he turtle eats:
   Nobbs prints blue — claret crowns his cup:
Nokes outdares Stokes in azure feats —
   Both gorge.   Who fished the murex up?
What porridge had John Keats?   65

INCIDENT OF THE FRENCH CAMP

You know, we French stormed Ratisbon:
   A mile or so away,
On a little mound, Napoleon
   Stood on our storming-day;

With neck out-thrust, you fancy how,   5
 Legs wide, arms locked behind,
As if to balance the prone brow
 Oppressive with its mind.

Just as perhaps he mused "My plans
 That soar, to earth may fall,   10
Let once my army-leader Lannes
 Waver at yonder wall" —
Out 'twixt the battery-smokes there flew
 A rider, bound on bound
Full-galloping; nor bridle drew   15
 Until he reached the mound.

Then off there flung in smiling joy,
 And held himself erect
By just his horse's mane, a boy:
 You hardly could suspect —   20
(So tight he kept his lips compressed,
 Scarce any blood came through)
You looked twice ere you saw his breast
 Was all but shot in two.

"Well," cried he, "Emperor, by God's grace   25
 We've got you Ratisbon!
The Marshal's in the market-place,
 And you'll be there anon
To see your flag-bird flap his vans
 Where I, to heart's desire,   30
Perched him!"   The chief's eye flashed; his plans
 Soared up again like fire.

The chief's eye flashed; but presently
 Softened itself, as sheathes
A film the mother-eagle's eye   35
 When her bruised eaglet breathes;

"You're wounded!"   "Nay," the soldier's pride
    Touched to the quick, he said:
"I'm killed, Sire!"   And his chief beside
    Smiling the boy fell dead.   40

THE PATRIOT

AN OLD STORY

It was roses, roses, all the way,
    With myrtle mixed in my path like mad:
The house-roofs seemed to heave and sway,
    The church-spires flamed, such flags they had,
A year ago on this very day.   5

The air broke into a mist with bells,
    The old walls rocked with the crowd and cries.
Had I said, "Good folk, mere noise repels —
    But give me your sun from yonder skies!"
They had answered, "And afterward, what else?"   10

Alack, it was I who leaped at the sun
    To give it my loving friends to keep!
Naught man could do have I left undone:
    And you see my harvest, what I reap
This very day, now a year is run.   15

There's nobody on the house-tops now —
    Just a palsied few at the windows set;
For the best of the sight is, all allow,
    At the Shambles' Gate — or, better yet,
By the very scaffold's foot, I trow.   20

I go in the rain, and, more than needs,
    A rope cuts both my wrists behind;
And I think, by the feel, my forehead bleeds,
    For they fling, whoever has a mind,
Stones at me for my year's misdeeds.   25

Thus I entered, and thus I go!
  In triumphs, people have dropped down dead.
"Paid by the world, what dost thou owe
  Me?" — God might question; now instead,
'Tis God shall repay: I am safer so.   30

MY LAST DUCHESS

FERRARA

That's my last Duchess painted on the wall,
Looking as if she were alive. I call
That piece a wonder, now: Frà Pandolf's hands
Worked busily a day, and there she stands.
Will't please you sit and look at her? I said   5
"Frà Pandolf" by design, for never read
Strangers like you that pictured countenance,
The depth and passion of its earnest glance,
But to myself they turned (since none puts by
The curtain I have drawn for you, but I)   10
And seemed as they would ask me, if they durst,
How such a glance came there; so, not the first
Are you to turn and ask thus. Sir, 'twas not
Her husband's presence only, called that spot
Of joy into the Duchess' cheek: perhaps   15
Frà Pandolf chanced to say, "Her mantle laps
Over my lady's wrist too much," or "Paint
Must never hope to reproduce the faint
Half-flush that dies along her throat:" such stuff
Was courtesy, she thought, and cause enough   20
For calling up that spot of joy. She had
A heart — how shall I say? — too soon made glad,
Too easily impressed: she liked whate'er
She looked on, and her looks went everywhere.
Sir, 'twas all one! My favour at her breast,   25
The dropping of the daylight in the West,
The bough of cherries some officious fool
Broke in the orchard for her, the white mule

She rode with round the terrace --- all and each
Would draw from her alike the approving speech,   30
Or blush, at least.   She thanked men — good! but thanked
Somehow — I know not how — as if she ranked
My gift of a nine-hundred-years-old name
With anybody's gift.   Who'd stoop to blame
This sort of trifling?   Even had you skill   35
In speech — (which I have not) — to make your will
Quite clear to such an one, and say, "Just this
Or that in you disgusts me; here you miss,
Or there exceed the mark" — and if she let
Herself be lessoned so, nor plainly set   40
Her wits to yours, forsooth, and made excuse,
— E'en then would be some stooping; and I choose
Never to stoop.   Oh sir, she smiled, no doubt,
Whene'er I passed her; but who passed without
Much the same smile?   This grew; I gave commands;   45
Then all smiles stopped together.   There she stands
As if alive.   Will't please you rise?   We'll meet
The company below, then.   I repeat,
The Count your master's known munificence
Is ample warrant that no just pretence   50
Of mine for dowry will be disallowed;
Though his fair daughter's self, as I avowed
At starting, is my object.   Nay, we'll go
Together down, sir.   Notice Neptune, though,
Taming a sea-horse, thought a rarity,   55
Which Claus of Innsbruck cast in bronze for me!

THE BOY AND THE ANGEL

MORNING, evening, noon and night,
"Praise God!" sang Theocrite.

Then to his poor trade he turned,
Whereby the daily meal was earned.

Hard he laboured, long and well; 5
O'er his work the boy's curls fell.

But ever, at each period,
He stopped and sang, "Praise God!"

Then back again his curls he threw,
And cheerful turned to work anew. 10

Said Blaise, the listening monk, "Well done;
I doubt not thou art heard, my son:

"As well as if thy voice to-day
Were praising God, the Pope's great way.

"This Easter Day, the Pope at Rome 15
Praises God from Peter's dome."

Said Theocrite, "Would God that I
Might praise him that great way, and die!"

Night passed, day shone,
And Theocrite was gone. 20

With God a day endures alway,
A thousand years are but a day.

God said in heaven, "Nor day nor night
Now brings the voice of my delight."

Then Gabriel, like a rainbow's birth, 25
Spread his wings and sank to earth;

Entered, in flesh, the empty cell,
Lived there, and played the craftsman well;

And morning, evening, noon and night,
Praised God in place of Theocrite.   30

And from a boy, to youth he grew:
The man put off the stripling's hue:

The man matured and fell away
Into the season of decay:

And ever o'er the trade he bent,   35
And ever lived on earth content.

(He did God's will; to him, all one
If on the earth or in the sun.)

God said, "A praise is in mine ear;
There is no doubt in it, no fear: 40

"So sing old worlds, and so
New worlds that from my footstool go.

"Clearer loves sound other ways:
I miss my little human praise."

Then forth sprang Gabriel's wings, off fell   45
The flesh disguise, remained the cell.

'Twas Easter Day: he flew to Rome,
And paused above Saint Peter's dome.

In the tiring-room close by
The great outer gallery,   50

With his holy vestments dight,
Stood the new Pope, Theocrite:

And all his past career
Came back upon him clear.

Since when, a boy, he plied his trade,   **55**
Till on his life the sickness weighed;

And in his cell, when death drew near,
An angel in a dream brought cheer:

And rising from the sickness drear.
He grew a priest, and now stood here.   **60**

To the East with praise he turned,
And on his sight the angel burned.

"I bore thee from thy craftsman's cell,
And set thee here; I did not well.

"Vainly I left my angel-sphere,   **65**
Vain was thy dream of many a year.

"Thy voice's praise seemed weak; it dropped —
Creation's chorus stopped!

"Go back and praise again
The early way, while I remain.   **70**

"With that weak voice of our disdain,
Take up creation's pausing strain.

"Back to the cell and poor employ:
Resume the craftsman and the boy!"

Theocrite grew old at home;   **75**
A new Pope dwelt in Peter's dome.

One vanished as the other died:
They sought God side by side.

INSTANS TYRANNUS

I

Of the million or two, more or less,
I rule and possess,
One man, for some cause undefined,
Was least to my mind.

II

I struck him, he grovelled, of course —   5
For, what was his force?
I pinned him to earth with my weight
And persistence of hate:
And he lay, would not moan, would not curse,
As his lot might be worse.   10

III

"Were the object less mean, would he stand
At the swing of my hand!
For obscurity helps him and blots
The hole where he squats."
So, I set my five wits on the stretch   15
To inveigle the wretch.
All in vain!   Gold and jewels I threw,
Still he couched there perdue;
I tempted his blood and his flesh,
Hid in roses my mesh,   20
Choicest cates and the flagon's best spilth:
Still he kept to his filth.

IV

Had he kith now or kin, were access
To his heart, did I press:
Just a son or a mother to seize!   25
No such booty as these.

Were it simply a friend to pursue
'Mid my million or two,
Who could pay me in person or pelf
What he owes me himself!　　　　　30
No: I could not but smile through my chafe:
For the fellow lay safe
As his mates do, the midge and the nit,
— Through minuteness, to wit.

V

Then a humour more great took its place　　35
At the thought of his face,
The droop, the low cares of the mouth,
The trouble uncouth
'Twixt the brows, all that air one is fain
To put out of its pain.　　　　　40
And, "no!" I admonished myself,
"Is one mocked by an elf,
Is one baffled by toad or by rat?
The gravamen's in that!
How the lion, who crouches to suit　　45
His back to my foot,
Would admire that I stand in debate!
But the small turns the great
If it vexes you — that is the thing!
Toad or rat vex the king?　　　　50
Though I waste half my realm to unearth
Toad or rat, 'tis well worth!"

VI

So, I soberly laid my last plan
To extinguish the man.
Round his creep-hole, with never a break,　　55
Ran my fires for his sake;
Overhead, did my thunder combine
With my underground mine:

Till I looked from my labour content
To enjoy the event.   60

VII

When sudden . . . how think ye, the end?
Did I say "without friend"?
Say rather, from marge to blue marge
The whole sky grew his targe
With the sun's self for visible boss,   65
While an Arm ran across
Which the earth heaved beneath like a breast
Where the wretch was safe prest!
Do you see?   Just my vengeance complete,
The man sprang to his feet,   70
Stood erect, caught at God's skirts, and prayed!
— So, *I* was afraid!

THE GLOVE

(PETER RONSARD *loquitur*)

"HEIGHO," yawned one day King Francis,
"Distance all value enhances!
When a man's busy, why, leisure
Strikes him as wonderful pleasure:
'Faith, and at leisure once is he?   5
Straightway he wants to be busy.
Here we've got peace; and aghast I'm
Caught thinking war the true pastime.
Is there a reason in metre?
Give us your speech, master Peter!"   10
I who, if mortal dare say so,
Ne'er am at loss with my Naso,
"Sire," I replied, "joys prove cloudlets:
Men are the merest Ixions" —
Here the King whistled aloud, "Let's   15
— Heigho — go look at our lions!"

Such are the sorrowful chances
If you talk fine to King Francis.

And so, to the courtyard proceeding,
Our company, Francis was leading,   20
Increased by new followers tenfold
Before he arrived at the penfold:
Lords, ladies, like clouds which bedizen
At sunset the western horizon.
And Sir De Lorge pressed 'mid the foremost   25
With the dame he professed to adore most.
Oh, what a face!   One by fits eyed
Her, and the horrible pitside;
For the penfold surrounded a hollow
Which led where the eye scarce dared follow,   30
And shelved to the chamber secluded
Where Bluebeard, the great lion, brooded.
The King hailed his keeper, an Arab
As glossy and black as a scarab,
And bade him make sport and at once stir   35
Up and out of his den the old monster.
They opened a hole in the wire-work
Across it, and dropped there a firework,
And fled: one's heart's beating redoubled:
A pause, while the pit's mouth was troubled,   40
The blackness and silence so utter,
By the firework's slow sparkling and sputter;
Then earth in a sudden contortion
Gave out to our gaze her abortion.
Such a brute!   Were I friend Clement Marot   45
(Whose experience of Nature's but narrow,
And whose faculties move in no small mist
When he versifies David the Psalmist)
I should study that brute to describe you
Illum Juda Leonem de Tribu.   50
One's whole blood grew curdling and creepy
To see the black mane, vast and heapy,

The tail in the air stiff and straining,
The wide eyes, nor waxing nor waning,
As over the barrier which bounded   55
His platform, and us who surrounded
The barrier, they reached and they rested
On space that might stand him in best stead:
For who knew, he thought, what the amazement,
The eruption of clatter and blaze meant,   60
And if, in this minute of wonder,
No outlet, 'mid lightning and thunder,
Lay broad, and, his shackles all shivered,
The lion at last was delivered?
Ay, that was the open sky o'erhead!   65
And you saw by the flash on his forehead,
By the hope in those eyes wide and steady,
He was leagues in the desert already,
Driving the flocks up the mountain,
Or catlike couched hard by the fountain   70
To waylay the date-gathering negress:
So guarded he entrance or egress.
"How he stands!" quoth the King: "we may well swear,
(No novice, we've won our spurs elsewhere
And so can afford the confession,)   75
We exercise wholesome discretion
In keeping aloof from his threshold,
Once hold you, those jaws want no fresh hold,
Their first would too pleasantly purloin
The visitor's brisket or surloin: 80
But who's he would prove so foolhardy?
Not the best man of Marignan, pardie!"

The sentence no sooner was uttered,
Than over the rails a glove fluttered,
Fell close to the lion, and rested: 85
The dame 'twas, who flung it and jested
With life so, De Lorge had been wooing
For months past; he sat there pursuing

His suit, weighing out with nonchalance
Fine speeches like gold from a balance.   90

Sound the trumpet, no true knight's a tarrier!
De Lorge made one leap at the barrier,
Walked straight to the glove — while the lion
Ne'er moved, kept his far-reaching eye on
The palm-tree-edged desert-spring's sapphire,   95
And the musky oiled skin of the Kaffir —
Picked it up, and as calmly retreated,
Leaped back where the lady was seated,
And full in the face of its owner
Flung the glove.

    "Your heart's queen, you dethrone her?   100
So should I!" — cried the King — "'twas mere vanity,
Not love, set that task to humanity!"
Lords and ladies alike turned with loathing
From such a proved wolf in sheep's clothing

Not so, I; for I caught an expression   105
In her brow's undisturbed self-possession
Amid the Court's scoffing and merriment —
As if from no pleasing experiment
She rose, yet of pain not much heedful
So long as the process was needful —   110
As if she had tried in a crucible,
To what "speeches like gold" were reducible,
And, finding the finest prove copper,
Felt the smoke in her face was but proper;
To know what she had *not* to trust to,   115
Was worth all the ashes and dust too.
She went out 'mid hooting and laughter;
Clement Marot stayed; I followed after,
And asked, as a grace, what it all meant?
If she wished not the rash deed's recallment?   120
"For I" — so I spoke — "am a poet:
Human nature — behoves that I know it!"

She told me, "Too long had I heard
Of the deed proved alone by the word:
For my love — what De Lorge would not dare! 125
With my scorn — what De Lorge could compare!
And the endless descriptions of death
He would brave when my lip formed a breath,
I must reckon as braved, or, of course,
Doubt his word — and moreover, perforce, 130
For such gifts as no lady could spurn,
Must offer my love in return.
When I looked on your lion, it brought
All the dangers at once to my thought,
Encountered by all sorts of men, 135
Before he was lodged in his den —
From the poor slave whose club or bare hands
Dug the trap, set the snare on the sands,
With no King and no Court to applaud,
By no shame, should he shrink, overawed, 140
Yet to capture the creature made shift,
That his rude boys might laugh at the gift,
— To the page who last leaped o'er the fence
Of the pit, on no greater pretence
Than to get back the bonnet he dropped, 145
Lest his pay for a week should be stopped.
So, wiser I judged it to make
One trial what 'death for my sake'
Really meant, while the power was yet mine,
Than to wait until time should define 150
Such a phrase not so simply as I,
Who took it to mean just 'to die.'
The blow a glove gives is but weak:
Does the mark yet discolour my cheek?
But when the heart suffers a blow, 155
Will the pain pass so soon, do you know?"

I looked, as away she was sweeping,
And saw a youth eagerly keeping

As close as he dared to the doorway.
No doubt that a noble should more weigh　　**160**
His life than befits a plebeian;
And yet, had our brute been Nemean —
(I judge by a certain calm fervour
The youth stepped with, forward to serve her)　**164**
— He'd have scarce thought you did him the worst turn
If you whispered, "Friend, what you'd get, first earn!"
And when, shortly after, she carried
Her shame from the Court, and they married,
To that marriage some happiness, maugre
The voice of the Court, I dared augur.　　**170**

For De Lorge, he made women with men vie,
Those in wonder and praise, these in envy;
And in short stood so plain a head taller
That he wooed and won . . . how do you call her?
The beauty, that rose in the sequel　　**175**
To the King's love, who loved her a week well.
And 'twas noticed he never would honour
De Lorge (who looked daggers upon her)
With the easy commission of stretching
His legs in the service, and fetching　　**180**
His wife, from her chamber, those straying
Sad gloves she was always mislaying,
While the King took the closet to chat in, —
But of course this adventure came pat in.
And never the King told the story,　　**185**
How bringing a glove brought such glory,
But the wife smiled — "His nerves are grown firmer:
Mine he brings now and utters no murmur."

meet the coming evil or attack is the best offence

Venienti occurrite morbo!
With which moral I drop my theorbo.　　**190**

THE ITALIAN IN ENGLAND

THAT second time they hunted me
From hill to plain, from shore to sea,
And Austria, hounding far and wide
Her bloodhounds through the countryside,
Breathed hot and instant on my trace —   5
I made six days a hiding-place
Of that dry green old aqueduct
Where I and Charles, when boys, have plucked
The fireflies from the roof above,
Bright creeping through the moss they love: 10
— How long it seems since Charles was lost!
Six days the soldiers crossed and crossed
The country in my very sight;
And when that peril ceased at night,
The sky broke out in red dismay   15
With signal fires; well, there I lay
Close covered o'er in my recess,
Up to the neck in ferns and cress,
Thinking on Metternich our friend,
And Charles's miserable end,   20
And much beside, two days; the third,
Hunger o'ercame me when I heard
The peasants from the village go
To work among the maize; you know,
With us in Lombardy, they bring   25
Provisions packed on mules, a string
With little bells that cheer their task,
And casks, and boughs on every cask
To keep the sun's heat from the wine;
These I let pass in jingling line,   30
And, close on them, dear noisy crew,
The peasants from the village, too:
For at the very rear would troop
Their wives and sisters in a group
To help, I knew.   When these had passed,   35

I threw my glove to strike the last,
Taking the chance: she did not start,
Much less cry out, but stooped apart,
One instant rapidly glanced round,
And saw me beckon from the ground;   40
A wild bush grows and hides my crypt;
She picked my glove up while she stripped
A branch off, then rejoined the rest
With that; my glove lay in her breast.
Then I drew breath: they disappeared: 45
It was for Italy I feared.

An hour, and she returned alone
Exactly where my glove was thrown.
Meanwhile came many thoughts; on me
Rested the hopes of Italy;   50
I had devised a certain tale
Which, when 'twas told her, could not fail
Persuade a peasant of its truth;
I meant to call a freak of youth
This hiding, and give hopes of pay,   55
And no temptation to betray.
But when I saw that woman's face,
Its calm simplicity of grace,
Our Italy's own attitude
In which she walked thus far, and stood,   60
Planting each naked foot so firm,
To crush the snake and spare the worm —
At first sight of her eyes, I said,
"I am that man upon whose head
They fix the price, because I hate   65
The Austrians over us: the State
Will give you gold — oh, gold so much! —
If you betray me to their clutch,
And be your death, for aught I know,
If once they find you saved their foe.   70
Now, you must bring me food and drink,

And also paper, pen and ink,
And carry safe what I shall write
To Padua, which you'll reach at night
Before the duomo shuts; go in,   75
And wait till Tenebræ begin;
Walk to the third confessional,
Between the pillar and the wall,
And kneeling whisper, *Whence comes peace?*
Say it a second time, then cease;   80
And if the voice inside returns,
From Christ and Freedom; what concerns
The cause of Peace? — for answer, slip
My letter where you placed your lip;
Then come back happy we have done   85
Our mother service — I, the son,
As you the daughter of our land!"

    Three mornings more, she took her stand
In the same place, with the same eyes:
I was no surer of sunrise   90
Than of her coming.   We conferred
Of her own prospects, and I heard
She had a lover — stout and tall,
She said — then let her eyelids fall,
"He could do much" — as if some doubt   95
Entered her heart — then, passing out,
"She could not speak for others, who
Had other thoughts; herself she knew:"
And so she brought me drink and food.
After four days, the scouts pursued   100
Another path; at last arrived
The help my Paduan friends contrived
To furnish me: she brought the news.
For the first time I could not choose
But kiss her hand, and lay my own   105
Upon her head —"This faith was shown
To Italy, our mother; she

Uses my hand and blesses thee."
She followed down to the seashore;
I left and never saw her more.   110

   How very long since I have thought
Concerning — much less wished for — aught
Beside the good of Italy,
For which I live and mean to die!
I never was in love; and since   115
Charles proved false, what shall now convince
My inmost heart I have a friend?
However, if I pleased to spend
Real wishes on myself — say, three —
I know at least what one should be.   120
I would grasp Metternich until
I felt his red wet throat distil
In blood through these two hands.   And next
— Nor much for that am I perplexed —
Charles, perjured traitor, for his part,   125
Should die slow of a broken heart
Under his new employers.   Last
— Ah, there, what should I wish?   For fast
Do I grow old and out of strength.
If I resolved to seek at length   130
My father's house again, how scared
They all would look, and unprepared!
My brothers live in Austria's pay
— Disowned me long ago, men say;
And all my early mates who used   135
To praise me so — perhaps induced
More than one early step of mine —
Are turning wise: while some opine
"Freedom grows License," some suspect
"Haste breeds Delay," and recollect   140
They always said, such premature
Beginnings never could endure!
So, with a sullen "All's for best,"

The land seems settling to its rest.
I think then, I should wish to stand   **145**
This evening in that dear, lost land,
Over the sea the thousand miles,
And know if yet that woman smiles
With the calm smile; some little farm
She lives in there, no doubt: what harm   **150**
If I sat on the door-side bench,
And, while her spindle made a trench
Fantastically in the dust,
Inquired of all her fortunes — just
Her children's ages and their names,   **155**
And what may be the husband's aims
For each of them.   I'd talk this out,
And sit there, for an hour about,
Then kiss her hand once more, and lay
Mine on her head, and go my way.   **160**

So much for idle wishing — how
It steals the time!   To business now.

THE ENGLISHMAN IN ITALY

PIANO DI SORRENTO

FORTÙ, Fortù, my beloved one, sit here by my side,
On my knees put up both little feet!   I was sure, if I tried,
I could make you laugh spite of Scirocco.   Now, open your
    eyes,
Let me keep you amused till he vanish in black from the
    skies,
With telling my memories over as you tell your beads;   **5**
All the Plain saw me gather, I garland — the flowers or the
    weeds.

Time for rain! for your long hot dry Autumn had net-worked
    with brown

The white skin of each grape on the bunches, marked like a
    quail's crown,
Those creatures you make such account of, whose heads —
    speckled white
Over brown like a great spider's back, as I told you last
    night —   10
Your mother bites off for her supper.   Red-ripe as could be,
Pomegranates were chapping and splitting in halves on the
    tree:
And betwixt the loose walls of great flintstone, or in the thick
    dust
On the path, or straight out of the rock-side, wherever could
    thrust
Some burnt sprig of bold hardy rock-flower its yellow face
    up,   15
For the prize were great butterflies fighting, some five for
    one cup.
So, I guessed, ere I got up this morning, what change was in
    store,
By the quick rustle-down of the quail-nets which woke me
    before
I could open my shutter, made fast with a bough and a stone,
And look through the twisted dead vine-twigs, sole lattice
    that's known.   20
Quick and sharp rang the rings down the net-poles, while,
    busy beneath,
Your priest and his brother tugged at them, the rain in their
    teeth.
And out upon all the flat house-roofs where split figs lay
    drying,
The girls took the frails under cover: nor use seemed in try-
    ing
To get out the boats and go fishing, for, under the cliff,   25
Fierce the black water frothed o'er the blind-rock. No see-
    ing our skiff
Arrive about noon from Amalfi — our fisher arrive,
And pitch down his basket before us, all trembling alive

With pink and grey jellies, your sea-fruit; you touch the
    strange lumps,
And mouths gape there, eyes open, all manner of horns
    and of humps,   30
Which only the fisher looks grave at, while round him like
    imps
Cling screaming the children as naked and brown as his
    shrimps;
Himself too as bare to the middle — you see round his neck
The string and its brass coin suspended, that saves him from
    wreck.
But to-day not a boat reached Salerno, so back, to a man, 35
Came our friends, with whose help in the vineyards grape-
    harvest began.
In the vat, halfway up in our house-side, like blood the
    juice spins,
While your brother all bare-legged is dancing till breathless
    he grins
Dead-beaten in effort on effort to keep the grapes under,
Since still when he seems all but master, in pours the fresh
    plunder   40
From girls who keep coming and going with basket on
    shoulder,
And eyes shut against the rain's driving; your girls that are
    older —
For under the hedges of aloe, and where, on its bed
Of the orchard's black mould, the love-apple lies pulpy and
    red,
All the young ones are kneeling and filling their laps with
    the snails   45
Tempted out by this first rainy weather — your best of
    regales,
As to-night will be proved to my sorrow, when, supping in
    state,
We shall feast our grape-gleaners (two dozen, three over one
    plate)
With lasagne so tempting to swallow in slippery ropes,

And gourds fried in great purple slices, that colour of
    popes.   50
Meantime, see the grape bunch they've brought you: the
    rain-water slips
O'er the heavy blue bloom on each globe which the wasp to
    your lips
Still follows with fretful persistence: nay, taste, while awake.
This half of a curd-white smooth cheese-ball that peels,
    flake by flake,
Like an onion, each smoother and whiter; next, sip this
    weak wine   55
From the thin green glass flask, with its stopper, a leaf of the
    vine;
And end with the prickly-pear's red flesh that leaves through
    its juice
The stony black seeds on your pearl-teeth. Scirocco is
    loose!
Hark, the quick, whistling pelt of the olives which, thick in
    one's track,
Tempt the stranger to pick up and bite them, though not yet
    half black!   60
How the old twisted olive trunks shudder, the medlars let fall
Their hard fruit, and the brittle great fig-trees snap off, figs
    and all,
For here comes the whole of the tempest! No refuge, but
    creep
Back again to my side and my shoulder, and listen or sleep.

Oh, how will your country show next week, when all the
    vine-boughs   65
Have been stripped of their foliage to pasture the mules and
    the cows?
Last eve, I rode over the mountains; your brother, my guide,
Soon left me, to feast on the myrtles that offered, each side,
Their fruit-balls, black, glossy and luscious — or strip from
    the sorbs
A treasure, or, rosy and wondrous, those hairy gold orbs!   70

But my mule picked his sure sober path out, just stopping
    to neigh
When he recognized down in the valley his mates on their
    way
With the faggots and barrels of water; and soon we emerged
From the plain, where the woods could scarce follow; and
    still as we urged
Our way, the woods wondered, and left us, as up still we
    trudged,   75
Though the wild path grew wilder each instant, and place
    was e'en grudged
'Mid the rock-chasms and piles of loose stones like the loose
    broken teeth
Of some monster which climbed there to die from the ocean
    beneath —
Place was grudged to the silver-grey fume-weed that clung
    to the path,
And dark rosemary ever a-dying that, 'spite the wind's
    wrath,   80
So loves the salt rock's face to seaward, and lentisks as
    staunch
To the stone where they root and bear berries, and . . . what
    shows a branch
Coral-coloured, transparent, with circlets of pale sea-green
    leaves;
Over all trod my mule with the caution of gleaners o'er
    sheaves,
Still, foot after foot like a lady, till, round after round,   85
He climbed to the top of Calvano, and God's own profound
Was above me, and round me the mountains, and under, the
    sea,
And within me my heart to bear witness what was and shall
    be.
Oh, heaven and the terrible crystal!   No rampart excludes
Your eye from the life to be lived in the blue solitudes.   90
Oh, those mountains, their infinite movement!   Still moving
    with you;

For, ever some new head and breast of them thrusts into
    view
To observe the intruder; you see it if quickly you turn
And, before they escape you, surprise them.   They grudge
    you should learn
How the soft plains they look on, lean over and love (they
    pretend)   95
— Cower beneath them, the flat sea-pine crouches, the wild
    fruit-trees bend,
E'en the myrtle-leaves curl, shrink and shut: all is silent and
    grave:
'Tis a sensual and timorous beauty, how fair! but a slave.
So, I turned to the sea; and there slumbered as greenly as
    ever
Those isles of the siren, your Galli; no ages can sever   100
The Three, nor enable their sister to join them — halfway
On the voyage, she looked at Ulysses — no farther to-
    day,
Though the small one, just launched in the wave, watches
    breast-high and steady
From under the rock, her bold sister swum halfway al-
    ready.
Fortù, shall we sail there together and see from the sides 105
Quite new rocks show their faces, new haunts where the
    siren abides?
Shall we sail round and round them, close over the rocks,
    though unseen,
That ruffle the grey glassy water to glorious green?
Then scramble from splinter to splinter, reach land and
    explore,
On the largest, the strange square black turret with never a
    door,   110
Just a loop to admit the quick lizards; then, stand there and
    hear
The birds' quiet singing, that tells us what life is, so clear?
- — The secret they sang to Ulysses when, ages ago,
He heard and he knew this life's secret I hear and I know.

Ah, see!   The sun breaks o'er Calvano; he strikes the great
      gloom   115
And flutters it o'er the mount's summit in airy gold fume.
All is over.   Look out, see the gipsy, our tinker and smith,
Has arrived, set up bellows and forge, and down-squatted
      forthwith
To his hammering, under the wall there; one eye keeps aloof
The urchins that itch to be putting his jews'-harps to proof,
While the other, through locks of curled wire, is watching
      how sleek   121
Shines the hog, come to share in the windfall — chew, abbot's
      own cheek!
All is over.   Wake up and come out now, and down let us go,
And see the fine things got in order at church for the show
Of the Sacrament, set forth this evening; to-morrow's the
      Feast   125
Of the Rosary's Virgin, by no means of Virgins the least,
As you'll hear in the off-hand discourse which (all nature, no
      art)
The Dominican brother, these three weeks, was getting by
      heart.
Not a pillar nor post but is dizened with red and blue papers;
All the roof waves with ribbons, each altar ablaze with long
      tapers;   130
But the great masterpiece is the scaffold rigged glorious to
      hold
All the fiddlers and fifers and drummers and trumpeters
      bold,
Not afraid of Bellini nor Auber, who, when the priest's
      hoarse,
Will strike us up something that's brisk for the feast's second
      course.
And then will the flaxen-wigged Image be carried in pomp
Through the plain, while in gallant procession the priests
      mean to stomp.   136
All round the glad church lie old bottles with gunpowder
      stopped,

Which will be, when the Image re-enters, religiously popped;
And at night from the crest of Calvano great bonfires will
      hang,
On the plain will the trumpets join chorus, and more poppers
      bang.   140
At all events, come — to the garden as far as the wall;
See me tap with a hoe on the plaster till out there shall fall
A scorpion with wide angry nippers!

              — "Such trifles!" you say?
Fortù, in my England at home, men meet gravely to-day 144
And debate, if abolishing Corn-laws be righteous and wise
— If 'twere proper, Scirocco should vanish in black from the
      skies!

IN A GONDOLA

He sings

I SEND my heart up to thee, all my heart
   In this my singing.
For the stars help me, and the sea bears part;
   The very night is clinging
Closer to Venice' streets to leave one space   5
   Above me, whence thy face
May light my joyous heart to thee its dwelling-place.

She speaks

Say after me, and try to say
My very words, as if each word
Came from you of your own accord,   10
In your own voice, in your own way:
"This woman's heart and soul and brain
Are mine as much as this gold chain
She bids me wear; which" (say again)
"I choose to make by cherishing   15

A precious thing, or choose to fling
Over the boat-side, ring by ring."
And yet once more say . . . no word more
Since words are only words.   Give o'er!

Unless you call me, all the same,   20
Familiarly by my pet name,
Which if the Three should hear you call,
And me reply to, would proclaim
At once our secret to them all.
Ask of me, too, command me, blame —   25
Do, break down the partition-wall
'Twixt us, the daylight world beholds
Curtained in dusk and splendid folds!   ·
What's left but — all of me to take?
I am the Three's: prevent them, slake   30
Your thirst!   'Tis said, the Arab sage,
In practising with gems, can loose
Their subtle spirit in his cruce
And leave but ashes: so, sweet mage,
Leave them my ashes when thy use   35
Sucks out my soul, thy heritage!

He sings

Past we glide, and past, and past!
   What's that poor Agnese doing
Where they make the shutters fast?
   Gray Zanobi's just a-wooing   40
To his couch the purchased bride:
   Past we glide!

Past we glide, and past, and past!
   Why's the Pucci Palace flaring
Like a beacon to the blast?   45
   Guests by hundreds, not one caring
If the dear host's neck were wried:
   Past we glide!

She sings

The moth's kiss, first!
Kiss me as if you made believe   50
You were not sure, this eve,
How my face, your flower, had pursed
Its petals up; so, here and there
You brush it, till I grow aware
Who wants me, and wide ope I burst.   55

The bee's kiss, now!
Kiss me as if you entered gay
My heart at some noonday,
A bud that dares not disallow
The claim, so all is rendered up,   60
And passively its shattered cup
Over your head to sleep I bow.

He sings

What are we two?
I am a Jew,
And carry thee, farther than friends can pursue,   65
To a feast of our tribe;
Where they need thee to bribe
The devil that blasts them unless he imbibe
Thy . . . Scatter the vision for ever!   And now,
As of old, I am I, thou art thou!   70

Say again, what we are?
The sprite of a star,
I lure thee above where the destinies bar
My plumes their full play
Till a ruddier ray   75
Than my pale one announce there is withering away
Some . . . Scatter the vision for ever!   And now,
As of old, I am I, thou art thou!

He muses

Oh, which were best, to roam or rest?
The land's lap or the water's breast?   80
To sleep on yellow millet-sheaves,
Or swim in lucid shallows just
Eluding water-lily leaves,
An inch from Death's black fingers, thrust
To lock you, whom release he must;   85
Which life were best on Summer eves?

He speaks, musing

Lie back; could thought of mine improve you?
From this shoulder let there spring
A wing; from this, another wing;
Wings, not legs and feet, shall move you!   90
Snow-white must they spring, to blend
With your flesh, but I intend
They shall deepen to the end,
Broader, into burning gold,
Till both wings crescent-wise enfold   95
Your perfect self, from 'neath your feet
To o'er your head, where, lo, they meet
As if a million sword-blades hurled
Defiance from you to the world!

Rescue me thou, the only real!   100
And scare away this mad ideal
That came, nor motions to depart!
Thanks!   Now, stay ever as thou art!

Still he muses

What if the Three should catch at last
Thy serenader?   While there's cast   105
Paul's cloak about my head, and fast
Gian pinions me, Himself has past
His stylet through my back; I reel;
And . . . is it thou I feel?

They trail me, these three godless knaves,   110
Past every church that saints and saves,
Nor stop till, where the cold sea raves
By Lido's wet accursed graves,
They scoop mine, roll me to its brink,
And ... on thy breast I sink!   115

She replies, musing

Dip your arm o'er the boat-side, elbow-deep,
As I do: thus: were death so unlike sleep,
Caught this way? Death's to fear from flame or steel,
Or poison doubtless; but from water — feel!
Go find the bottom! Would you stay me? There! 120
Now pluck a great blade of that ribbon-grass
To plait in where the foolish jewel was,
I flung away: since you have praised my hair,
'Tis proper to be choice in what I wear.

He speaks

Row home? must we row home? Too surely   125
Know I where its front's demurely
Over the Giudecca piled;
Window just with window mating,
Door on door exactly waiting,
All's the set face of a child: 130
But behind it, where's a trace
Of the staidness and reserve,
And formal lines without a curve,
In the same child's playing-face?
No two windows look one way   135
O'er the small sea-water thread
Below them. Ah, the autumn day
I, passing, saw you overhead!
First, out a cloud of curtain blew,
Then a sweet cry, and last came you —   140
To catch your lory that must needs
Escape just then, of all times then.

To peck a tall plant's fleecy seeds,
And make me happiest of men.
I scarce could breathe to see you reach   **145**
So far back o'er the balcony
To catch him ere he climbed too high
Above you in the Smyrna peach,
That quick the round smooth cord of gold,
This coiled hair on your head, unrolled,   **150**
Fell down you like a gorgeous snake
The Roman girls were wont, of old,
When Rome there was, for coolness' sake,
To let lie curling o'er their bosoms.
Dear lory, may his beak retain   **155**
Ever its delicate rose stain
As if the wounded lotus-blossoms
Had marked their thief to know again!

Stay longer yet, for others' sake
Than mine!   What should your chamber do?   **160**
— With all its rarities that ache
In silence while day lasts, but wake
At night-time and their life renew,
Suspended just to pleasure you
Who brought against their will together   **165**
These objects, and, while day lasts, weave
Around them such a magic tether
That dumb they look: your harp, believe,
With all the sensitive tight strings
Which dare not speak, now to itself   **170**
Breathes slumberously, as if some elf
Went in and out the chords, his wings
Make murmur wheresoe'er they graze,
As an angel may, between the maze
Of midnight palace-pillars, on   **175**
And on, to sow God's plagues, have gone
Through guilty glorious Babylon.
And while such murmurs flow, the nymph

Bends o'er the harp-top from her shell
As the dry limpet for the lymph   180
Come with a tune he knows so well.
And how your statues' hearts must swell!
And how your pictures must descend
To see each other, friend with friend!
Oh, could you take them by surprise,   185
You'd find Schidone's eager Duke
Doing the quaintest courtesies
To that prim saint by Haste-thee-Luke!
And, deeper into her rock den,
Bold Castelfranco's Magdalen   190
You'd find retreated from the ken
Of that robed counsel-keeping Ser —
As if the Tizian thinks of her,
And is not, rather, gravely bent
On seeing for himself what toys   195
Are these, his progeny invent,
What litter now the board employs
Whereon he signed a document
That got him murdered! Each enjoys
Its night so well, you cannot break   200
The sport up, so, indeed must make
More stay with me, for others' sake.

She speaks

To-morrow, if a harp-string, say,
Is used to tie the jasmine back
That overfloods my room with sweets,   205
Contrive your Zorzi somehow meets
My Zanze! If the ribbon's black,
The Three are watching: keep away!

Your gondola — let Zorzi wreathe
A mesh of water-weeds about   210
Its prow, as if he unaware
Had struck some quay or bridge-foot stair!

That I may throw a paper out
As you and he go underneath.

There's Zanze's vigilant taper; safe are we.   215
Only one minute more to-night with me?
Resume your past self of a month ago!
Be you the bashful gallant, I will be
The lady with the colder breast than snow.
Now bow you, as becomes, nor touch my hand   220
More than I touch yours when I step to land,
And say, "All thanks, Siora!" —

                           Heart to heart
And lips to lips!   Yet once more, ere we part,
Clasp me and make me thine, as mine thou art!

                      [He is surprised, and stabbed.

It was ordained to be so, sweet! — and best   225
Comes now, beneath thine eyes, upon thy breast.
Still kiss me!   Care not for the cowards!   Care
Only to put aside thy beauteous hair
My blood will hurt!   The Three, I do not scorn
To death, because they never lived: but I   230
Have lived indeed, and so — (yet one more kiss) — can die!

WARING

I

I

WHAT'S become of Waring
Since he gave us all the slip,
Chose land-travel or seafaring,
Boots and chest or staff and scrip,
Rather than pace up and down   5
Any longer London town?

II

Who'd have guessed it from his lip
Or his brow's accustomed bearing,

On the night he thus took ship
Or started landward? — little caring   10
For us, it seems, who supped together

(Friends of his too, I remember)
And walked home through the merry weather,
The snowiest in all December.
I left his arm that night myself   15
For what's-his-name's, the new prose-poet
Who wrote the book there, on the shelf —
How, forsooth, was I to know it
If Waring meant to glide away
Like a ghost at break of day?   20
Never looked he half so gay!

III

He was prouder than the Devil:
How he must have cursed our revel!
Ay, and many other meetings,
Indoor visits, outdoor greetings,   25
As up and down he paced this London,
With no work done, but great works undone,
Where scarce twenty knew his name.
Why not, then, have earlier spoken,
Written, bustled?   Who's to blame   30
If your silence kept unbroken?
"True, but there were sundry jottings,
Stray-leaves, fragments, blurs and blottings,
Certain first steps were achieved
Already which" — (is that your meaning?)   35
"Had well borne out whoe'er believed
In more to come!"   But who goes gleaning
Hedgeside chance-blades, while full-sheaved
Stand cornfields by him?   Pride, o'erweening
Pride alone, puts forth such claims   40
O'er the day's distinguished names.

IV

Meantime, how much I loved him,
I find out now I've lost him.
I who cared not if I moved him,
Who could so carelessly accost him,   45
Henceforth never shall get free
Of his ghostly company.
His eyes that just a little wink
As deep I go into the merit
Of this and that distinguished spirit —   50
His cheeks' raised colour, soon to sink,
As long I dwell on some stupendous
And tremendous (Heaven defend us!)
Monstr'-inform'-ingens-horrend-ous
Demoniaco-seraphic   55
Penman's latest piece of graphic.
Nay, my very wrist grows warm
With his dragging weight of arm.
E'en so, swimmingly appears,
Through one's after-supper musings,   60
Some lost lady of old years
With her beauteous vain endeavour
And goodness unrepaid as ever,
The face, accustomed to refusings,
We, puppies that we were . . . Oh, never   65
Surely, nice of conscience, scrupled
Being aught like false, forsooth, to?
Telling aught but honest truth to?
What a sin, had we centupled
Its possessor's grace and sweetness!   70
No! she heard in its completeness
Truth, for truth's a weighty matter,
And truth, at issue, we can't flatter!
Well, 'tis done with; she's exempt
From damning us through such a sally;   75
And so she glides, as down a valley,
Taking up with her contempt,

Past our reach; and in, the flowers
Shut her unregarded hours.

V

Oh, could I have him back once more,   80
This Waring, but one half-day more!
Back, with the quiet face of yore,
So hungry for acknowledgement
Like mine! I'd fool him to his bent!
Feed, should not he, to heart's content?   85
I'd say, "to only have conceived,
Planned your great works, apart from progress,
Surpasses little works achieved!"
I'd lie so, I should be believed.
I'd make such havoc of the claims   90
Of the day's distinguished names
To feast him with, as feasts an ogress
Her feverish sharp-toothed gold-crowned child!
Or as one feasts a creature rarely
Captured here, unreconciled   95
To capture; and completely gives
Its pettish humours license, barely
Requiring that it lives.

VI

Ichabod, Ichabod,
The glory is departed!   100
Travels Waring East away?
Who, of knowledge, by hearsay,
Reports a man upstarted
Somewhere as a god,
Hordes grown European-hearted,   105
Millions of the wild made tame
On a sudden at his fame?
In Vishnu-land what Avatar?
Or who in Moscow, toward the Czar,
With the demurest of footfalls   110

Over the Kremlin's pavement bright
With serpentine and syenite,
Steps, with five other Generals
That simultaneously take snuff,
For each to have pretext enough   115
And kerchiefwise unfold his sash
Which, softness' self, is yet the stuff
To hold fast where a steel chain snaps,
And leave the grand white neck no gash?
Waring in Moscow, to those rough   120
Cold northern natures born perhaps,
Like the lambwhite maiden dear
From the circle of mute kings
Unable to repress the tear,
Each as his sceptre down he flings,   125
To Dian's fane at Taurica,
Where now a captive priestess, she alway
Mingles her tender grave Hellenic speech
With theirs, tuned to the hailstone-beaten beach
As pours some pigeon, from the myrrhy lands   130
Rapt by the whirlblast to fierce Scythian strands
Where breed the swallows, her melodious cry
Amid their barbarous twitter!
In Russia?   Never!   Spain were fitter!
Ay, most likely 'tis in Spain   135
That we and Waring meet again
Now, while he turns down that cool narrow lane
Into the blackness, out of grave Madrid
All fire and shine, abrupt as when there's slid
Its stiff gold blazing pall   140
From some black coffin-lid.
Or, best of all,
I love to think
The leaving us was just a feint;
Back here to London did he slink,   145
And now works on without a wink
Of sleep, and we are on the brink

Of something great in fresco-paint:
Some garret's ceiling, walls and floor,   150
Up and down and o'er and o'er
He splashes, as none splashed before
Since great Caldara Polidore.
Or Music means this land of ours
Some favour yet, to pity won
By Purcell from his Rosy Bowers —   155
"Give me my so-long promised son,
Let Waring end what I begun!"
Then down he creeps and out he steals
Only when the night conceals
His face; in Kent 'tis cherry-time,   160
Or hops are picking: or at prime
Of March he wanders as, too happy,
Years ago when he was young,
Some mild eve when woods grew sappy
And the early moths had sprung   165
To life from many a trembling sheath
Woven the warm boughs beneath;
While small birds said to themselves
What should soon be actual song,
And young gnats, by tens and twelves,   170
Made as if they were the throng
That crowd around and carry aloft
The sound they have nursed, so sweet and pure,
Out of a myriad noises soft,
Into a tone that can endure   175
Amid the noise of a July noon
When all God's creatures crave their boon,
All at once and all in tune,
And get it, happy as Waring then,
Having first within his ken   180
What a man might do with men:
And far too glad, in the even-glow,
To mix with the world he meant to take
Into his hand, he told you, so —

And out of it his world to make,   185
To contract and to expand
As he shut or oped his hand.
O Waring, what's to really be?
A clear stage and a crowd to see!
Some Garrick, say, out shall not he   190
The heart of Hamlet's mystery pluck?
Or, where most unclean beasts are rife,
Some Junius — am I right? — shall tuck
His sleeve, and forth with flaying-knife!
Some Chatterton shall have the luck   195
Of calling Rowley into life!
Some one shall somehow run amuck
With this old world for want of strife
Sound asleep.   Contrive, contrive
To rouse us, Waring!   Who's alive?   200
Our men scarce seem in earnest now.
Distinguished names! — but 'tis, somehow,
As if they played at being names
Still more distinguished, like the games
Of children.   Turn our sport to earnest   205
With a visage of the sternest!
Bring the real times back, confessed
Still better than our very best!

                            II

                             I

"When I last saw Waring ..."
(How all turned to him who spoke!   210
You saw Waring?   Truth or joke?
In land-travel or sea-faring?)

                             II

"We were sailing by Triest
Where a day or two we harboured:
A sunset was in the West,   215

When, looking over the vessel's side,
One of our company espied
A sudden speck to larboard.
And as a sea-duck flies and swims
At once, so came the light craft up,   220
With its sole lateen sail that trims
And turns (the water round its rims
Dancing, as round a sinking cup)
And by us like a fish it curled,
And drew itself up close beside,   225
Its great sail on the instant furled,
And o'er its thwarts a shrill voice cried,
(A neck as bronzed as a Lascar's)
'Buy wine of us, you English Brig?
Or fruit, tobacco and cigars?   230
A pilot for you to Triest?
Without one, look you ne'er so big,
They'll never let you up the bay!
We natives should know best.'
I turned, and 'just those fellows' way,'   235
Our captain said, 'The 'long-shore thieves
Are laughing at us in their sleeves.'

III

"In truth, the boy leaned laughing back;
And one, half-hidden by his side
Under the furled sail, soon I spied,   240
With great grass hat and kerchief black,
Who looked up with his kingly throat,
Said somewhat, while the other shook
His hair back from his eyes to look
Their longest at us; then the boat,   245
I know not how, turned sharply round,
Laying her whole side on the sea
As a leaping fish does; from the lee
Into the weather, cut somehow
Her sparkling path beneath our bow   250

And so went off, as with a bound.
Into the rosy and golden half
O' the sky, to overtake the sun
And reach the shore, like the sea-calf
Its singing cave; yet I caught one   255
Glance ere away the boat quite passed,
And neither time nor toil could mar
Those features: so I saw the last
Of Waring!" — You?   Oh, never star
Was lost here but it rose afar!   260
Look East, where whole new thousands are!
In Vishnu-land what Avatar?

THE TWINS

"Give" and "It-shall-be-given-unto-you."

GRAND rough old Martin Luther
    Bloomed fables — flowers on furze,
The better the uncouther:
    Do roses stick like burrs?

A beggar asked an alms   5
    One day at an abbey-door,
Said Luther; but, seized with qualms,
    The Abbot replied, "We're poor!

"Poor, who had plenty once,
    When gifts fell thick as rain: 10
But they give us naught, for the nonce,
    And how should we give again?"

Then the beggar, "See your sins!
    Of old, unless I err,
Ye had brothers for inmates, twins,   15
    Date and Dabitur.

"While Date was in good case
　　Dabitur flourished too:
For Dabitur's lenten face
　　No wonder if Date rue.　　　　　　　　　20

"Would ye retrieve the one?
　　Try and make plump the other!
When Date's penance is done,
　　Dabitur helps his brother.

"Only, beware relapse!"　　　　　　　　　　25
　　The Abbot hung his head.
This beggar might be perhaps
　　An angel, Luther said.

THE LAST RIDE TOGETHER

I SAID — Then, dearest, since 'tis so,
Since now at length my fate I know,
Since nothing all my love avails,
Since all, my life seemed meant for, fails,
　　Since this was written and needs must be —　　5
My whole heart rises up to bless
Your name in pride and thankfulness!
Take back the hope you gave — I claim
Only a memory of the same
— And this beside, if you will not blame,　　　10
　　Your leave for one more last ride with me.

My mistress bent that brow of hers;
Those deep dark eyes where pride demurs
When pity would be softening through,
Fixed me a breathing-while or two　　　　　　15
　　With life or death in the balance: right!
The blood replenished me again;
My last thought was at least not vain:

I and my mistress, side by side
Shall be together, breathe and ride,   20
So, one day more am I deified.
    Who knows but the world may end to-night?

Hush! if you saw some western cloud
All billowy-bosomed, over-bowed
By many benedictions — sun's   25
And moon's and evening-star's at once —
    And so, you, looking and loving best,
Conscious grew, your passion drew
Cloud, sunset, moonrise, star-shine too,
Down on you, near and yet more near,   30
Till flesh must fade for heaven was here! —
Thus leant she and lingered — joy and fear!
    Thus lay she a moment on my breast.

Then we began to ride.   My soul
Smoothed itself out, a long-cramped scroll   35
Freshening and fluttering in the wind.
Past hopes already lay behind.
    What need to strive with a life awry?
Had I said that, had I done this,
So might I gain, so might I miss.   40
Might she have loved me? just as well
She might have hated, who can tell!
Where had I been now if the worst befell?
    And here we are riding, she and I.

Fail I alone, in words and deeds?   45
Why, all men strive, and who succeeds?
We rode; it seemed my spirit flew,
Saw other regions, cities new,
    As the world rushed by on either side.
I thought — All labour, yet no less   50
Bear up beneath their unsuccess.

Look at the end of work, contrast
The petty done, the undone vast,
This present of theirs with the hopeful past!
    I hoped she would love me; here we ride.   **55**

What hand and brain went ever paired?
What heart alike conceived and dared?
What act proved all its thought had been?
What will but felt the fleshly screen?
    We ride and I see her bosom heave.   **60**
There's many a crown for who can reach.
Ten lines, a statesman's life in each!
The flag stuck on a heap of bones,
A soldier's doing! what atones?
They scratch his name on the Abbey-stones.   **65**
    My riding is better, by their leave.

What does it all mean, poet?   Well,
Your brains beat into rhythm, you tell
What we felt only; you expressed
You hold things beautiful the best,   **70**
    And pace them in rhyme so, side by side.
'Tis something, nay 'tis much: but then,
Have you yourself what's best for men?
Are you — poor, sick, old ere your time —
Nearer one whit your own sublime   **75**
Than we who never have turned a rhyme?
    Sing, riding's a joy! For me, I ride.

And you, great sculptor — so, you gave
A score of years to Art, her slave,
And that's your Venus, whence we turn   **80**
To yonder girl that fords the burn!
    You acquiesce, and shall I repine?
What, man of music, you grown grey
With notes and nothing else to say,

Is this your sole praise from a friend,   85
"Greatly his opera's strains intend,
But in music we know how fashions end!"
    I gave my youth; but we ride, in fine.

    Who knows what's fit for us?   Had fate
Proposed bliss here should sublimate   90
My being — had I signed the bond —
Still one must lead some life beyond,
    Have a bliss to die with, dim-descried.
This foot once planted on the goal,
This glory-garland round my soul,   95
Could I descry such?   Try and test!
I sink back shuddering from the quest.
Earth being so good, would heaven seem best?
    Now, heaven and she are beyond this ride.

And yet — she has not spoke so long!   100
What if heaven be that, fair and strong
At life's best, with our eyes upturned
Whither life's flower is first discerned,
    We, fixed so, ever should so abide?
What if we still ride on, we two,   105
With life for ever old yet new,
Changed not in kind but in degree,
The instant made eternity, —
And heaven just prove that I and she
    Ride, ride together, for ever ride?   110

A GRAMMARIAN'S FUNERAL

SHORTLY AFTER THE REVIVAL OF LEARNING
IN EUROPE

LET us begin and carry up this corpse,
    Singing together.
Leave we the common crofts, the vulgar thorpes
    Each in its tether

Sleeping safe on the bosom of the plain,   5
    Cared-for till cock-crow:
Look out if yonder be not day again
    Rimming the rock-row!
That's the appropriate country; there, man's thought,
    Rarer, intenser,   10
Self-gathered for an outbreak, as it ought,
    Chafes in the censer.
Leave we the unlettered plain its herd and crop;
    Seek we sepulture
On a tall mountain, cited to the top,   15
    Crowded with culture!
All the peaks soar, but one the rest excels;
    Clouds overcome it;
No! yonder sparkle is the citadel's
    Circling its summit.   20
Thither our path lies; wind we up the heights;
    Wait ye the warning?
Our low life was the level's and the night's;
    He's for the morning.
Step to a tune, square chests, erect each head,   25
    'Ware the beholders!
This is our master, famous, calm and dead,
    Borne on our shoulders.

Sleep, crop and herd! sleep, darkling thorpe and croft,
    Safe from the weather!   30
He, whom we convoy to his grave aloft,
    Singing together,
He was a man born with thy face and throat,
    Lyric Apollo!
Long he lived nameless: how should Spring take note 35
    Winter would follow?
Till lo, the little touch, and youth was gone!
    Cramped and diminished,
Moaned he, "New measures, other feet anon!
    My dance is finished"?   40

No, that's the world's way: (keep the mountain-side,
    Make for the city!)
He knew the signal, and stepped on with pride
    Over men's pity;
Left play for work, and grappled with the world   **45**
    Bent on escaping:
"What's in the scroll," quoth he, "thou keepest furled?
    Show me their shaping,
Theirs who most studied man, the bard and sage —
    Give!" — So, he gowned him,   **50**
Straight got by heart that book to its last page:
    Learned, we found him.
Yea, but we found him bald too, eyes like lead,
    Accents uncertain:
"Time to taste life," another would have said,   **55**
    "Up with the curtain!"
This man said rather, "Actual life comes next?
    Patience a moment!
Grant I have mastered learning's crabbed text,
    Still there's the comment.   **60**
Let me know all!   Prate not of most or least,
    Painful or easy!
Even to the crumbs I'd fain eat up the feast,
    Ay, nor feel queasy."
Oh, such a life as he resolved to live,   **65**
    When he had learned it,
When he had gathered all books had to give!
    Sooner, he spurned it.
Image the whole, then execute the parts —
    Fancy the fabric   **70**
Quite, ere you build, ere steel strike fire from quartz,
    Ere mortar dab brick!

(Here's the town-gate reached: there's the market-place
    Gaping before us.)
Yea, this in him was the peculiar grace   **75**
    (Hearten our chorus!)

That before living he'd learn how to live —
    No end to learning:
Earn the means first — God surely will contrive
    Use for our earning.   80
Others mistrust and say, "But time escapes
    Live now or never!"
He said, "What's time?   Leave Now for dogs and apes!
    Man has Forever."
Back to his book then: deeper drooped his head: 85
    Calculus racked him:
Leaden before, his eyes grew dross of lead:
    Tussis attacked him.
"Now, master, take a little rest!" — not he!
    (Caution redoubled,   90
Step two abreast, the way winds narrowly!)
    Not a whit troubled,
Back to his studies, fresher than at first,
    Fierce as a dragon
He (soul-hydroptic with a sacred thirst)   95
    Sucked at the flagon.
Oh, if we draw a circle premature,
    Heedless of far gain,
Greedy for quick returns of profit, sure
    Bad is our bargain!   100
Was it not great? did not he throw on God,
    (He loves the burthen) —
God's task to make the heavenly period
    Perfect the earthen?
Did not he magnify the mind, show clear   105
    Just what it all meant?
He would not discount life, as fools do here,
    Paid by instalment.
He ventured neck or nothing — heaven's success
    Found, or earth's failure: 110
"Wilt thou trust death or not?"   He answered "Yes:
    Hence with life's pale lure!"
That low man seeks a little thing to do,
    Sees it and does it:

This high man, with a great thing to pursue,   115
　　Dies ere he knows it.
That low man goes on adding one to one,
　　His hundred's soon hit:
This high man, aiming at a million,
　　Misses an unit.   120
That, has the world here — should he need the next,
　　Let the world mind him!
This, throws himself on God, and unperplexed
　　Seeking shall find him.
So, with the throttling hands of death at strife,   125
　　Ground he at grammar;
Still, through the rattle, parts of speech were rife:
　　While he could stammer
He settled *Hoti's* business — let it be! —
　　Properly based *Oun* —   130
Gave us the doctrine of the enclitic *De*,
　　Dead from the waist down.
Well, here's the platform, here's the proper place:
　　Hail to your purlieus,
All ye highfliers of the feathered race,   135
　　Swallows and curlews!
Here's the top-peak; the multitude below
　　Live, for they can, there:
This man decided not to Live but Know —
　　Bury this man there?   140
Here — here's his place, where meteors shoot, clouds form,
　　Lightnings are loosened,
Stars come and go!   Let joy break with the storm,
　　Peace let the dew send!
Lofty designs must close in like effects: 145
　　Loftily lying,
Leave him — still loftier than the world suspects,
　　Living and dying.

"CHILDE ROLAND TO THE DARK TOWER CAME"

(See Edgar's song in *Lear*)

My first thought was, he lied in every word,
 That hoary cripple, with malicious eye
 Askance to watch the working of his lie
On mine, and mouth scarce able to afford
Suppression of the glee, that pursed and scored   5
 Its edge, at one more victim gained thereby.

What else should he be set for, with his staff?
 What, save to waylay with his lies, ensnare
 All travellers who might find him posted there,
And ask the road?   I guessed what skull-like laugh   10
Would break, what crutch 'gin write my epitaph
 For pastime in the dusty thoroughfare,

If at his counsel I should turn aside
 Into that ominous tract which, all agree,
 Hides the Dark Tower.   Yet acquiescingly   15
I did turn as he pointed: neither pride
Nor hope rekindling at the end descried,
 So much as gladness that some end might be.

For, what with my whole world-wide wandering,
 What with my search drawn out through years, my hope
 Dwindled into a ghost not fit to cope   21
With that obstreperous joy success would bring,
I hardly tried now to rebuke the spring
 My heart made, finding failure in its scope.

As when a sick man very near to death   25
 Seems dead indeed, and feels begin and end
 The tears, and takes the farewell of each friend,
And hears one bid the other go, draw breath

Freelier outside, ("since all is o'er," he saith,
  "And the blow fallen no grieving can amend";)   30

While some discuss if near the other graves
  Be room enough for this, and when a day
  Suits best for carrying the corpse away,
With care about the banners, scarves and staves;
And still the man hears all, and only craves   35
  He may not shame such tender love and stay.

Thus, I had so long suffered in this quest,
  Heard failure prophesied so oft, been writ
  So many times among "The Band" — to wit,
The knights who to the Dark Tower's search addressed 40
Their steps — that just to fail as they, seemed best,
  And all the doubt was now — should I be fit?

So, quiet as despair, I turned from him,
  That hateful cripple, out of his highway
  Into the path he pointed.   All the day   45
Had been a dreary one at best, and dim
Was settling to its close, yet shot one grim
  Red leer to see the plain catch its estray.

For mark! no sooner was I fairly found
  Pledged to the plain, after a pace or two,   50
  Than, pausing to throw backward a last view
O'er the safe road, 'twas gone; gray plain all round:
Nothing but plain to the horizon's bound.
  I might go on; naught else remained to do.

So, on I went.   I think I never saw   55
  Such starved ignoble nature; nothing throve:
  For flowers — as well expect a cedar grove!
But cockle, spurge, according to their law
Might propagate their kind, with none to awe,
  You'd think; a burr had been a treasure-trove.   60

No! penury, inertness and grimace,
  In some strange sort, were the land's portion. "See
  Or shut your eyes," said Nature peevishly,
"It nothing skills: I cannot help my case:
'Tis the Last Judgement's fire must cure this place,   65
  Calcine its clods and set my prisoners free."

If there pushed any ragged thistle-stalk
  Above its mates, the head was chopped; the bents
  Were jealous else. What made those holes and rents
In the dock's harsh swarth leaves, bruised as to balk   70
All hope of greenness? 'tis a brute must walk
  Pashing their life out, with a brute's intents.

As for the grass, it grew as scant as hair
  In leprosy; thin dry blades pricked the mud
  Which underneath looked kneaded up with blood.   75
One stiff blind horse, his every bone a-stare,
Stood stupefied, however he came there:
  Thrust out past service from the devil's stud!

Alive? he might be dead for aught I know,
  With that red gaunt and colloped neck a-strain,   80
  And shut eyes underneath the rusty mane;
Seldom went such grotesqueness with such woe;
I never saw a brute I hated so;
  He must be wicked to deserve such pain.

I shut my eyes and turned them on my heart.   85
  As a man calls for wine before he fights,
  I asked one draught of earlier, happier sights,
Ere fitly I could hope to play my part.
Think first, fight afterwards — the soldier's art:
  One taste of the old time sets all to rights.   90

Not it! I fancied Cuthbert's reddening face
  Beneath its garniture of curly gold,

Dear fellow, till I almost felt him fold
An arm in mine to fix me to the place,
That way he used. Alas, one night's disgrace!   95
    Out went my heart's new fire and left it cold.

Giles then, the soul of honour — there he stands
    Frank as ten years ago when knighted first.
    What honest man should dare (he said) he durst.
Good — but the scene shifts — faugh! what hangman
        hands   100
Pin to his breast a parchment? His own bands
    Read it. Poor traitor, spit upon and curst!

Better this present than a past like that;
    Back therefore to my darkening path again!
    No sound, no sight as far as eye could strain.   105
Will the night send a howlet or a bat?
I asked: when something on the dismal flat
    Came to arrest my thoughts and change their train.

A sudden little river crossed my path
    As unexpected as a serpent comes.   110
    No sluggish tide congenial to the glooms;
This, as it frothed by, might have been a bath
For the fiend's glowing hoof — to see the wrath
    Of its black eddy bespate with flakes and spumes.

So petty yet so spiteful! All along,   115
    Low scrubby alders kneeled down over it;
    Drenched willows flung them headlong in a fit
Of mute despair, a suicidal throng:
The river which had done them all the wrong,
    Whate'er that was, rolled by, deterred no whit.   120

Which, while I forded — good saints, how I feared
    To set my foot upon a dead man's cheek,

Each step, or feel the spear I thrust to seek
For hollows, tangled in his hair or beard!
— It may have been a water-rat I speared,   125
    But, ugh! it sounded like a baby's shriek.

Glad was I when I reached the other bank.
    Now for a better country.   Vain presage!
    Who were the strugglers, what war did they wage,
Whose savage trample thus could pad the dank   130
Soil to a plash?   Toads in a poisoned tank,
    Or wild cats in a red-hot iron cage —

The fight must so have seemed in that fell cirque.
    What penned them there, with all the plain to choose?
    No footprint leading to that horrid mews,   135
None out of it.   Mad brewage set to work
Their brains, no doubt, like galley-slaves the Turk
    Pits for his pastime, Christians against Jews.

And more than that — a furlong on — why, there!
    What bad use was that engine for, that wheel,   140
    Or brake, not wheel — that harrow fit to reel
Men's bodies out like silk? with all the air
Of Tophet's tool, on earth left unaware,
    Or brought to sharpen its rusty teeth of steel.

Then came a bit of stubbed ground, once a wood,   145
    Next a marsh, it would seem, and now mere earth
    Desperate and done with; (so a fool finds mirth,
Makes a thing and then mars it, till his mood
Changes and off he goes!) within a rood —
    Bog, clay and rubble, sand and stark black dearth.   150

Now blotches rankling, coloured gay and grim,
    Now patches where some leanness of the soil's
    Broke into moss or substances like boils:
Then came some palsied oak, a cleft in him

Like a distorted mouth that splits its rim   **155**
   Gaping at death, and dies while it recoils.

And just as far as ever from the end!
   Naught in the distance but the evening, naught
   To point my footstep further!   At the thought,
A great black bird, Apollyon's bosom-friend,   **160**
Sailed past, nor beat his wide wing dragon-penned
   That brushed my cap — perchance the guide I sought.

For, looking up, aware I somehow grew,
   'Spite of the dusk, the plain had given place
   All round to mountains — with such name to grace   **165**
Mere ugly heights and heaps now stolen in view.
How thus they had surprised me, — solve it, you!
   How to get from them was no clearer case.

Yet half I seemed to recognize some trick
   Of mischief happened to me, God knows when —   **170**
   In a bad dream perhaps.   Here ended, then,
Progress this way.   When, in the very nick
Of giving up, one time more, came a click
   As when a trap shuts — you're inside the den!

Burningly it came on me all at once,   **175**
   This was the place! those two hills on the right,
   Crouched like two bulls locked horn in horn in fight;
While to the left, a tall scalped mountain . . . Dunce,
Dotard, a-dozing at the very nonce,
   After a life spent training for the sight!   **180**

What in the midst lay but the Tower itself?
   The round squat turret, blind as the fool's heart,
   Built of brown stone, without a counterpart
In the whole world.   The tempest's mocking elf
Points to the shipman thus the unseen shelf   **185**
   He strikes on, only when the timbers start.

Not see? because of night perhaps? — why, day
   Came back again for that! before it left,
   The dying sunset kindled through a cleft:
The hills, like giants at a hunting, lay,   190
Chin upon hand, to see the game at bay —
   "Now stab and end the creature — to the heft!"

Not hear? when noise was everywhere! it tolled
   Increasing like a bell. Names in my ears
   Of all the lost adventurers my peers —   195
How such a one was strong, and such was bold,
And such was fortunate, yet each of old
   Lost, lost! one moment knelled the woe of years.

There they stood, ranged along the hillsides, met
   To view the last of me, a living frame   200
   For one more picture! in a sheet of flame
I saw them and I knew them all.   And yet
Dauntless the slug-horn to my lips I set,
   And blew.   *"Childe Roland to the Dark Tower came."*

HOW IT STRIKES A CONTEMPORARY

I ONLY knew one poet in my life:
And this, or something like it, was his way.

  You saw go up and down Valladolid,
A man of mark, to know next time you saw.
His very serviceable suit of black
Was courtly once and conscientious still,
And many might have worn it, though none did:
The cloak, that somewhat shone and showed the threads,
Had purpose, and the ruff, significance.
He walked and tapped the pavement with his cane,   10
Scenting the world, looking it full in face,
An old dog, bald and blindish, at his heels.

They turned up, now, the alley by the church,
That leads nowhither; now, they breathed themselves
On the main promenade just at the wrong time: 15
You'd come upon his scrutinizing hat,
Making a peaked shade blacker than itself
Against the single window spared some house
Intact yet with its mouldered Moorish work, —
Or else surprise the ferrel of his stick   20
Trying the mortar's temper 'tween the chinks
Of some new shop a-building, French and fine.
He stood and watched the cobbler at his trade,
The man who slices lemons into drink,
The coffee-roaster's brazier, and the boys   25
That volunteer to help him turn its winch.
He glanced o'er books on stalls with half an eye,
And fly-leaf ballads on the vendor's string,
And broad-edge bold-print posters by the wall.
He took such cognizance of men and things,   30
If any beat a horse, you felt he saw;
If any cursed a woman, he took note;
Yet stared at nobody — you stared at him,
And found, less to your pleasure than surprise,
He seemed to know you and expect as much.   35
So, next time that a neighbour's tongue was loosed,
It marked the shameful and notorious fact.
We had among us, not so much a spy,
As a recording chief-inquisitor,
The town's true master if the town but knew!   40
We merely kept a governor for form,
While this man walked about and took account
Of all thought, said and acted, then went home,
And wrote it fully to our Lord the King,
Who has an itch to know things, he knows why,   45
And reads them in his bedroom of a night.
Oh, you might smile! there wanted not a touch,
A tang of . . . well, it was not wholly ease
As back into your mind the man's look came.

Stricken in years a little — such a brow   50
His eyes had to live under! — clear as flint
On either side the formidable nose
Curved, cut and coloured like an eagle's claw.
Had he to do with A.'s surprising fate?
When altogether old B. disappeared   55
And young C. got his mistress — was't our friend,
His letter to the King, that did it all?
What paid the bloodless man for so much pains?
Our Lord the King has favourites manifold,
And shifts his ministry some once a month;   60
Our city gets new governors at whiles —
But never word or sign, that I could hear,
Notified to this man about the streets
The King's approval of those letters conned
The last thing duly at the dead of night.   65
Did the man love his office?   Frowned our Lord,
Exhorting when none heard — "Beseech me not!
Too far above my people — beneath me!
I set the watch — how should the people know?
Forget them, keep me all the more in mind!"   70
Was some such understanding 'twixt the two?

   I found no truth in one report at least —
That if you tracked him to his home, down lanes
Beyond the Jewry, and as clean to pace,
You found he ate his supper in a room   75
Blazing with lights, four Titians on the wall,
And twenty naked girls to change his plate!
Poor man, he lived another kind of life
In that new stuccoed third house by the bridge,
Fresh-painted, rather smart than otherwise!   80
The whole street might o'erlook him as he sat,
Leg crossing leg, one foot on the dog's back,
Playing a decent cribbage with his maid
(Jacynth, you're sure her name was) o'er the cheese
And fruit, three red halves of starved winter-pears, 85

Or treat of radishes in April.   Nine,
Ten, struck the church clock, straight to bed went he.

    My father, like the man of sense he was,
Would point him out to me a dozen times;
"'St —'St," he'd whisper, "the Corregidor!"   90
I had been used to think that personage
Was one with lacquered breeches, lustrous belt,
And feathers like a forest in his hat,
Who blew a trumpet and proclaimed the news,
Announced the bull-fights, gave each church its turn, 95
And memorized the miracle in vogue!
He had a great observance from us boys;
We were in error; that was not the man.

    I'd like now, yet had haply been afraid,
To have just looked, when this man came to die,   100
And seen who lined the clean gay garret-sides
And stood about the neat low truckle-bed,
With the heavenly manner of relieving guard.
Here had been, mark, the general-in-chief,
Through a whole campaign of the world's life and death, 105
Doing the King's work all the dim day long,
In his old coat and up to knees in mud,
Smoked like a herring, dining on a crust, —
And, now the day was won, relieved at once!
No further show or need for that old coat,   110
You are sure, for one thing!   Bless us, all the while
How sprucely we are dressed out, you and I!
A second, and the angels alter that.
Well, I could never write a verse, — could you?
Let's to the Prado and make the most of time.   115

AN EPISTLE

CONTAINING THE STRANGE MEDICAL EXPERIENCE OF KARSHISH, THE ARAB PHYSICIAN

KARSHISH, the picker-up of learning's crumbs,
The not-incurious in God's handiwork
(This man's-flesh he hath admirably made,
Blown like a bubble, kneaded like a paste,
To coop up and keep down on earth a space   5
That puff of vapour from his mouth, man's soul)
— To Abib, all-sagacious in our art,
Breeder in me of what poor skill I boast,
Like me inquisitive how pricks and cracks
Befall the flesh through too much stress and strain,   10
Whereby the wily vapour fain would slip
Back and rejoin its source before the term, —
And aptest in contrivance (under God)
To baffle it by deftly stopping such: —
The vagrant Scholar to his Sage at home   15
Sends greeting (health and knowledge, fame with peace)
Three samples of true snake-stone — rarer still,
One of the other sort, the melon-shaped,
(But fitter, pounded fine, for charms than drugs,)
And writeth now the twenty-second time.   20

My journeyings were brought to Jericho:
Thus I resume.   Who studious in our art
Shall count a little labour unrepaid?
I have shed sweat enough, left flesh and bone
On many a flinty furlong of this land.   25
Also, the countryside is all on fire
With rumours of a marching hitherward:
Some say Vespasian cometh, some, his son.
A black lynx snarled and pricked a tufted ear;
Lust of my blood inflamed his yellow balls: 30
I cried and threw my staff and he was gone.
Twice have the robbers stripped and beaten me.

And once a town declared me for a spy;
But at the end, I reach Jerusalem,
Since this poor covert where I pass the night,   35
This Bethany, lies scarce the distance thence
A man with plague-sores at the third degree
Runs till he drops down dead.   Thou laughest here!
'Sooth, it elates me, thus reposed and safe,
To void the stuffing of my travel-scrip   40
And share with thee whatever Jewry yields.
A viscid choler is observable
In tertians, I was nearly bold to say;
And falling-sickness hath a happier cure
Than our school wots of: there's a spider here   45
Weaves no web, watches on the ledge of tombs,
Sprinkled with mottles on an ash-grey back;
Take five and drop them . . . but who knows his mind,
The Syrian runagate I trust this to?
His service payeth me a sublimate   50
Blown up his nose to help the ailing eye
Best wait: I reach Jerusalem at morn,
There set in order my experiences,
Gather what most deserves, and give thee all —
Or I might add, Judæa's gum-tragacanth   55
Scales off in purer flakes, shines clearer-grained,
Cracks 'twixt the pestle and the porphyry,
In fine exceeds our produce.   Scalp-disease
Confounds me, crossing so with leprosy —
Thou hadst admired one sort I gained at Zoar —   60
But zeal outruns discretion.   Here I end.

   Yet stay: my Syrian blinketh gratefully,
Protesteth his devotion is my price —
Suppose I write what harms not, though he steal?
I half resolve to tell thee, yet I blush,   65
What set me off a-writing first of all.
An itch I had, a sting to write, a tang!
For be it this town's barrenness — or else

The Man had something in the look of him —
His case has struck me far more than 'tis worth.   70
So, pardon if — (lest presently I lose
In the great press of novelty at hand
The care and pains this somehow stole from me)
I bid thee take the thing while fresh in mind,
Almost in sight — for, wilt thou have the truth?   75
The very man is gone from me but now,
Whose ailment is the subject of discourse.
Thus then, and let thy better wit help all!

'Tis but a case of mania — subinduced
By epilepsy, at the turning-point   80
Of trance prolonged unduly some three days:
When, by the exhibition of some drug
Or spell, exorcisation, stroke of art
Unknown to me and which 'twere well to know,
The evil thing out-breaking all at once   85
Left the man whole and sound of body indeed, —
But, flinging (so to speak) life's gates too wide,
Making a clear house of it too suddenly,
The first conceit that entered might inscribe
Whatever it was minded on the wall   90
So plainly at that vantage, as it were,
(First come, first served) that nothing subsequent
Attaineth to erase those fancy-scrawls
The just-returned and new-established soul
Hath gotten now so thoroughly by heart   95
That henceforth she will read or these or none.
And first — the man's own firm conviction rests
That he was dead (in fact they buried him)
— That he was dead and then restored to life
By a Nazarene physician of his tribe: 100
— 'Sayeth, the same bade "Rise," and he did rise.
"Such cases are diurnal," thou wilt cry
Not so this figment! — not, that such a fume,
Instead of giving way to time and health,

Should eat itself into the life of life,   105
As saffron tingeth flesh, blood, bones and all!
For see, how he takes up the after-life.
The man — it is one Lazarus a Jew,
Sanguine, proportioned, fifty years of age,
The body's habit wholly laudable,   110
As much, indeed, beyond the common health
As he were made and put aside to show.
Think, could we penetrate by any drug
And bathe the wearied soul and worried flesh,
And bring it clear and fair, by three days' sleep!   115
Whence has the man the balm that brightens all?
This grown man eyes the world now like a child.
Some elders of his tribe, I should premise,
Led in their friend, obedient as a sheep,
To bear my inquisition.   While they spoke,   120
Now sharply, now with sorrow — told the case —
He listened not except I spoke to him,
But folded his two hands and let them talk,
Watching the flies that buzzed: and yet no fool.
And that's a sample how his years must go.   125
Look, if a beggar, in fixed middle-life,
Should find a treasure, — can he use the same
With straitened habits and with tastes starved small,
And take at once to his impoverished brain
The sudden element that changes things,   130
That sets the undreamed-of rapture at his hand
And puts the cheap old joy in the scorned dust?
Is he not such an one as moves to mirth —
Warily parsimonious, when no need,
Wasteful as drunkenness at undue times?   135
All prudent counsel as to what befits
The golden mean, is lost on such an one:
The man's fantastic will is the man's law.
So here — we call the treasure knowledge, say,
Increased beyond the fleshly faculty —   140
Heaven opened to a soul while yet on earth,

Earth forced on a soul's use while seeing heaven:
The man is witless of the size, the sum,
The value in proportion of all things,
Or whether it be little or be much.   145
Discourse to him of prodigious armaments
Assembled to besiege his city now,
And of the passing of a mule with gourds —
'Tis one! Then take it on the other side,
Speak of some trifling fact, — he will gaze rapt   150
With stupor at its very littleness,
(Far as I see) as if in that indeed
He caught prodigious import, whole results;
And so will turn to us the bystanders
In ever the same stupor (note this point)   155
That we too see not with his opened eyes.
Wonder and doubt come wrongly into play,
Preposterously, at cross purposes.
Should his child sicken unto death — why, look
For scarce abatement of his cheerfulness,   160
Or pretermission of the daily craft!
While a word, gesture, glance from that same child
At play or in the school or laid asleep,
Will startle him to an agony of fear,
Exasperation, just as like. Demand   165
The reason why — "'tis but a word," object —
"A gesture" — he regards thee as our lord
Who lived there in the pyramid alone,
Looked at us (dost thou mind?) when, being young,
We both would unadvisedly recite   170
Some charm's beginning, from that book of his,
Able to bid the sun throb wide and burst
All into stars, as suns grown old are wont.
Thou and the child have each a veil alike
Thrown o'er your heads, from under which ye both   175
Stretch your blind hands and trifle with a match
Over a mine of Greek fire, did ye know!
He holds on firmly to some thread of life —

(It is the life to lead perforcedly)
Which runs across some vast distracting orb   180
Of glory on either side that meagre thread,
Which, conscious of, he must not enter yet —
The spiritual life around the earthly life:
The law of that is known to him as this,
His heart and brain move there, his feet stay here. 185
So is the man perplext with impulses
Sudden to start off crosswise, not straight on,
Proclaiming what is right and wrong across,
And not along, this black thread through the blaze —
"It should be" balked by "here it cannot be."   190
And oft the man's soul springs into his face
As if he saw again and heard again
His sage that bade him "Rise" and he did rise.
Something, a word, a tick o' the blood within
Admonishes: then back he sinks at once   195
To ashes, who was very fire before,
In sedulous recurrence to his trade
Whereby he earneth him the daily bread;
And studiously the humbler for that pride,
Professedly the faultier that he knows   200
God's secret, while he holds the thread of life.
Indeed the especial marking of the man
Is prone submission to the heavenly will —
Seeing it, what it is, and why it is.
'Sayeth, he will wait patient to the last   205
For that same death which must restore his being
To equilibrium, body loosening soul
Divorced even now by premature full growth:
He will live, nay, it pleaseth him to live
So long as God please, and just how God please.   210
He even seeketh not to please God more
(Which meaneth, otherwise) than as God please.
Hence, I perceive not he affects to preach
The doctrine of his sect whate'er it be,
Make proselytes as madmen thirst to do: 215

How can he give his neighbour the real ground,
His own conviction?   Ardent as he is —
Call his great truth a lie, why, still the old
"Be it as God please" reassureth him.
I probed the sore as thy disciple should: 220
"How, beast," said I, "this stolid carelessness
Sufficeth thee, when Rome is on her march
To stamp out like a little spark thy town,
Thy tribe, thy crazy tale and thee at once?"
He merely looked with his large eyes on me.   225
The man is apathetic, you deduce?
Contrariwise, he loves both old and young,
Able and weak, affects the very brutes
And birds — how say I? flowers of the field —
As a wise workman recognizes tools   230
In a master's workshop, loving what they make.
Thus is the man as harmless as a lamb:
Only impatient, let him do his best,
At ignorance and carelessness and sin —
An indignation which is promptly curbed: 235
As when in certain travel I have feigned
To be an ignoramus in our art
According to some preconceived design,
And happed to hear the land's practitioners,
Steeped in conceit sublimed by ignorance,   240
Prattle fantastically on disease,
Its cause and cure — and I must hold my peace!

    Thou wilt object — Why have I not ere this
Sought out the sage himself, the Nazarene
Who wrought this cure, inquiring at the source,   245
Conferring with the frankness that befits?
Alas! it grieveth me, the learned leech
Perished in a tumult many years ago,
Accused — our learning's fate — of wizardry,
Rebellion, to the setting up a rule   250
And creed prodigious as described to me.

His death, which happened when the earthquake fell
(Prefiguring, as soon appeared, the loss
To occult learning in our lord the sage
Who lived there in the pyramid alone)   255
Was wrought by the mad people — that's their wont!
On vain recourse, as I conjecture it,
To his tried virtue, for miraculous help —
How could he stop the earthquake?   That's their way!
The other imputations must be lies;   260
But take one, though I loathe to give it thee,
In mere respect for any good man's fame.
(And after all, our patient Lazarus
Is stark mad; should we count on what he says?
Perhaps not: though in writing to a leech   265
'Tis well to keep back nothing of a case.)
This man so cured regards the curer, then,
As — God forgive me! who but God himself,
Creator and sustainer of the world,
That came and dwelt in flesh on it awhile!   270
— 'Sayeth that such an one was born and lived,
Taught, healed the sick, broke bread at his own house,
Then died, with Lazarus by, for aught I know,
And yet was . . . what I said nor choose repeat,
And must have so avouched himself, in fact,   275
In hearing of this very Lazarus
Who saith — but why all this of what he saith?
Why write of trivial matters, things of price
Calling at every moment for remark?
I noticed on the margin of a pool   280
Blue-flowering borage, the Aleppo sort,
Aboundeth, very nitrous.   It is strange!

    Thy pardon for this long and tedious case,
Which, now that I review it, needs must seem
Unduly dwelt on, prolixly set forth!   285
Nor I myself discern in what is writ
Good cause for the peculiar interest

And awe indeed this man has touched me with.
Perhaps the journey's end, the weariness
Had wrought upon me first. I met him thus: 290
I crossed a ridge of short sharp broken hills
Like an old lion's cheek teeth. Out there came
A moon made like a face with certain spots
Multiform, manifold, and menacing:
Then a wind rose behind me. So we met   295
In this old sleepy town at unaware,
The man and I. I send thee what is writ.
Regard it as a chance, a matter risked
To this ambiguous Syrian — he may lose,
Or steal, or give it thee with equal good.   300
Jerusalem's repose shall make amends
For time this letter wastes, thy time and mine;
Till when, once more thy pardon and farewell!

The very God! think, Abib; dost thou think?
So, the All-Great, were the All-Loving too —   305
So, through the thunder comes a human voice
Saying, "O heart I made, a heart beats here!
Face, my hands fashioned, see it in myself!
Thou hast no power nor mayst conceive of mine,
But love I gave thee, with myself to love,   310
And thou must love me who have died for thee!"
The madman saith He said so: it is strange.

PICTOR IGNOTUS

FLORENCE, 15—

I COULD have painted pictures like that youth's
  Ye praise so. How my soul springs up! No bar
Stayed me — ah, thought which saddens while it soothes!
  — Never did fate forbid me, star by star,
To outburst on your night with all my gift   5
  Of fires from God: nor would my flesh have shrunk

From seconding my soul, with eyes uplift
   And wide to heaven, or, straight like thunder, sunk
To the centre, of an instant; or around
   Turned calmly and inquisitive, to scan   10
The license and the limit, space and bound,
   Allowed to truth made visible in man.
And, like that youth ye praise so, all I saw,
   Over the canvas could my hand have flung,
Each face obedient to its passion's law,   15
   Each passion clear proclaimed without a tongue;
Whether Hope rose at once in all the blood,
   A-tiptoe for the blessing of embrace,
Or Rapture drooped the eyes, as when her brood
   Pull down the nesting dove's heart to its place;   20
Or Confidence lit swift the forehead up,
   And locked the mouth fast, like a castle braved, —
O human faces, hath it spilt, my cup?
   What did ye give me that I have not saved?
Nor will I say I have not dreamed (how well!)   25
   Of going — I, in each new picture, — forth,
As, making new hearts beat and bosoms swell,
   To Pope or Kaiser, East, West, South, or North,
Bound for the calmly satisfied great State,
   Or glad aspiring little burgh, it went,   30
Flowers cast upon the car which bore the freight,
   Through old streets named afresh from the event,
Till it reached home, where learned age should greet
   My face, and youth, the star not yet distinct
Above his hair, lie learning at my feet! —   35
   Oh, thus to live, I and my picture, linked
With love about, and praise, till life should end,
   And then not go to heaven, but linger here,
Here on my earth, earth's every man my friend, —
   The thought grew frightful, 'twas so wildly dear! 40
But a voice changed it.   Glimpses of such sights
   Have scared me, like the revels through a door
Of some strange house of idols at its rites!
This world seemed not the world it was before:

Mixed with my loving trusting ones, there trooped   45
   ... Who summoned those cold faces that begun
To press on me and judge me?   Though I stooped
   Shrinking, as from the soldiery a nun,
They drew me forth, and spite of me ... enough!
   These buy and sell our pictures, take and give,   50
Count them for garniture and household-stuff,
   And where they live needs must our pictures live
And see their faces, listen to their prate,
   Partakers of their daily pettiness,
Discussed of —"This I love, or this I hate,   55
   This likes me more, and this affects me less!"
Wherefore I chose my portion.   If at whiles
   My heart sinks, as monotonous I paint
These endless cloisters and eternal aisles
   With the same series, Virgin, Babe and Saint,   60
With the same cold calm beautiful regard, —
   At least no merchant traffics in my heart;
The sanctuary's gloom at least shall ward
   Vain tongues from where my pictures stand apart:
Only prayer breaks the silence of the shrine   65
   While, blackening in the daily candle-smoke,
They moulder on the damp wall's travertine,
   'Mid echoes the light footstep never woke.
So, die my pictures! surely, gently die!
   O youth, men praise so, — holds their praise its worth? 70
Blown harshly, keeps the trump its golden cry?
   Tastes sweet the water with such specks of earth?

FRA LIPPO LIPPI

I AM poor brother Lippo, by your leave!
You need not clap your torches to my face.
Zooks, what's to blame? you think you see a monk!
What, 'tis past midnight, and you go the rounds,
And here you catch me at an alley's end   5
Where sportive ladies leave their doors ajar?

The Carmine's my cloister: hunt it up,
Do, — harry out, if you must show your zeal,
Whatever rat, there, haps on his wrong hole,
And nip each softling of a wee white mouse,   10
Weke, weke, that's crept to keep him company!
Aha, you know your betters!   Then, you'll take
Your hand away that's fiddling on my throat,
And please to know me likewise.   Who am I?
Why, one, sir, who is lodging with a friend   15
Three streets off — he's a certain . . . how d'ye call?
Master — a . . . Cosimo of the Medici,
I' the house that caps the corner.   Boh! you were best!
Remember and tell me, the day you're hanged,
How you affected such a gullet's-gripe!   20
But you, sir, it concerns you that your knaves
Pick up a manner nor discredit you:
Zooks, are we pilchards, that they sweep the streets
And count fair prize what comes into their net?
He's Judas to a tittle, that man is!   25
Just such a face!   Why, sir, you make amends.
Lord, I'm not angry!   Bid your hangdogs go
Drink out this quarter-florin to the health
Of the munificent House that harbours me
(And many more beside, lads! more beside!)   30
And all's come square again.   I'd like his face —
His, elbowing on his comrade in the door
With the pike and lantern — for the slave that holds
John Baptist's head a-dangle by the hair
With one hand ("Look you, now," as who should say)   35
And his weapon in the other, yet unwiped!
It's not your chance to have a bit of chalk,
A wood-coal or the like? or you should see!
Yes, I'm the painter, since you style me so.
What, brother Lippo's doings, up and down,   40
You know them and they take you? like enough!
I saw the proper twinkle in your eye —
'Tell you, I liked your looks at very first.

Let's sit and set things straight now, hip to haunch.
Here's spring come, and the nights one makes up bands 45
To roam the town and sing out carnival,
And I've been three weeks shut within my mew,
A-painting for the great man, saints and saints
And saints again. I could not paint all night —
Ouf! I leaned out of window for fresh air. 50
There came a hurry of feet and little feet,
A sweep of lute-strings, laughs, and whiffs of song —
Flower o' the broom,
Take away love, and our earth is a tomb!
Flower o' the quince, 55
I let Lisa go, and what good in life since?
Flower o' the thyme — and so on. Round they went.
Scarce had they turned the corner when a titter
Like the skipping of rabbits by moonlight, — three slim
     shapes,
And a face that looked up . . . zooks, sir, flesh and blood, 60
That's all I'm made of! Into shreds it went,
Curtain and counterpane and coverlet,
All the bed-furniture — a dozen knots,
There was a ladder! Down I let myself,
Hands and feet, scrambling somehow, and so dropped, 65
And after them. I came up with the fun
Hard by Saint Laurence, hail fellow, well met, —
Flower o' the rose,
If I've been merry, what matter who knows?
And so, as I was stealing back again 70
To get to bed and have a bit of sleep
Ere I rise up to-morrow and go work
On Jerome knocking at his poor old breast
With his great round stone to subdue the flesh,
You snap me of the sudden. Ah, I see! 75
Though your eye twinkles still, you shake your head —
Mine's shaved — a monk, you say — the sting's in that!
If Master Cosimo announced himself,
Mum's the word naturally; but a monk!

Come, what am I a beast for? tell us, now!   80
I was a baby when my mother died
And father died and left me in the street.
I starved there, God knows how, a year or two
On fig-skins, melon-parings, rinds and shucks,
Refuse and rubbish.   One fine frosty day,   85
My stomach being empty as your hat,
The wind doubled me up and down I went.
Old Aunt Lapaccia trussed me with one hand,
(Its fellow was a stinger as I knew,)
And so along the wall, over the bridge,   90
By the straight cut to the convent.   Six words there,
While I stood munching my first bread that month:
"So, boy, you're minded," quoth the good fat father,
Wiping his own mouth, 'twas refection-time —
"To quit this very miserable world?   95
Will you renounce" . . . "the mouthful of bread?" thought I;
By no means!   Brief, they made a monk of me;
I did renounce the world, its pride and greed,
Palace, farm, villa, shop, and banking-house,
Trash, such as these poor devils of Medici   100
Have given their hearts to — all at eight years old.
Well, sir, I found in time, you may be sure,
'Twas not for nothing — the good bellyful,
The warm serge and the rope that goes all round,
And day-long blessed idleness beside!   105
"Let's see what the urchin's fit for" — that came next.
Not overmuch their way, I must confess.
Such a to-do!   They tried me with their books;
Lord, they'd have taught me Latin in pure waste!
Flower o' the clove,   110
All the Latin I construe is "amo," I love!
But, mind you, when a boy starves in the streets
Eight years together, as my fortune was,
Watching folk's faces to know who will fling
The bit of half-stripped grape-bunch he desires,   115
And who will curse or kick him for his pains, —

Which gentleman processional and fine,
Holding a candle to the Sacrament,
Will wink and let him lift a plate and catch
The droppings of the wax to sell again, 120
Or holla for the Eight and have him whipped, —
How say I? — nay, which dog bites, which lets drop
His bone from the heap of offal in the street, —
Why, soul and sense of him grow sharp alike,
He learns the look of things, and none the less 125
For admonition from the hunger-pinch.
I had a store of such remarks, be sure,
Which, after I found leisure, turned to use.
I drew men's faces on my copy-books,
Scrawled them within the antiphonary's marge, 130
Joined legs and arms to the long music-notes,
Found eyes and nose and chin for A's and B's,
And made a string of pictures of the world
Betwixt the ins and outs of verb and noun,
On the wall, the bench, the door. The monks looked black.
"Nay," quoth the Prior, "turn him out, d'ye say? 136
In no wise. Lose a crow and catch a lark.
What if at last we get our man of parts,
We Carmelites, like those Camaldolese
And Preaching Friars, to do our church up fine 140
And put the front on it that ought to be!"
And hereupon he bade me daub away.
Thank you! my head being crammed, the walls a blank,
Never was such prompt disemburdening.
First, every sort of monk, the black and white, 145
I drew them, fat and lean: then, folk at church,
From good old gossips waiting to confess
Their cribs of barrel-droppings, candle-ends, —
To the breathless fellow at the altar-foot,
Fresh from his murder, safe and sitting there 150
With the little children round him in a row
Of admiration, half for his beard and half
For that white anger of his victim's son

Shaking a fist at him with one fierce arm,
Signing himself with the other because of Christ   155
(Whose sad face on the cross sees only this
After the passion of a thousand years)
Till some poor girl, her apron o'er her head,
(Which the intense eyes looked through) came at eve
On tiptoe, said a word, dropped in a loaf,   160
Her pair of earrings and a bunch of flowers
('The brute took growling), prayed, and so was gone.
I painted all, then cried "'Tis ask and have;
Choose, for more's ready!" — laid the ladder flat,
And showed my covered bit of cloister-wall.   165
The monks closed in a circle and praised loud
Till checked, taught what to see and not to see,
Being simple bodies, — "That's the very man!
Look at the boy who stoops to pat the dog!
That woman's like the Prior's niece who comes   170
To care about his asthma: it's the life!"
But there my triumph's straw-fire flared and funked;
Their betters took their turn to see and say:
The Prior and the learned pulled a face
And stopped all that in no time. "How? what's here?   175
Quite from the mark of painting, bless us all!
Faces, arms, legs and bodies like the true
As much as pea and pea! it's devil's-game!
Your business is not to catch men with show,
With homage to the perishable clay,   180
But lift them over it, ignore it all,
Make them forget there's such a thing as flesh.
Your business is to paint the souls of men —
Man's soul, and it's a fire, smoke . . . no, it's not . . .
It's vapour done up like a new-born babe —   185
(In that shape when you die it leaves your mouth)
It's . . . well, what matters talking, it's the soul!
Give us no more of body than shows soul!
Here's Giotto, with his Saint a-praising God,
That sets us praising, — why not stop with him?   190

Why put all thoughts of praise out of our head
With wonder at lines, colours, and what not?
Paint the soul, never mind the legs and arms!
Rub all out, try at it a second time.
Oh, that white smallish female with the breasts,   195
She's just my niece . . . Herodias, I would say —
Who went and danced and got men's heads cut off!
Have it all out!"   Now, is this sense, I ask?
A fine way to paint soul, by painting body
So ill, the eye can't stop there, must go further   200
And can't fare worse!   Thus, yellow does for white
When what you put for yellow's simply black,
And any sort of meaning looks intense
When all beside itself means and looks naught.
Why can't a painter lift each foot in turn,   205
Left foot and right foot, go a double step,
Make his flesh liker and his soul more like,
Both in their order?   Take the prettiest face,
The Prior's niece . . . patron-saint — is it so pretty
You can't discover if it means hope, fear,   210
Sorrow or joy? won't beauty go with these?
Suppose I've made her eyes all right and blue,
Can't I take breath and try to add life's flash,
And then add soul and heighten them three-fold?
Or say there's beauty with no soul at all —   215
(I never saw it — put the case the same —)
If you get simple beauty and naught else,
You get about the best thing God invents:
That's somewhat: and you'll find the soul you have missed,
Within yourself, when you return him thanks.   220
"Rub all out!"   Well, well, there's my life, in short,
And so the thing has gone on ever since.
I'm grown a man no doubt, I've broken bounds:
You should not take a fellow eight years old
And make him swear to never kiss the girls.   225
I'm my own master, paint now as I please —
Having a friend, you see, in the Corner-house!

Lord, it's fast holding by the rings in front —
Those great rings serve more purposes than just
To plant a flag in, or tie up a horse!   230
And yet the old schooling sticks, the old grave eyes
Are peeping o'er my shoulder as I work,
The heads shake still — "It's art's decline, my son!
You're not of the true painters, great and old;
Brother Angelico's the man, you'll find;   235
Brother Lorenzo stands his single peer:
Fag on at flesh, you'll never make the third!"
Flower o' the pine,
You keep your mistr . . . manners, and I'll stick to mine!
I'm not the third, then: bless us, they must know!   240
Don't you think they're the likeliest to know,
They with their Latin? So, I swallow my rage,
Clench my teeth, suck my lips in tight, and paint
To please them — sometimes do and sometimes don't;
For, doing most, there's pretty sure to come   245
A turn, some warm eve finds me at my saints —
A laugh, a cry, the business of the world —
(*Flower o' the peach,*
Death for us all, and his own life for each!)
And my whole soul revolves, the cup runs over,   250
The world and life's too big to pass for a dream,
And I do these wild things in sheer despite,
And play the fooleries you catch me at,
In pure rage! The old mill-horse, out at grass
After hard years, throws up his stiff heels so,   255
Although the miller does not preach to him
The only good of grass is to make chaff.
What would men have? Do they like grass or no —
May they or mayn't they? all I want's the thing
Settled for ever one way. As it is,   260
You tell too many lies and hurt yourself:
You don't like what you only like too much,
You do like what, if given you at your word,
You find abundantly detestable.

For me, I think I speak as I was taught;   265
I always see the garden and God there
A-making man's wife: and, my lesson learned,
The value and significance of flesh,
I can't unlearn ten minutes afterwards.

    You understand me: I'm a beast, I know.   270
But see, now — why, I see as certainly
As that the morning-star's about to shine,
What will hap some day.   We've a youngster here
Comes to our convent, studies what I do,
Slouches and stares and lets no atom drop: 275
His name is Guidi — he'll not mind the monks —
They call him Hulking Tom, he lets them talk —
He picks my practice up — he'll paint apace,
I hope so — though I never live so long,
I know what's sure to follow.   You be judge!   280
You speak no Latin more than I, belike;
However, you're my man, you've seen the world   *memoring*
— The beauty and the wonder and the power,
The shapes of things, their colours, lights and shades,
Changes, surprises — and God made it all! ✓   285
— For what?   Do you feel thankful, ay or no,
For this fair town's face, yonder river's line,
The mountain round it and the sky above,
Much more the figures of man, woman, child,
These are the frame to?   What's it all about?   290
To be passed over, despised? or dwelt upon,
Wondered at? oh, this last of course! — you say.
But why not do as well as say, — paint these
Just as they are, careless what comes of it?
God's works — paint any one, and count it crime   295
To let a truth slip.   Don't object, "His works
Are here already; Nature is complete:
Suppose you reproduce her — (which you can't)
There's no advantage! you must beat her, then."
For, don't you mark? we're made so that we love   300

First when we see them painted, things we have passed
Perhaps a hundred times nor cared to see;
And so they are better, painted — better to us,
Which is the same thing.   Art was given for that;
God uses us to help each other so,   305
Lending our minds out.   Have you noticed, now,
Your cullion's hanging face?   A bit of chalk,
And trust me but you should, though!   How much more,
If I drew higher things with the same truth!
That were to take the Prior's pulpit-place,   310
Interpret God to all of you!   Oh, oh,
It makes me mad to see what men shall do
And we in our graves!   This world's no blot for us,
Nor blank; it means intensely, and means good:
To find its meaning is my meat and drink.   315
"Ay, but you don't so instigate to prayer!"
Strikes in the Prior: "when your meaning's plain
It does not say to folk — remember matins,
Or, mind you fast next Friday!"   Why, for this
What need of art at all?   A skull and bones,   320
Two bits of stick nailed crosswise, or, what's best,
A bell to chime the hour with, does as well.
I painted a Saint Laurence six months since
At Prato, splashed the fresco in fine style:
"How looks my painting, now the scaffold's down?"   325
I ask a brother: "Hugely," he returns —
"Already not one phiz of your three slaves
Who turn the Deacon off his toasted side,
But's scratched and prodded to our heart's content,
The pious people have so eased their own   330
With coming to say prayers there in a rage:
We get on fast to see the bricks beneath.
Expect another job this time next year,
For pity and religion grow i' the crowd —
Your painting serves its purpose!"   Hang the fools!   335

    — That is — you'll not mistake an idle word

Spoke in a huff by a poor monk, God wot.
Tasting the air this spicy night which turns
The unaccustomed head like Chianti wine!
Oh, the church knows! don't misreport me, now!   340
It's natural a poor monk out of bounds
Should have his apt word to excuse himself:
And hearken how I plot to make amends.
I have bethought me: I shall paint a piece
. . . There's for you!   Give me six months, then go, see   345
Something in Sant' Ambrogio's!   Bless the nuns!
They want a cast o' my office.   I shall paint
God in the midst, Madonna and her babe,
Ringed by a bowery, flowery angel-brood,
Lilies and vestments and white faces, sweet   350
As puff on puff of grated orris-root
When ladies crowd to Church at midsummer.
And then i' the front, of course a saint or two —
Saint John, because he saves the Florentines,
Saint Ambrose, who puts down in black and white   355
The convent's friends and gives them a long day,
And Job, I must have him there past mistake,
The man of Uz (and Us without the z,
Painters who need his patience).   Well, all these
Secured at their devotion, up shall come   360
Out of a corner when you least expect,
As one by a dark stair into a great light,
Music and talking, who but Lippo! I! —
Mazed, motionless, and moonstruck — I'm the man!
Back I shrink — what is this I see and hear?   365
I, caught up with my monk's-things by mistake,
My old serge gown and rope that goes all round,
I, in this presence, this pure company!
Where's a hole, where's a corner for escape?
Then steps a sweet angelic slip of a thing   370
Forward, puts out a soft palm — "Not so fast!"
— Addresses the celestial presence, "nay —
He made you and devised you, after all,

Though he's none of you!   Could Saint John there draw —
His camel-hair make up a painting-brush?   375
We come to brother Lippo for all that,
Iste perfecit opus!"   So, all smile —
I shuffle sideways with my blushing face
Under the cover of a hundred wings
Thrown like a spread of kirtles when you're gay   380
And play hot cockles, all the doors being shut,
Till, wholly unexpected, in there pops
The hothead husband!   Thus I scuttle off
To some safe bench behind, not letting go
The palm of her, the little lily thing   385
That spoke the good word for me in the nick,
Like the Prior's niece . . . Saint Lucy, I would say.
And so all's saved for me, and for the church
A pretty picture gained.   Go, six months hence!
Your hand, sir, and good-bye: no lights, no lights!   390
The street's hushed, and I know my own way back,
Don't fear me!   There's the gray beginning.   Zooks!

ANDREA DEL SARTO

(CALLED "THE FAULTLESS PAINTER")

BUT do not let us quarrel any more,
No, my Lucrezia; bear with me for once:
Sit down and all shall happen as you wish.
You turn your face, but does it bring your heart?
I'll work then for your friend's friend, never fear,   5
Treat his own subject after his own way,
Fix his own time, accept too his own price,
And shut the money into this small hand
When next it takes mine.   Will it? tenderly?
Oh, I'll content him — but to-morrow, Love!   10
I often am much wearier than you think,
This evening more than usual, and it seems
As if — forgive now — should you let me sit
Here by the window with your hand in mine

And look a half-hour forth on Fiesole, 15
Both of one mind, as married people use,
Quietly, quietly the evening through,
I might get up to-morrow to my work
Cheerful and fresh as ever.   Let us try.
To-morrow, how you shall be glad for this! 20
Your soft hand is a woman of itself,
And mine the man's bared breast she curls inside.
Don't count the time lost, neither; you must serve
For each of the five pictures we require:
It saves a model.   So! keep looking so — 25
My serpentining beauty, rounds on rounds!
— How could you ever prick those perfect ears,
Even to put the pearl there! oh, so sweet —
My face, my moon, my everybody's moon,
Which everybody looks on and calls his, 30
And, I suppose, is looked on by in turn,
While she looks — no one's: very dear, no less.
You smile? why, there's my picture ready made,
There's what we painters call our harmony!
A common grayness silvers everything, — 35
All in a twilight, you and I alike
— You, at the point of your first pride in me
(That's gone you know), — but I, at every point;
My youth, my hope, my art, being all toned down
To yonder sober pleasant Fiesole. 40
There's the bell clinking from the chapel-top;
That length of convent-wall across the way
Holds the trees safer, huddled more inside;
The last monk leaves the garden; days decrease,
And autumn grows, autumn in everything. 45
Eh? the whole seems to fall into a shape
As if I saw alike my work and self
And all that I was born to be and do,
A twilight-piece.   Love, we are in God's hand.
How strange now looks the life he makes us lead; 50
So free we seem, so fettered fast we are!

I feel he laid the fetter: let it lie!
This chamber for example — turn your head —
All that's behind us!   You don't understand
Nor care to understand about my art,   55
But you can hear at least when people speak:
And that cartoon, the second from the door
— It is the thing, Love! so such thing should be —
Behold Madonna! — I am bold to say.
I can do with my pencil what I know,   60
What I see, what at bottom of my heart
I wish for, if I ever wish so deep —
Do easily, too — when I say, perfectly,
I do not boast, perhaps: yourself are judge,
Who listened to the Legate's talk last week,   65
And just as much they used to say in France.
At any rate 'tis easy, all of it!
No sketches first, no studies, that's long past:
I do what many dream of all their lives,
— Dream? strive to do, and agonize to do,   70
And fail in doing.   I could count twenty such
On twice your fingers, and not leave this town,
Who strive — you don't know how the others strive
To paint a little thing like that you smeared
Carelessly passing with your robes afloat, —   75
Yet do much less, so much less, Someone says,
(I know his name, no matter) — so much less!
Well, less is more, Lucrezia: I am judged.
There burns a truer light of God in them,
In their vexed beating stuffed and stopped-up brain,   80
Heart, or whate'er else, than goes on to prompt
This low-pulsed forthright craftsman's hand of mine.
Their works drop groundward, but themselves, I know,
Reach many a time a heaven that's shut to me,
Enter and take their place there sure enough,   85
Though they come back and cannot tell the world.
My works are nearer heaven, but I sit here.
The sudden blood of these men! at a word —

Praise them, it boils, or blame them, it boils **too.**
I, painting from myself and to myself,   90
Know what I do, am unmoved by men's blame
Or their praise either.   Somebody remarks
Morello's outline there is wrongly traced,
His hue mistaken; what of that? or else,
Rightly traced and well ordered; what of that?   95
Speak as they please, what does the mountain **care?**
Ah, but a man's reach should exceed his grasp,
Or what's a heaven for?   All is silver-gray
Placid and perfect with my art: the worse!
I know both what I want and what might **gain,**   100
And yet how profitless to know, to sigh
"Had I been two, another and myself,
Our head would have o'erlooked the world!"   No doubt.
Yonder's a work now, of that famous youth
The Urbinate who died five years ago.   105
('Tis copied, George Vasari sent it me.)
Well, I can fancy how he did it all,
Pouring his soul, with kings and popes to see,
Reaching, that heaven might so replenish him,
Above and through his art — for it gives way;   110
That arm is wrongly put — and there again —
A fault to pardon in the drawing's lines,
Its body, so to speak: its soul is right,
He means right — that, a child may understand.
Still, what an arm! and I could alter it: 115
But all the play, the insight and the stretch —
Out of me, out of me!   And wherefore out?
Had you enjoined them on me, given me soul,
We might have risen to Rafael, I and you!
Nay, Love, you did give all I asked, I think —   120
More than I merit, yes, by many times.
But had you — oh, with the same perfect brow,
And perfect eyes, and more than perfect mouth,
And the low voice my soul hears, as a bird
The fowler's pipe, and follows to the snare —   125

Had you, with these the same, but brought a mind!
Some women do so.   Had the mouth there urged
"God and the glory! never care for gain.
The present by the future, what is that?
Live for fame, side by side with Agnolo!   130
Rafael is waiting: up to God, all three!"
I might have done it for you.   So it seems:
Perhaps not.   All is as God overrules.
Beside, incentives come from the soul's self;
The rest avail not.   Why do I need you?   135
What wife had Rafael, or has Agnolo?
In this world, who can do a thing, will not;
And who would do it, cannot, I perceive:
Yet the will's somewhat — somewhat, too, the power —
And thus we half-men struggle.   At the end,   140
God, I conclude, compensates, punishes.
'Tis safer for me, if the award be strict,
That I am something underrated here,
Poor this long while, despised, to speak the truth.
I dared not, do you know, leave home all day,   145
For fear of chancing on the Paris lords.
The best is when they pass and look aside;
But they speak sometimes; I must bear it all.
Well may they speak!   That Francis, that first time,
And that long festal year at Fontainebleau!   150
I surely then could sometimes leave the ground,
Put on the glory, Rafael's daily wear,
In that humane great monarch's golden look, —
One finger in his beard or twisted curl
Over his mouth's good mark that made the smile,   155
One arm about my shoulder, round my neck,
The jingle of his gold chain in my ear,
I painting proudly with his breath on me,
All his Court round him, seeing with his eyes,
Such frank French eyes, and such a fire of souls   160
Profuse, my hand kept plying by those hearts, —
And, best of all, this, this, this face beyond,

This in the background, waiting on my work,
To crown the issue with a last reward!
A good time, was it not, my kingly days? 165
And had you not grown restless . . . but I know —
'Tis done and past; 'twas right, my instinct said;
Too live the life grew, golden and not gray,
And I'm the weak-eyed bat no sun should tempt
Out of the grange whose four walls make his world. 170
How could it end in any other way?
You called me, and I came home to your heart.
The triumph was — to reach and stay there; since
I reached it ere the triumph, what is lost?
Let my hands frame your face in your hair's gold, 175
You beautiful Lucrezia that are mine!
"Rafael did this, Andrea painted that;
The Roman's is the better when you pray,
But still the other's Virgin was his wife" —
Men will excuse me.   I am glad to judge 180
Both pictures in your presence; clearer grows
My better fortune, I resolve to think.
For, do you know, Lucrezia, as God lives,
Said one day Agnolo, his very self,
To Rafael . . . I have known it all these years . . . 185
(When the young man was flaming out his thoughts
Upon a palace-wall for Rome to see,
Too lifted up in heart because of it)
"Friend, there's a certain sorry little scrub
Goes up and down our Florence, none cares how, 190
Who, were he set to plan and execute
As you are, pricked on by your popes and kings,
Would bring the sweat into that brow of yours!"
To Rafael's! — And indeed the arm is wrong.
I hardly dare . . . yet, only you to see, 195
Give the chalk here — quick, thus the line should go!
Ay, but the soul! he's Rafael! rub it out!
Still, all I care for, if he spoke the truth,
(What he? why, who but Michel Agnolo?

Do you forget already words like those?)   206
If really there was such a chance, so lost, —
Is, whether you're — not grateful — but more pleased.
Well, let me think so.   And you smile indeed!
This hour has been an hour!   Another smile?
If you would sit thus by me every night   205
I should work better, do you comprehend?
I mean that I should earn more, give you more.
See, it is settled dusk now; there's a star;
Morello's gone, the watch-lights show the wall,
The cue-owls speak the name we call them by.   210
Come from the window, love, — come in, at last,
Inside the melancholy little house
We built to be so gay with.   God is just.
King Francis may forgive me: oft at nights
When I look up from painting, eyes tired out,   215
The walls become illumined, brick from brick
Distinct, instead of mortar, fierce bright gold
That gold of his I did cement them with!
Let us but love each other.   Must you go?
That Cousin here again? he waits outside?   220
Must see you — you, and not with me?   Those loans?
More gaming debts to pay? you smiled for that?
Well, let smiles buy me! have you more to spend?
While hand and eye and something of a heart
Are left me, work's my ware, and what's it worth?   225
I'll pay my fancy.   Only let me sit
The gray remainder of the evening out,
Idle, you call it, and muse perfectly
How I could paint, were I but back in France,
One picture, just one more — the Virgin's face   230
Not yours this time!   I want you at my side
To hear them — that is, Michel Agnolo —
Judge all I do and tell you of its worth.
Will you?   To-morrow, satisfy your friend.
I take the subjects for his corridor,   235
Finish the portrait out of hand — there, there,

And throw him in another thing or two
If he demurs: the whole should prove enough
To pay for this same Cousin's freak.   Beside,
What's better and what's all I care about,   240
Get you the thirteen scudi for the ruff!
Love, does that please you?   Ah, but what does he,
The Cousin! what does he to please you more?

    I am grown peaceful as old age to-night.
I regret little, I would change still less.   245
Since there my past life lies, why alter it?
The very wrong to Francis! — it is true
I took his coin, was tempted and complied,
And built this house and sinned, and all is said.
My father and my mother died of want.   250
Well, had I riches of my own? you see
How one gets rich!   Let each one bear his lot.
They were born poor, lived poor, and poor they died:
And I have laboured somewhat in my time
And not been paid profusely.   Some good son   255
Paint my two hundred pictures — let him try!
No doubt, there's something strikes a balance.   Yes,
You loved me quite enough, it seems to-night.
This must suffice me here.   What would one have?
In heaven, perhaps, new chances, one more chance —   260
Four great walls in the New Jerusalem,
Meted on each side by the angel's reed,
For Leonard, Rafael, Agnolo and me
To cover — the three first without a wife,
While I have mine!   So — still they overcome   265
Because there's still Lucrezia, — as I choose.

    Again the Cousin's whistle!   Go, my Love.

THE BISHOP ORDERS HIS TOMB AT SAINT PRAXED'S CHURCH

ROME, 15 —

VANITY, saith the preacher, vanity!
Draw round my bed: is Anselm keeping back?
Nephews — sons mine . . . ah, God, I know not! Well —
She, men would have to be your mother once,
Old Gandolf envied me, so fair she was!   5
What's done is done, and she is dead beside,
Dead long ago, and I am Bishop since,
And as she died so must we die ourselves,
And thence ye may perceive the world's a dream.
Life, how and what is it? As here I lie   10
In this state-chamber, dying by degrees,
Hours and long hours in the dead night, I ask
"Do I live, am I dead?" Peace, peace seems all.
Saint Praxed's ever was the church for peace;
And so, about this tomb of mine. I fought   15
With tooth and nail to save my niche, ye know:
— Old Gandolf cozened me, despite my care;
Shrewd was that snatch from out the corner South
He graced his carrion with, God curse the same!
Yet still my niche is not so cramped but thence   20
One sees the pulpit o' the epistle-side,
And somewhat of the choir, those silent seats,
And up into the aery dome where live
The angels, and a sunbeam's sure to lurk:
And I shall fill my slab of basalt there,   25
And 'neath my tabernacle take my rest,
With those nine columns round me, two and two,
The odd one at my feet where Anselm stands:
Peach-blossom marble all, the rare, the ripe,
As fresh-poured red wine of a mighty pulse.   30
— Old Gandolf with his paltry onion-stone,
Put me where I may look at him! True peach,
Rosy and flawless: how I earned the prize!

Draw close: that conflagration of my church
— What then?   So much was saved if aught were missed! 35
My sons, ye would not be my death?   Go dig
The white-grape vineyard where the oil-press stood.
Drop water gently till the surface sink,
And if ye find . . . Ah, God, I know not, I! . . .
Bedded in store of rotten fig-leaves soft, 40
And corded up in a tight olive-frail,
Some lump, ah God, of *lapis lazuli,*
Big as a Jew's head cut off at the nape,
Blue as a vein o'er the Madonna's breast . . .
Sons, all have I bequeathed you, villas, all, 45
That brave Frascati villa with its bath,
So, let the blue lump poise between my knees,
Like God the Father's globe on both his hands
Ye worship in the Jesu Church so gay,
For Gandolf shall not choose but see and burst! 50
Swift as a weaver's shuttle fleet our years:
Man goeth to the grave, and where is he?
Did I say basalt for my slab, sons?   Black —
'Twas ever antique-black I meant!   How else
Shall ye contrast my frieze to come beneath? 55
The bas-relief in bronze ye promised me.
Those Pans and Nymphs ye wot of, and perchance
Some tripod, thyrsus, with a vase or so,
The Saviour at his sermon on the mount,
Saint Praxed in a glory, and one Pan 60
Ready to twitch the Nymph's last garment off,
And Moses with the tables . . . but I know
Ye mark me not!   What do they whisper thee,
Child of my bowels, Anselm?   Ah, ye hope
To revel down my villas while I gasp 65
Bricked o'er with beggar's mouldy travertine
Which Gandolf from his tomb-top chuckles at!
Nay, boys, ye love me — all of jasper, then!
'Tis jasper ye stand pledged to, lest I grieve
My bath must needs be left behind, alas! 70

One block, pure green as a pistachio-nut,
There's plenty jasper somewhere in the world —
And have I not Saint Praxed's ear to pray
Horses for ye, and brown Greek manuscripts,
And mistresses with great smooth marbly limbs?   75
— That's if ye carve my epitaph aright,
Choice Latin, picked phrase, Tully's every word,
No gaudy ware like Gandolf's second line —
Tully, my masters?   Ulpian serves his need!
And then how I shall lie through centuries,   80
And hear the blessed mutter of the mass,
And see God made and eaten all day long,
And feel the steady candle-flame, and taste
Good strong thick stupefying incense-smoke!
For as I lie here, hours of the dead night,   85
Dying in state and by such slow degrees,
I fold my arms as if they clasped a crook,
And stretch my feet forth straight as stone can point,
And let the bedclothes, for a mortcloth, drop
Into great laps and folds of sculptor's-work: 90
And as yon tapers dwindle, and strange thoughts
Grow, with a certain humming in my ears,
About the life before I lived this life,
And this life too, popes, cardinals and priests
Saint Praxed at his sermon on the mount,   95
Your tall pale mother with her talking eyes,
And new-found agate urns as fresh as day,
And marble's language, Latin pure, discreet,
— Aha, ELUCESCEBAT quoth our friend?
No Tully, said I, Ulpian at the best!   100
Evil and brief hath been my pilgrimage.
All *lapis*, all, sons!   Else I give the Pope
My villas!   Will ye ever eat my heart?
Ever your eyes were as a lizard's quick,
They glitter like your mother's for my soul,   105
Or ye would heighten my impoverished frieze,
Piece out its starved design, and fill my vase

With grapes, and add a visor and a Term,
And to the tripod ye would tie a lynx
That in his struggle throws the thyrsus down,   110
To comfort me on my entablature
Whereon I am to lie till I must ask
"Do I live, am I dead?"   There, leave me, there!
For ye have stabbed me with ingratitude
To death — ye wish it — God, ye wish it!   Stone —   115
Gritstone, a-crumble!   Clammy squares which sweat
As if the corpse they keep were oozing through —
And no more *lapis* to delight the world!
Well, go!   I bless ye.   Fewer tapers there,
But in a row: and, going, turn your backs   120
— Ay, like departing altar-ministrants,
And leave me in my church, the church for peace,
That I may watch at leisure if he leers —
Old Gandolf — at me, from his onion-stone,
As still he envied me, so fair she was!   125

CLEON

"As certain also of your own poets have said" —

CLEON the poet (from the sprinkled isles,
Lily on lily, that o'erlace the sea,
And laugh their pride when the light wave lisps "Greece")—
To Protus in his Tyranny: much health!

They give thy letter to me, even now: 5
I read and seem as if I heard thee speak.
The master of thy galley still unlades
Gift after gift; they block my court at last
And pile themselves along its portico
Royal with sunset, like a thought of thee: 10
And one white she-slave from the group dispersed
Of black and white slaves (like the chequer-work
Pavement, at once my nation's work and gift,
Now covered with this settle-down of doves).

One lyric woman, in her crocus vest   15
Woven of sea-wools, with her two white hands
Commends to me the strainer and the cup
Thy lip hath bettered ere it blesses mine.

Well-counselled, king, in thy munificence!
For so shall men remark, in such an act   20
Of love for him whose song gives life its joy,
Thy recognition of the use of life;
Nor call thy spirit barely adequate
To help on life in straight ways, broad enough
For vulgar souls, by ruling and the rest.   25
Thou, in the daily building of thy tower —
Whether in fierce and sudden spasms of toil,
Or through dim lulls of unapparent growth,
Or when the general work 'mid good acclaim
Climbed with the eye to cheer the architect —   30
Didst ne'er engage in work for mere work's sake,
Hadst ever in thy heart the luring hope
Of some eventual rest a-top of it,
Whence, all the tumult of the building hushed,
Thou first of men mightst look out to the East: 35
The vulgar saw thy tower, thou sawest the sun.
For this, I promise on thy festival
To pour libation, looking o'er the sea,
Making this slave narrate thy fortunes, speak
Thy great words, and describe thy royal face —   40
Wishing thee wholly where Zeus lives the most,
Within the eventual element of calm.

Thy letter's first requirement meets me here.
It is as thou hast heard: in one short life
I, Cleon, have effected all those things   45
Thou wonderingly dost enumerate.
That epos on thy hundred plates of gold
Is mine, — and also mine the little chant,
So sure to rise from every fishing-bark

When, lights at prow, the seamen haul their net. 50
The image of the sun-god on the phare,
Men turn from the sun's self to see, is mine;
The Pœcile, o'er-storied its whole length,
As thou didst hear, with painting, is mine too.
I know the true proportions of a man 55
And woman also, not observed before;
And I have written three books on the soul,
Proving absurd all written hitherto,
And putting us to ignorance again.
For music — why, I have combined the moods, 60
Inventing one.   In brief, all arts are mine;
Thus much the people know and recognize,
Throughout our seventeen islands.   Marvel not.
We of these latter days, with greater mind
Than our forerunners, since more composite, 65
Look not so great, beside their simple way,
To a judge who only sees one way at once,
One mind-point and no other at a time, —
Compares the small part of a man of us
With some whole man of the heroic age, 70
Great in his way — not ours, nor meant for ours.
And ours is greater, had we skill to know:
For, what we call this life of men on earth,
This sequence of the soul's achievements here
Being, as I find much reason to conceive, 75
Intended to be viewed eventually
As a great whole, not analyzed to parts,
But each part having reference to all, —
How shall a certain part, pronounced complete,
Endure effacement by another part? 80
Was the thing done? — then, what's to do again?
See, in the chequered pavement opposite,
Suppose the artist made a perfect rhomb,
And next a lozenge, then a trapezoid —
He did not overlay them, superimpose 85
The new upon the old and blot it out,

But laid them on a level in his work,
Making at last a picture; there it lies.
So, first the perfect separate forms were made,
The portions of mankind; and after, so,   90
Occurred the combination of the same.
For where had been a progress, otherwise?
Mankind, made up of all the single men, —
In such a synthesis the labour ends.
Now mark me! those divine men of old time   95
Have reached, thou sayest well, each at one point
The outside verge that rounds our faculty;
And where they reached, who can do more than reach?
It takes but little water just to touch
At some one point the inside of a sphere,   100
And, as we turn the sphere, touch all the rest
In due succession: but the finer air
Which not so palpably nor obviously,
Though no less universally, can touch
The whole circumference of that emptied sphere   105
Fills it more fully than the water did;
Holds thrice the weight of water in itself
Resolved into a subtler element.
And yet the vulgar call the sphere first full
Up to the visible height — and after, void;   110
Not knowing air's more hidden properties.
And thus our soul, misknown, cries out to Zeus
To vindicate his purpose in our life.
Why stay we on the earth unless to grow?
Long since, I imaged, wrote the fiction out,   115
That he or other god descended here
And, once for all, showed simultaneously
What, in its nature, never can be shown,
Piecemeal or in succession; — showed, I say,
The worth both absolute and relative   120
Of all his children from the birth of time,
His instruments for all appointed work.
I now go on to image — might we hear

The judgement which should give the due to each,
Show where the labour lay and where the ease,   125
And prove Zeus' self, the latent everywhere!
This is a dream: — but no dream, let us hope,
That years and days, the summers and the springs,
Follow each other with unwaning powers.
The grapes which dye thy wine are richer far,   130
Through culture, than the wild wealth of the rock;
The suave plum than the savage-tasted drupe;
The pastured honey-bee drops choicer sweet;
The flowers turn double, and the leaves turn flowers;
That young and tender crescent-moon, thy slave,   135
Sleeping above her robe as buoyed by clouds,
Refines upon the women of my youth.
What, and the soul alone deteriorates?
I have not chanted verse like Homer, no —
Nor swept string like Terpander, no — no carved   140
And painted men like Phidias and his friend:
I am not great as they are, point by point.
But I have entered into sympathy
With these four, running these into one soul,
Who, separate, ignored each other's art.   145
Say, is it nothing that I know them all?
The wild flower was the larger; I have dashed
Rose-blood upon its petals, pricked its cup's
Honey with wine, and driven its seed to fruit,
And show a better flower if not so large: 150
I stand myself.   Refer this to the gods
Whose gift alone it is! which, shall I dare
(All pride apart) upon the absurd pretext
That such a gift by chance lay in my hand,
Discourse of lightly or depreciate?   155
It might have fallen to another's hand: what then?
I pass too surely: let at least truth stay!

    And next, of what thou followest on to ask.
This being with me as I declare, O king,

My works, in all these varicoloured kinds,   160
So done by me, accepted so by men —
Thou askest, if (my soul thus in men's hearts)
I must not be accounted to attain
The very crown and proper end of life?
Inquiring thence how, now life closeth up,   165
I face death with success in my right hand:
Whether I fear death less than dost thyself
The fortunate of men?   "For" (writest thou)
"Thou leavest much behind, while I leave naught.
Thy life stays in the poems men shall sing,   170
The pictures men shall study; while my life,
Complete and whole now in its power and joy,
Dies altogether with my brain and arm,
Is lost indeed; since, what survives myself?
The brazen statue to o'erlook my grave,   175
Set on the promontory which I named.
And that — some supple courtier of my heir
Shall use its robed and sceptred arm, perhaps,
To fix the rope to, which best drags it down.
I go then: triumph thou, who dost not go!"   180

  Nay, thou art worthy of hearing my whole mind.
Is this apparent, when thou turn'st to muse
Upon the scheme of earth and man in chief,
That admiration grows as knowledge grows?
That imperfection means perfection hid,   185
Reserved in part, to grace the after-time?
If, in the morning of philosophy,
Ere aught had been recorded, nay perceived,
Thou, with the light now in thee, couldst have looked
On all earth's tenantry, from worm to bird,   190
Ere man, her last, appeared upon the stage —
Thou wouldst have seen them perfect, and deduced
The perfectness of others yet unseen.
Conceding which — had Zeus then questioned thee,
"Shall I go on a step, improve on this,   195

Do more for visible creatures than is done?"
Thou wouldst have answered, "Ay, by making each
Grow conscious in himself — by that alone.
All's perfect else: the shell sucks fast the rock,
The fish strikes through the sea, the snake both swims   200
And slides, forth range the beasts, the birds take flight,
Till life's mechanics can no further go —
And all this joy in natural life is put
Like fire from off thy finger into each,
So exquisitely perfect is the same.   205
But 'tis pure fire, and they mere matter are;
It has them, not they it: and so I choose
For man, thy last premeditated work,
(If I might add a glory to the scheme),
That a third thing should stand apart from both,   210
A quality arise within his soul,
Which, intro-active, made to supervise
And feel the force it has, may view itself,
And so be happy."   Man might live at first
The animal life: but is there nothing more?   215
In due time, let him critically learn
How he lives; and, the more he gets to know
Of his own life's adaptabilities,
The more joy-giving will his life become.
Thus man, who hath this quality, is best.   220

    But thou, king, hadst more reasonably said:
"Let progress end at once, — man make no step
Beyond the natural man, the better beast,
Using his senses, not the sense of sense."
In man there's failure, only since he left   225
The lower and inconscious forms of life.
We called it an advance, the rendering plain
Man's spirit might grow conscious of man's life,
And, by new lore so added to the old,
Take each step higher over the brute's head.   230
This grew the only life, the pleasure-house,

Watch-tower and treasure-fortress of the soul,
Which whole surrounding flats of natural life
Seemed only fit to yield subsistence to;
A tower that crowns a country.   But alas,   235
The soul now climbs it just to perish there!
For thence we have discovered ('tis no dream —
We know this, which we had not else perceived)
That there's a world of capability
For joy, spread round about us, meant for us,   240
Inviting us; and still the soul craves all,
And still the flesh replies, "Take no jot more
Than ere thou clomb'st the tower to look abroad!
Nay, so much less as that fatigue has brought
Deduction to it."   We struggle, fain to enlarge   245
Our bounded physical recipiency,
Increase our power, supply fresh oil to life,
Repair the waste of age and sickness: no,
It skills not! life's inadequate to joy,
As the soul sees joy, tempting life to take.   250
They praise a fountain in my garden here
Wherein a Naiad sends the water-bow
Thin from her tube: she smiles to see it rise.
What if I told her, it is just a thread
From that great river which the hills shut up,   255
And mock her with my leave to take the same?
The artificer has given her one small tube
Past power to widen or exchange — what boot.
To know she might spout oceans if she could?
She cannot lift beyond her first thin thread: 260
And so a man can use but a man's joy
While he sees God's.   Is it for Zeus to boast,
"See, man, how happy I live, and despair —
That I may be still happier — for thy use!"
If this were so, we could not thank our Lord,   265
As hearts beat on to doing; 'tis not so —
Malice it is not.   Is it carelessness?
Still, no.   If care — where is the sign?   I ask,

And get no answer, and agree in sum,
O king, with thy profound discouragement,   270
Who seest the wider but to sigh the more.
Most progress is most failure: thou sayest well.

    The last point now: — thou dost except a case —
Holding joy not impossible to one
With artist-gifts — to such a man as I   275
Who leave behind me living works indeed;
For, such a poem, such a painting lives.
What? dost thou verily trip upon a word,
Confound the accurate view of what joy is
(Caught somewhat clearer by my eyes than thine) 280
With feeling joy? confound the knowing how
And showing how to live (my faculty)
With actually living? — Otherwise
Where is the artist's vantage o'er the king?
Because in my great epos I display   285
How divers men, young, strong, fair, wise, can act —
Is this as though I acted? if I paint,
Carve the young Phœbus, am I therefore young?
Methinks I'm older that I bowed myself
The many years of pain that taught me art!   290
Indeed, to know is something, and to prove
How all this beauty might be enjoyed, is more.
But, knowing naught, to enjoy is something too.
Yon rower, with the moulded muscles there,
Lowering the sail, is nearer it than I.   295
I can write love-odes: thy fair slave's an ode.
I get to sing of love, when grown too grey
For being beloved: she turns to that young man,
The muscles all a-ripple on his back.
I know the joy of kingship: well, thou art king!   300

    "But," sayest thou — (and I marvel, I repeat,
To find thee trip on such a mere word) "what
Thou writest, paintest, stays; that does not die:

Sappho survives, because we sing her songs,
And Æschylus, because we read his plays!"   **305**
Why, if they live still, let them come and take
Thy slave in my despite, drink from thy cup,
Speak in my place. Thou diest while I survive?
Say rather that my fate is deadlier still,
In this, that every day my sense of joy   **310**
Grows more acute, my soul (intensified
By power and insight) more enlarged, more keen;
While every day my hairs fall more and more,
My hand shakes, and the heavy years increase —
The horror quickening still from year to year,   **315**
The consummation coming past escape
When I shall know most, and yet least enjoy —
When all my works wherein I prove my worth,
Being present still to mock me in men's mouths,
Alive still, in the praise of such as thou,   **320**
I, I the feeling, thinking, acting man,
The man who loved his life so over-much,
Sleep in my urn. It is so horrible,
I dare at times imagine to my need
Some future state revealed to us by Zeus.   **325**
Unlimited in capability
For joy, as this is in desire for joy,
— To seek which, the joy-hunger forces us:
That, stung by straitness of our life, made strait
On purpose to make prized the life at large —   **330**
Freed by the throbbing impulse we call death,
We burst there as the worm into the fly,
Who, while a worm still, wants his wings. But no!
Zeus has not yet revealed it; and alas,
He must have done so, were it possible!   **335**

   Live long and happy, and in that thought die:
Glad for what was! Farewell. And for the rest,
I cannot tell thy messenger aright
Where to deliver what he bears of thine

To one called Paulus; we have heard his fame   340
Indeed, if Christus be not one with him —
I know not, nor am troubled much to know.
Thou canst not think a mere barbarian Jew,
As Paulus proves to be, one circumcised,
Hath access to a secret shut from us?   345
Thou wrongest our philosophy, O king,
In stooping to inquire of such an one,
As if his answer could impose at all!
He writeth, doth he? well, and he may write.
Oh, the Jew findeth scholars! certain slaves   350
Who touched on this same isle, preached him and Christ;
And (as I gathered from a bystander)
Their doctrine could be held by no sane man.

RUDEL TO THE LADY OF TRIPOLI

I

I KNOW a Mount, the gracious Sun perceives
First, when he visits, last, too, when he leaves
The world; and, vainly favoured, it repays
The day-long glory of his steadfast gaze
By no change of its large calm front of snow.   5
And underneath the Mount, a Flower I know,
He cannot have perceived, that changes ever
At his approach; and, in the lost endeavour
To live his life, has parted, one by one,
With all a flower's true graces, for the grace   10
Of being but a foolish mimic sun,
With ray-like florets round a disk-like face.
Men nobly call by many a name the Mount
As over many a land of theirs its large
Calm front of snow like a triumphal targe   15
Is reared, and still with old names, fresh names vie,
Each to its proper praise and own account:
Men call the Flower the Sunflower, sportively.

II

Oh, Angel of the East, one, one gold look
Across the waters to this twilight nook,   20
— The far sad waters, Angel, to this nook!

III

Dear Pilgrim, art thou for the East indeed?
Go! — saying ever as thou dost proceed,
That I, French Rudel, choose for my device
A sunflower outspread like a sacrifice   25
Before its idol.   See!   These inexpert
And hurried fingers could not fail to hurt
The woven picture; 'tis a woman's skill
Indeed; but nothing baffled me, so, ill
Or well, the work is finished.   Say, men feed   30
On songs I sing, and therefore bask the bees
On my flower's breast as on a platform broad:
But, as the flower's concern is not for these
But solely for the sun, so men applaud
In vain this Rudel, he not looking here   35
But to the East — the East!   Go, say this, Pilgrim dear!

ONE WORD MORE

TO E. B. B.

I

THERE they are, my fifty men and women
Naming me the fifty poems finished!
Take them, Love, the book and me together:
Where the heart lies, let the brain lie also.

II

Rafael made a century of sonnets,   5
Made and wrote them in a certain volume
Dinted with the silver-pointed pencil
Else he only used to draw Madonnas:

These, the world might view — but one, the volume.
Who that one, you ask?   Your heart instructs you.   10
Did she live and love it all her lifetime?
Did she drop, his lady of the sonnets,
Die, and let it drop beside her pillow
Where it lay in place of Rafael's glory,
Rafael's cheek so duteous and so loving —   15
Cheek, the world was wont to hail a painter's,
Rafael's cheek, her love had turned a poet's?

III

You and I would rather read that volume,
(Taken to his beating bosom by it),
Lean and list the bosom-beats of Rafael,   20
Would we not? than wonder at Madonnas —
Her, San Sisto names, and Her, Foligno,
Her, that visits Florence in a vision,
Her, that's left with lilies in the Louvre —
Seen by us and all the world in circle.   25

IV

You and I will never read that volume.
Guido Reni, like his own eye's apple
Guarded long the treasure-book and loved it.
Guido Reni dying, all Bologna
Cried, and the world cried too, "Ours, the treasure!"   30
Suddenly, as rare things will, it vanished.

V

Dante once prepared to paint an angel:
Whom to please?   You whisper "Beatrice."
While he mused and traced it and retraced it,
(Peradventure with a pen corroded   35
Still by drops of that hot ink he dipped for,
When, his left-hand i' the hair o' the wicked,
Back he held the brow and pricked its stigma,

Bit into the live man's flesh for parchment,
Loosed him, laughed to see the writing rankle,   40
Let the wretch go festering through Florence) —
Dante, who loved well because he hated,
Hated wickedness that hinders loving,
Dante standing, studying his angel, —
In there broke the folk of his Inferno.   45
Says he — "Certain people of importance"
(Such he gave his daily dreadful line to)
"Entered and would sieze, forsooth, the poet."
Says the poet — "Then I stopped my painting."

VI

You and I would rather see that angel,   50
Painted by the tenderness of Dante,
Would we not? — than read a fresh Inferno.

VII

You and I will never see that picture.
While he mused on love and Beatrice,
While he softened o'er his outlined angel,   55
In they broke, those "people of importance":
We and Bice bear the loss for ever.

VIII

What of Rafael's sonnets, Dante's picture?
This: no artist lives and loves, that longs not
Once, and only once, and for one only,   60
(Ah, the prize!) to find his love a language
Fit and fair and simple and sufficient —
Using nature that's an art to others,
Not, this one time, art that's turned his nature.
Ay, of all the artists living, loving,   65
None but would forego his proper dowry, —
Does he paint? he fain would write a poem, —
Does he write? he fain would paint a picture,

Put to proof art alien to the artist's,
Once, and only once, and for one only,   70
So to be the man and leave the artist,
Gain the man's joy, miss the artist's sorrow.

IX

Wherefore? Heaven's gift takes earth's abatement!
He who smites the rock and spreads the water,
Bidding drink and live a crowd beneath him,   75
Even he, the minute makes immortal,
Proves, perchance, but mortal in the minute,
Desecrates, belike, the deed in doing.
While he smites, how can he but remember,
So he smote before, in such a peril,   80
When they stood and mocked — "Shall smiting help us?"
When they drank and sneered — "A stroke is easy!"
When they wiped their mouths and went their journey,
Throwing him for thanks — "But drought was pleasant."
Thus old memories mar the actual triumph;   85
Thus the doing savours of disrelish;
Thus achievement lacks a gracious somewhat;
O'er-importuned brows becloud the mandate,
Carelessness or consciousness — the gesture.
For he bears an ancient wrong about him,   90
Sees and knows again those phalanxed faces,
Hears, yet one time more, the 'customed prelude —
"How shouldst thou, of all men, smite, and save us?"
Guesses what is like to prove the sequel —
"Egypt's flesh-pots — nay, the drought was better."   95

X

Oh, the crowd must have emphatic warrant!
Theirs, the Sinai-forehead's cloven brilliance.
Right-arm's rod-sweep, tongue's imperial fiat.
Never dares the man put off the prophet.

XI

Did he love one face from out the thousands,　　　100
(Were she Jethro's daughter, white and wifely,
Were she but the Æthiopian bondslave,)
He would envy yon dumb patient camel,
Keeping a reserve of scanty water
Meant to save his own life in the desert;　　　105
Ready in the desert to deliver
(Kneeling down to let his breast be opened)
Hoard and life together for his mistress.

XII

I shall never, in the years remaining,
Paint you pictures, no, nor carve you statues,　　　110
Make you music that should all-express me;
So it seems: I stand on my attainment.
This of verse alone, one life allows me:
Verse and nothing else have I to give you.
Other heights in other lives, God willing:　　　115
All the gifts from all the heights, your own, Love!

XIII

Yet a semblance of resource avails us —
Shade so finely touched, love's sense must seize it.
Take these lines, look lovingly and nearly,
Lines I write the first time and the last time.　　　120
He who works in fresco, steals a hairbrush,
Curbs the liberal hand, subservient proudly,
Cramps his spirit, crowds its all in little,
Makes a strange art of an art familiar,
Fills his lady's missal-marge with flowerets.　　　125
He who blows through bronze, may breathe through silver,
Fitly serenade a slumbrous princess.
He who writes, may write for once as I do.

XIV

Love, you saw me gather men and women,
Live or dead or fashioned by my fancy,
Enter each and all, and use their service,
Speak from every mouth, — the speech, a poem.
Hardly shall I tell my joys and sorrows,
Hopes and fears, belief and disbelieving:
I am mine and yours — the rest be all men's,
Karshish, Cleon, Norbert, and the fifty.
Let me speak this once in my true person,
Not as Lippo, Roland, or Andrea,
Though the fruit of speech be just this sentence:
Pray you, look on these my men and women,
Take and keep my fifty poems finished;
Where my heart lies, let my brain lie also!
Poor the speech; be how I speak, for all things.

130

135

140

XV

Not but that you know me!   Lo, the moon's self!
Here in London, yonder late in Florence,
Still we find her face, the thrice-transfigured.
Curving on a sky imbrued with colour,
Drifted over Fiesole by twilight,
Came she, our new crescent of a hair's-breadth.
Full she flared it, lamping Samminiato,
Rounder 'twixt the cypresses and rounder,
Perfect till the nightingales applauded.
Now, a piece of her old self, impoverished,
Hard to greet, she traverses the house-roofs,
Hurries with unhandsome thrift of silver,
Goes dispiritedly, glad to finish.

145

150

155

XVI

What, there's nothing in the moon noteworthy?
Nay: for if that moon could love a mortal,
Use, to charm him (so to fit a fancy),

All her magic ('tis the old sweet mythos),   160
She would turn a new side to her mortal,
Side unseen of herdsman, huntsman, steersman —
Blank to Zoroaster on his terrace,
Blind to Galileo on his turret,
Dumb to Homer, dumb to Keats — him, even!   165
Think, the wonder of the moonstruck mortal —
When she turns round, comes again in heaven,
Opens out anew for worse or better!
Proves she like some portent of an iceberg
Swimming full upon the ship it founders,   170
Hungry with huge teeth of splintered crystals?
Proves she as the paved work of a sapphire
Seen by Moses when he climbed the mountain?
Moses, Aaron, Nadab and Abihu
Climbed and saw the very God, the Highest,   175
Stand upon the paved work of a sapphire.
Like the bodied heaven in his clearness
Shone the stone, the sapphire of that paved work,
When they ate and drank and saw God also!

XVII

What were seen?   None knows, none ever shall know.   180
Only this is sure — the sight were other,
Not the moon's same side, born late in Florence,
Dying now impoverished here in London.
God be thanked, the meanest of his creatures
Boasts two soul-sides, one to face the world with,   185
One to show a woman when he loves her!

XVIII

This I say of me, but think of you, Love!
This to you — yourself my moon of poets!
Ah, but that's the world's side, there's the wonder,
Thus they see you, praise you, think they know you!   190
There, in turn I stand with them and praise you —

Out of my own self, I dare to phrase it.
But the best is when I glide from out them,
Cross a step or two of dubious twilight,
Come out on the other side, the novel   195
Silent silver lights and darks undreamed of,
Where I hush and bless myself with silence.

XIX

Oh, their Rafael of the dear Madonnas,
Oh, their Dante of the dread Inferno,
Wrote one song — and in my brain I sing it,   200
Drew one angel — borne, see, on my bosom!

                                              R. B.

BEN KARSHOOK'S WISDOM

"WOULD a man 'scape the rod?"
    Rabbi Ben Karshook saith,
"See that he turn to God
    The day before his death."

"Ay, could a man inquire   5
    When it shall come!" I say.
The Rabbi's eye shoots fire —
    "Then let him turn to-day!"

II

Quoth a young Sadducee:
    "Reader of many rolls,   10
Is it so certain we
    Have, as they tell us, souls?"

"Son, there is no reply!"
    The Rabbi bit his beard;
"Certain, a soul have I —   15
    We may have none," he sneer'd.

      .   .   .   .   .   .

Thus Karshook, the Hiram's-Hammer
  The Right-hand Temple-column,
Taught babes in grace their grammar,
  And struck the simple, solemn.   20

JAMES LEE'S WIFE

I. JAMES LEE'S WIFE SPEAKS AT THE WINDOW

Ah, Love, but a day
  And the world has changed!
The sun's away,
  And the bird estranged;
The wind has dropped,   5
  And the sky's deranged:
Summer has stopped.

Look in my eyes!
  Wilt thou change too?
Should I fear surprise?   10
  Shall I find aught new
In the old and dear,
  In the good and true,
With the changing year?

Thou art a man,   15
  But I am thy love.
For the lake, its swan;
  For the dell, its dove;
And for thee — (oh, haste!)
  Me, to bend above,   20
Me, to hold embraced.

II. BY THE FIRESIDE

Is all our fire of shipwreck wood,
  Oak and pine?

Oh, for the ills half-understood,
  The dim dead woe
  Long ago   **5**
Befallen this bitter coast of France!
Well, poor sailors took their chance;
  I take mine.

A ruddy shaft our fire must shoot
  O'er the sea: **10**
Do sailors eye the casement — mute,
  Drenched and stark,
  From their bark —
And envy, gnash their teeth for hate
O' the warm safe house and happy freight **15**
  — Thee and me?

God help you, sailors, at your need!
  Spare the curse!
For some ships, safe in port indeed,
  Rot and rust,   **20**
  Run to dust,
All through worms i' the wood, which crept,
Gnawed our hearts out while we slept:
  That is worse.

Who lived here before us two?   **25**
  Old-world pairs.
Did a woman ever — would I knew! —
  Watch the man
  With whom began
Love's voyage full-sail, — (now, gnash your teeth!) **30**
When planks start, open hell beneath
  Unawares?

III. IN THE DOORWAY

The swallow has set her six young on the rail,
  And looks seaward:

The water's in stripes like a snake, olive-pale
    To the leeward, —
On the weather-side, black, spotted white with the wind. 5
"Good fortune departs, and disaster's behind," —
Hark, the wind with its wants and its infinite wail!

Our fig-tree, that leaned for the saltness, has furled
    Her five fingers,
Each leaf like a hand opened wide to the world   10
    Where there lingers
No glint of the gold, Summer sent for her sake:
How the vines writhe in rows, each impaled on its stake!
My heart shrivels up and my spirit shrinks curled.

Yet here are we two; we have love, house enough,   15
    With the field there,
This house of four rooms, that field red and rough,
    Though it yield there,
For the rabbit that robs, scarce a blade or a bent;
If a magpie alight now, it seems an event;   20
And they both will be gone at November's rebuff.

But why must cold spread? but wherefore bring change
    To the spirit,
God meant should mate his with an infinite range,
    And inherit   25
His power to put life in the darkness and cold?
Oh, live and love worthily, bear and be bold!
Whom Summer made friends of, let Winter estrange!

IV. ALONG THE BEACH

I will be quiet and talk with you,
    And reason why you are wrong.
You wanted my love — is that much true?
And so I did love, so I do:
    What has come of it all along?   5

I took you — how could I otherwise?
    For a world to me, and more;
For all, love greatens and glorifies
Till God's aglow, to the loving eyes,
    In what was mere earth before.   10

Yes, earth — yes, mere ignoble earth!
    Now do I mis-state, mistake?
Do I wrong your weakness and call it worth?
Expect all harvest, dread no dearth,
    Seal my sense up for your sake?   15

Oh, Love, Love, no, Love! not so, indeed!
    You were just weak earth, I knew:
With much in you waste, with many a weed,
And plenty of passions run to seed,
    But a little good grain too.   20

And such as you were, I took you for mine:
    Did not you find me yours,
To watch the olive and wait the vine,
And wonder when rivers of oil and wine
    Would flow, as the Book assures?   25

Well, and if none of these good things came,
    What did the failure prove?
The man was my whole world, all the same,
With his flowers to praise or his weeds to blame,
    And, either or both, to love.   30

Yet this turns now to a fault — there! there!
    That I do love, watch too long,
And wait too well, and weary and wear;
And 'tis all an old story, and my despair
    Fit subject for some new song: 35

"How the light, light love, he has wings to fly
    At suspicion of a bond:

My wisdom has bidden your pleasure good-bye,
Which will turn up next in a laughing eye,
And why should you look beyond?"   40

V. ON THE CLIFF

I leaned on the turf,
I looked at a rock
Left dry by the surf;
For the turf, to call it grass were to mock:
Dead to the roots, so deep was done   5
The work of the summer sun.

And the rock lay flat
As an anvil's face:
No iron like that!
Baked dry; of a weed, of a shell, no trace: 10
Sunshine outside, but ice at the core,
Death's altar by the lone shore.

On the turf, sprang gay
With his films of blue,
No cricket, I'll say,   15
But a warhorse, barded and chanfroned too,
The gift of a quixote-mage to his knight,
Real fairy, with wings all right

On the rock, they scorch
Like a drop of fire   20
From a brandished torch,
Fall two red fans of a butterfly:
No turf, no rock: in their ugly stead,
See, wonderful blue and red!

Is it not so   25
With the minds of men?
The level and low-

The burnt and bare, in themselves; but then
With such a blue and red grace, not theirs, —
Love settling unawares!   30

VI. READING A BOOK, UNDER THE CLIFF

"Still ailing, Wind?   Wilt be appeased or no?
    Which needs the other's office, thou or I?
Dost want to be disburthened of a woe,
    And can, in truth, my voice untie
Its links, and let it go?   5

"Art thou a dumb, wronged thing that would be righted,
    Entrusting thus thy cause to me?   Forbear!
No tongue can mend such pleadings; faith, requited
    With falsehood, — love, at last awar
Of scorn, — hopes, early blighted, —   10

"We have them; but I know not any tone
    So fit as thine to falter forth a sorrow:
Dost think men would go mad without a moan,
    If they knew any way to borrow
A pathos like thy own?   15

"Which sigh wouldst mock, of all the sighs?   The one
    So long escaping from lips starved and blue,
That lasts while on her pallet-bed the nun
    Stretches her length; her foot comes through
The straw she shivers on;   20

"You had not thought she was so tall: and spent,
    Her shrunk lids open, her lean fingers shut
Close, close, their sharp and livid nails indent
    The clammy palm; then all is mute:
That way, the spirit went.   25

"Or wouldst thou rather that I understand
    Thy will to help me? — like the dog I found

Once, pacing sad this solitary strand,
   Who would not take my food, poor hound,
But whined and licked my hand."   30

All this, and more, comes from some young man's pride
   Of power to see — in failure and mistake,
Relinquishment, disgrace, on every side —
   Merely examples for his sake,
Helps to his path untried: 35

Instances he must — simply recognize?
   Oh, more than so! — must, with a learner's zeal,
Make doubly prominent, twice emphasize,
   By added touches that reveal
The god in babe's disguise.   40

Oh, he knows what defeat means, and the rest!
   Himself the undefeated that shall be:
Failure, disgrace, he flings them you to test, —
   His triumph, in eternity
Too plainly manifest!   45

Whence, judge if he learn forthwith what the wind
   Means in its moaning — by the happy prompt
Instinctive way of youth, I mean; for kind
   Calm years, exacting their accompt
Of pain, mature the mind: 50

And some midsummer morning, at the lull
   Just about daybreak, as he looks across
A sparkling foreign country, wonderful
   To the sea's edge for gloom and gloss,
Next minute must annul, —   55

Then, when the wind begins among the vines,
   So low, so low, what shall it say but this?

"Here is the change beginning, here the lines
    Circumscribe beauty, set to bliss
The limit time assigns."   60

Nothing can be as it has been before;
    Better, so call it, only not the same.
To draw one beauty into our hearts' core,
    And keep it changeless! such our claim;
So answered — Never more!   65

Simple?   Why, this is the old woe o' the world;
    Tune, to whose rise and fall we live and die.
Rise with it, then!   Rejoice that man is hurled
    From change to change unceasingly.
His soul's wings never furled!   70

That's a new question; still replies the fact,
    Nothing endures: the wind moans, saying so;
We moan in acquiescence: there's life's pact,
    Perhaps probation — do *I* know?
God does: endure his act!   75

Only, for man, how bitter not to grave
    On his soul's hands' palms one fair good wise thing
Just as he grasped it!   For himself, death's wave;
    While time first washes — ah, the sting! —
O'er all he'd sink to save.   80

VII. AMONG THE ROCKS

Oh, good gigantic smile o' the brown old earth,
    This autumn morning!   How he sets his bones
To bask i' the sun, and thrusts out knees and feet
For the ripple to run over in its mirth;
    Listening the while, where on the heap of stones   5
The white breast of the sea-lark twitters sweet.

That is the doctrine, simple, ancient, true;
    Such is life's trial, as old earth smiles and knows.
If you loved only what were worth your love,
Love were clear gain, and wholly well for you: 10
    Make the low nature better by your throes!
Give earth yourself, go up for gain above!

VIII. BESIDE THE DRAWING-BOARD

I

"As like as a Hand to another Hand!"
    Whoever said that foolish thing,
Could not have studied to understand
    The counsels of God in fashioning,
Out of the infinite love of his heart,   5
This Hand, whose beauty I praise, apart
From the world of wonder left to praise,
If I tried to learn the other ways
Of love in its skill, or love in its power.
    "As like as a Hand to another Hand":   10
    Who said that, never took his stand,
Found and followed, like me, an hour,
The beauty in this — how free, how fine
To fear, almost — of the limit-line!
As I looked at this, and learned and drew,   15
    Drew and learned, and looked again,
While fast the happy minutes flew,
    Its beauty mounted into my brain,
    And a fancy seized me; I was fain
To efface my work, begin anew,   20
Kiss what before I only drew;
Ay, laying the red chalk 'twixt my lips,
    With soul to help if the mere lips failed,
    I kissed all right where the drawing ailed,
Kissed fast the grace that somehow slips   25
Still from one's soulless finger-tips.

II

'Tis a clay cast, the perfect thing,
　　From Hand live once, dead long ago:
Princess-like it wears the ring
　　To fancy's eye, by which we know　　　　30
That here at length a master found
　　His match, a proud lone soul its mate,
As soaring genius sank to ground,
　　And pencil could not emulate
The beauty in this, — how free, how fine　　35
To fear almost! — of the limit-line.
Long ago the god, like me
The worm, learned, each in our degree:
Looked and loved, learned and drew,
　　Drew and learned and loved again,　　　40
While fast the happy minutes flew,
　　Till beauty mounted into his brain
And on the finger which outvied
　　His art he placed the ring that's there,
Still by fancy's eye descried,　　　　　　45
　　In token of a marriage rare:
　　For him on earth, his art's despair,
For him in heaven, his soul's fit bride.

III

Little girl with the poor coarse hand
　　I turned from to a cold clay cast —　　50
I have my lesson, understand
　　The worth of flesh and blood at last!
Nothing but beauty in a Hand?
　　Because he could not change the hue,
　　Mend the lines and make them true　　55
To this which met his soul's demand, —
　　Would Da Vinci turn from you?
　　I hear him laugh my woes to scorn —
"The fool forsooth is all forlorn

Because the beauty, she thinks best, 60
Lived long ago or was never born, —
Because no beauty bears the test
In this rough peasant Hand!   Confessed!
Art is null and study void!'
So sayest thou?   So said not I, 65
Who threw the faulty pencil by,
And years instead of hours employed,
Learning the veritable use
Of flesh and bone and nerve beneath
Lines and hue of the outer sheath, 70
If haply I might reproduce
One motive of the powers profuse,
Flesh and bone and nerve that make
The poorest coarsest human hand
An object worthy to be scanned 75
A whole life long for their sole sake.
Shall earth and the cramped moment-space
Yield the heavenly crowning grace?
Now the parts and then the whole!
Who art thou, with stinted soul 80
And stunted body, thus to cry,
'I love — shall that be life's strait dole?
I must live beloved or die!'
This peasant hand that spins the wool
And bakes the bread, why lives it on, 85
Poor and coarse with beauty gone, —
What use survives the beauty?''   Fool!

Go, little girl with the poor coarse hand!
I have my lesson, shall understand.

IX. ON DECK

There is nothing to remember in me,
    Nothing I ever said with a grace,
Nothing I did that you care to see,
    Nothing I was that deserves a place
In your mind, now I leave you, set you free. 5

Conceded!   In turn, concede to me,
    Such things have been as a mutual flame.
Your soul's locked fast; but, love for a key,
    You might let it loose, till I grew the same
In your eyes, as in mine you stand: strange plea!   10

For then, then, what would it matter to me
    That I was the harsh, ill-favoured one?
We both should be like as pea and pea;
    It was ever so since the world begun:
So, let me proceed with my reverie.   15

How strange it were if you had all me,
    As I have all you in my heart and brain,
You, whose least word brought gloom or glee,
    Who never lifted the hand in vain —
Will hold mine yet, from over the sea!   20

Strange, if a face, when you thought of me,
    Rose like your own face present now,
With eyes as dear in their due degree,
    Much such a mouth, and as bright a brow,
Till you saw yourself, while you cried "'Tis She!"   25

Well, you may, you must, set down to me
    Love that was life, life that was love;
A tenure of breath at your lips' decree,
    A passion to stand as your thoughts approve,
A rapture to fall where your foot might be.   30

But did one touch of such love for me
    Come in a word or a look of yours,
Whose words and looks will, circling, flee
    Round me and round while life endures, —
Could I fancy "As I feel, thus feels He";   35

Why, fade you might to a thing like me,
    And your hair grow these coarse hanks of hair,
Your skin, this bark of a gnarled tree, —
    You might turn myself! — should I know or care
When I should be dead of joy, James Lee?   40

ABT VOGLER

(AFTER HE HAS BEEN EXTEMPORIZING UPON THE MUSICAL INSTRUMENT OF HIS INVENTION)

WOULD that the structure brave, the manifold music I build,
    Bidding my organ obey, calling its keys to their work,
Claiming each slave of the sound, at a touch, as when
        Solomon willed
    Armies of angels that soar, legions of demons that lurk,
Man, brute, reptile, fly, — alien of end and of aim,   5
    Adverse, each from the other heaven-high, hell-deep re-
        moved, —
Should rush into sight at once as he named the ineffable
        Name,
    And pile him a palace straight, to pleasure the princess he
        loved!

Would it might tarry like his, the beautiful building of mine,
    This which my keys in a crowd pressed and importuned
        to raise!   10
Ah, one and all, how they helped, would dispart now and
        now combine,
    Zealous to hasten the work, heighten their master his
        praise!
And one would bury his brow with a blind plunge down to
        hell,
    Burrow awhile and build, broad on the roots of things,
Then up again swim into sight, having based me my palace
        well,   15
    Founded it, fearless of flame, flat on the nether springs.

And another would mount and march, like the excellent
    minion he was,
    Ay, another and yet another, one crowd but with many a
        crest,
Raising my rampired walls of gold as transparent as glass,
    Eager to do and die, yield each his place to the rest: 20
For higher still and higher (as a runner tips with fire,
    When a great illumination surprises a festal night —
Outlining round and round Rome's dome from space to spire)
    Up, the pinnacled glory reached, and the pride of my soul
        was in sight.

In sight? Not half! for it seemed, it was certain, to match
    man's birth,   25
    Nature in turn conceived, obeying an impulse as I;
And the emulous heaven yearned down, made effort to reach
    the earth,
    As the earth had done her best, in my passion, to scale the
        sky:
Novel splendours burst forth, grew familiar and dwelt with
    mine,
    Not a point nor peak but found and fixed its wandering
        star;   30
Meteor-moons, balls of blaze: and they did not pale nor
    pine,
    For earth had attained to heaven, there was no more near
        nor far.

Nay, more; for there wanted not who walked in the glare and
    glow,
    Presences plain in the place; or, fresh from the Protoplast,
Furnished for ages to come, when a kindlier wind should
    blow,   35
    Lured now to begin and live, in a house to their liking at
        last;
Or else the wonderful Dead who have passed through the
    body and gone,

But were back once more to breathe in an old world worth
    their new:
What never had been, was now; what was, as it shall be anon;
    And what is — shall I say, matched both? for I was made
      perfect too.   40

All through my keys that gave their sounds to a wish of my
    soul,
    All through my soul that praised as its wish flowed visibly
      forth,
All through music and me! For think, had I painted the
    whole,
    Why, there it had stood, to see, nor the process so wonder-
      worth:
Had I written the same, made verse — still, effect proceeds
    from cause,   45
    Ye know why the forms are fair, ye hear how the tale is
      told;
It is all triumphant art, but art in obedience to laws,
    Painter and poet are proud in the artist-list enrolled: —

But here is the finger of God, a flash of the will that can,
    Existent behind all laws, that made them and, lo, they
      are!   50
And I know not if, save in this, such gift be allowed to man,
    That out of three sounds he frame, not a fourth sound, but
      a star.
Consider it well: each tone of our scale in itself is naught:
    It is everywhere in the world — loud, soft, and all is said.
Give it to me to use! I mix it with two in my thought: 55
    And there! Ye have heard and seen: consider and bow the
      head!

Well, it is gone at last, the palace of music I reared:
    Gone! and the good tears start, the praises that come too
      slow;

For one is assured at first, one scarce can say that he feared,
That he even gave it a thought, the gone thing was to go.
Never to be again!   But many more of the kind   61
    As good, nay, better perchance: is this your comfort to me?
To me, who must be saved because I cling with my mind
    To the same, same self, same love, same God: ay, what
        was, shall be.

Therefore to whom turn I but to thee, the ineffable
        Name?   65
    Builder and maker, thou, of houses not made with hands!
What, have fear of change from thee who art ever the
        same?
    Doubt that thy power can fill the heart that thy power
        expands?
There shall never be one lost good!   What was, shall live as
        before;
    The evil is null, is naught, is silence implying sound;   70
What was good shall be good, with, for evil, so much good
        more;
    On the earth the broken arcs; in the heaven, a perfect
        round.

All we have willed or hoped or dreamed of good shall exist;
    Not its semblance, but itself; no beauty, nor good, nor
        power
Whose voice has gone forth, but each survives for the
        melodist   75
    When eternity affirms the conception of an hour.
The high that proved too high, the heroic for earth too hard,
    The passion that left the ground to lose itself in the sky,
Are music sent up to God by the lover and the bard;
    Enough that he heard it once: we shall hear it by-and-by.

And what is our failure here but a triumph's evidence   81
    For the fullness of the days?   Have we withered or
        agonized?

Why else was the pause prolonged but that singing might
    issue thence?
  Why rushed the discords in but that harmony should be
    prized?
Sorrow is hard to bear, and doubt is slow to clear,   85
  Each sufferer says his say, his scheme of the weal and woe:
But God has a few of us whom he whispers in the ear;
  The rest may reason and welcome: 'tis we musicians know.

Well, it is earth with me; silence resumes her reign:
  I will be patient and proud, and soberly acquiesce.   90
Give me the keys. I feel for the common chord again,
  Sliding by semitones till I sink to the minor, — yes,
And I blunt it into a ninth, and I stand on alien ground,
  Surveying awhile the heights I rolled from into the deep;
Which, hark, I have dared and done, for my resting-place is
    found,   95
  The C Major of this life: so, now I will try to sleep.

RABBI BEN EZRA

Grow old along with me!
  The best is yet to be,
The last of life, for which the first was made:
  Our times are in His hand
  Who saith "A whole I planned,   5
Youth shows but half; trust God: see all, nor be afraid!"

  Not that, amassing flowers,
  Youth sighed "Which rose make ours,
Which lily leave and then as best recall?"
  Not that, admiring stars,   10
  It yearned "Nor Jove, nor Mars;
Mine be some figured flame which blends, transcends them
    all!"

    Not for such hopes and fears
    Annulling youth's brief years,
Do I remonstrate: folly wide the mark!   15
    Rather I prize the doubt
    Low kinds exist without,
Finished and finite clods, untroubled by a spark.

    Poor vaunt of life indeed,
    Were man but formed to feed   20
On joy, to solely seek and find and feast;
    Such feasting ended, then
    As sure an end to men;
Irks care the crop-full bird?   Frets doubt the maw-crammed
    beast?

    Rejoice we are allied   25
    To That which doth provide
And not partake, effect and not receive!
    A spark disturbs our clod;
    Nearer we hold of God
Who gives, than of His tribes that take, I must believe. 30

    Then, welcome each rebuff
    That turns earth's smoothness rough,
Each sting that bids nor sit nor stand but go!
    Be our joys three-parts pain!
    Strive, and hold cheap the strain;   35
Learn, nor account the pang; dare, never grudge the throe!

    For thence — a paradox
    Which comforts while it mocks —
Shall life succeed in that it seems to fail:
    What I aspired to be,   40
    And was not, comforts me:
A brute I might have been, but would not sink i' the scale.

    What is he but a brute
    Whose flesh has soul to suit,

Whose spirit works lest arms and legs want play?   45
    To man, propose this test —
    Thy body at its best,
How far can that project thy soul on its lone way?

    Yet gifts should prove their use:
    I own the Past profuse   50
Of power each side, perfection every turn:
    Eyes, ears took in their dole,
    Brain treasured up the whole;
Should not the heart beat once "How good to live and
    learn"?

    Not once beat "Praise be Thine!   55
    I see the whole design,
I, who saw power, see now love perfect too:
    Perfect I call Thy plan:
    Thanks that I was a man!
Maker, remake, complete, — I trust what Thou shalt do!" 60

    For pleasant is this flesh;
    Our soul, in its rose-mesh
Pulled ever to the earth, still yearns for rest;
    Would we some prize might hold
    To match those manifold   65
Possessions of the brute, — gain most, as we did best!

    Let us not always say
    "Spite of this flesh to-day
I strove, made head, gained ground upon the whole!"
    As the bird wings and sings,   70
    Let us cry "All good things
Are ours, nor soul helps flesh more, now, than flesh helps
    soul!"

    Therefore I summon age
    To grant youth's heritage,

*a contemporary
Victorian fables*

Life's struggle having so far reached its term: 75
    Thence shall I pass, approved
    A man, for aye removed
From the developed brute; a god though in the germ.

    And I shall thereupon
    Take rest, ere I be gone   80
Once more on my adventure brave and new:
    Fearless and unperplexed,
    When I wage battle next,
What weapons to select, what armour to indue.

    Youth ended, I shall try   85
    My gain or loss thereby;
Leave the fire ashes, what survives is gold:
    And I shall weigh the same,
    Give life its praise or blame:
Young, all lay in dispute; I shall know, being old.   90

    For note, when evening shuts,
    A certain moment cuts
The deed off, calls the glory from the gray:
    A whisper from the west
    Shoots — "Add this to the rest,   95
Take it and try its worth: here dies another day."

    So, still within this life,
    Though lifted o'er its strife,
Let me discern, compare, pronounce at last,
    "This rage was right i' the main,   100
    That acquiescence vain:
The Future I may face now I have proved the Past."

    For more is not reserved
    To man, with soul just nerved
To act to-morrow what he learns to-day: 105
    Here, work enough to watch

The Master work, and catch
Hints of the proper craft, tricks of the tool's true play.

As it was better, youth
Should strive, through acts uncouth,   110
Toward making, than repose on aught found made:
So, better, age, exempt
From strife, should know, than tempt
Further.   Thou waitedst age: wait death nor be afraid!

Enough now, if the Right   115
And Good and Infinite
Be named here, as thou callest thy hand thine own.
With knowledge absolute,
Subject to no dispute
From fools that crowded youth, nor let thee feel alone.   120

Be there, for once and all,
Severed great minds from small,
Announced to each his station in the Past!
Was I, the world arraigned,
Were they, my soul disdained,   125
Right?   Let age speak the truth and give us peace at last!

Now, who shall arbitrate?
Ten men love what I hate,
Shun what I follow, slight what I receive;
Ten, who in ears and eyes   130
Match me: we all surmise,
They this thing, and I that: whom shall my soul believe?

Not on the vulgar mass
Called "work," must sentence pass,
Things done, that took the eye and had the price;   135
O'er which, from level stand,
The low world laid its hand,
Found straightway to its mind, could value in a trice:

But all, the world's coarse thumb
　And finger failed to plumb, 140
So passed in making up the main account,
　All instincts immature,
　All purposes unsure,
That weighed not as his work, yet swelled the man's amount:

Thoughts hardly to be packed 145
　Into a narrow act,
Fancies that broke through language and escaped;
　All I could never be,
　All, men ignored in me,
This, I was worth to God, whose wheel the pitcher shaped.

Ay, note that Potter's wheel, 151
　That metaphor! and feel
Why time spins fast, why passive lies our clay, —
　Thou, to whom fools propound,
　When the wine makes its round, 155
"Since life fleets, all is change; the Past gone, seize to-day!"

Fool!　All that is, at all,
　Lasts ever, past recall;
Earth changes, but thy soul and God stand sure:
　What entered into thee, 160
　That was, is, and shall be:
Time's wheel runs back or stops: Potter and clay endure.

He fixed thee 'mid this dance
　Of plastic circumstance,
This Present, thou, forsooth, would fain arrest: 165
　Machinery just meant
　To give thy soul its bent,
Try thee and turn thee forth, sufficiently impressed.

What though the earlier grooves
　Which ran the laughing loves 170

Around thy base, no longer pause and press?
    What though, about thy rim,
    Skull-things in order grim
Grow out, in graver mood, obey the sterner stress?

    Look not thou down but up!   **175**
    To uses of a cup,
The festal board, lamp's flash and trumpet's peal,
    The new wine's foaming flow,
    The Master's lips aglow!
Thou, heaven's consummate cup, what need'st thou with
        earth's wheel?   180

    But I need, now as then,
    Thee, God, who mouldest men;
And since, not even while the whirl was worst,
    Did I — to the wheel of life
    With shapes and colours rife,   185
Bound dizzily — mistake my end, to slake Thy thirst:

    So, take and use Thy work:
    Amend what flaws may lurk,
What strain o' the stuff, what warpings past the aim!
    My times be in Thy hand!   190
    Perfect the cup as planned!
Let age approve of youth, and death complete the same!

CALIBAN UPON SETEBOS;

OR, NATURAL THEOLOGY IN THE ISLAND

"Thou thoughtest that I was altogether such an one as thyself."

['WILL sprawl, now that the heat of day is best,
Flat on his belly in the pit's much mire,
With elbows wide, fists clenched to prop his chin.
And, while he kicks both feet in the cool slush,
And feels about his spine small eft-things course,   5
Run in and out each arm, and make him laugh:

And while above his head a pompion-plant,
Coating the cave-top as a brow its eye,
Creeps down to touch and tickle hair and beard,
And now a flower drops with a bee inside,   10
And now a fruit to snap at, catch and crunch, —
He looks out o'er yon sea which sunbeams cross
And recross till they weave a spider-web,
(Meshes of fire, some great fish breaks at times,)
And talks to his own self, howe'er he please,   15
Touching that other, whom his dam called God.
Because to talk about Him, vexes — ha,
Could He but know! and time to vex is now,
When talk is safer than in winter-time.
Moreover, Prosper and Miranda sleep   20
In confidence he drudges at their task,
And it is good to cheat the pair, and gibe,
Letting the rank tongue blossom into speech.]

Setebos, Setebos, and Setebos!
'Thinketh, He dwelleth i' the cold o' the moon.   25

'Thinketh He made it, with the sun to match,
But not the stars; the stars came otherwise;
Only made clouds, winds, meteors, such as that:
Also this isle, what lives and grows thereon,
And snaky sea which rounds and ends the same.   30

'Thinketh, it came of being ill at ease:
He hated that He cannot change His cold,
Nor cure its ache. 'Hath spied an icy fish
That longed to 'scape the rock-stream where she lived,
And thaw herself within the lukewarm brine   35
O' the lazy sea her stream thrusts far amid,
A crystal spike 'twixt two warm walls of wave;
Only, she ever sickened, found repulse
At the other kind of water, not her life,
(Green-dense and dim-delicious, bred o' the sun)   40

Flounced back from bliss she was not born to breathe,
And in her old bounds buried her despair,
Hating and loving warmth alike: so He.

'Thinketh, He made thereat the sun, this isle,
Trees and the fowls here, beast and creeping thing.   **45**
Yon otter, sleek-wet, black, lithe as a leech;
Yon auk, one fire-eye in a ball of foam,
That floats and feeds; a certain badger brown
He hath watched hunt with that slant white-wedge eye
By moonlight; and the pie with the long tongue   **50**
That pricks deep into oakwarts for a worm,
And says a plain word when she finds her prize,
But will not eat the ants; the ants themselves
That build a wall of seeds and settled stalks
About their hole — He made all these and more,   **55**
Made all we see, and us, in spite: how else?
He could not, Himself, make a second self
To be His mate; as well have made Himself:
He would not make what He mislikes or slights,
An eyesore to Him, or not worth His pains: **60**
But did, in envy, listlessness or sport,
Make what Himself would fain, in a manner, be —
Weaker in most points, stronger in a few,
Worthy, and yet mere playthings all the while,
Things He admires and mocks too, — that is it.   **65**
Because, so brave, so better though they be,
It nothing skills if He begin to plague.
Look now, I melt a gourd-fruit into mash,
Add honeycomb and pods, I have perceived,
Which bite like finches when they bill and kiss, —   **70**
Then, when froth rises bladdery, drink up all,
Quick, quick, till maggots scamper through my brain;
Last, throw me on my back i' the seeded thyme.
And wanton, wishing I were born a bird.
Put case, unable to be what I wish,   **75**
I yet could make a live bird out of clay:

Would not I take clay, pinch my Caliban
Able to fly? — for, there, see, he hath wings,
And great comb like the hoopoe's to admire,
And there, a sting to do his foes offence,
There, and I will that he begin to live,   80
Fly to yon rock-top, nip me off the horns
Of grigs high up that make the merry din,
Saucy through their veined wings, and mind me not.
In which feat, if his leg snapped, brittle clay,   85
And he lay stupid-like, — why, I should laugh;
And if he, spying me, should fall to weep,
Beseech me to be good, repair his wrong,
Bid his poor leg smart less or grow again, —
Well, as the chance were, this might take or else   90
Not take my fancy: I might hear his cry,
And give the mankin three sound legs for one,
Or pluck the other off, leave him like an egg,
And lessoned he was mine and merely clay.
Were this no pleasure, lying in the thyme,   95
Drinking the mash, with brain become alive,
Making and marring clay at will?   So He.

'Thinketh, such shows nor right nor wrong in Him,
Nor kind, nor cruel: He is strong and Lord.
'Am strong myself compared to yonder crabs   100
That march now from the mountain to the sea;
'Let twenty pass, and stone the twenty-first,
Loving not, hating not, just choosing so.
'Say, the first straggler that boasts purple spots
Shall join the file, one pincer twisted off;   105
'Say, this bruised fellow shall receive a worm,
And two worms he whose nippers end in red;
As it likes me each time, I do: so He.

Well then, 'supposeth He is good i' the main,
Placable if His mind and ways were guessed,   110
But rougher than His handiwork, be sure!

Oh, He hath made things worthier than Himself,
And envieth that, so helped, such things do more
Than He who made them!   What consoles but this?
That they, unless through Him, do naught at all,   115
And must submit: what other use in things?
'Hath cut a pipe of pithless elder-joint
That, blown through, gives exact the scream o' the jay
When from her wing you twitch the feathers blue:
Sound this, and little birds that hate the jay   120
Flock within stone's throw, glad their foe is hurt:
Put case such pipe could prattle and boast forsooth,
"I catch the birds, I am the crafty thing,
I make the cry my maker cannot make
With his great round mouth; he must blow through mine!"
Would not I smash it with my foot?   So He.   126

But wherefore rough, why cold and ill at ease?
Aha, that is a question!   Ask, for that,
What knows, — the something over Setebos
That made Him, or He, may be, found and fought,   130
Worsted, drove off and did to nothing, perchance.
There may be something quiet o'er His head,
Out of His reach, that feels nor joy nor grief,
Since both derive from weakness in some way.
I joy because the quails come; would not joy   135
Could I bring quails here when I have a mind:
This Quiet, all it hath a mind to, doth.
'Esteemeth stars the outposts of its couch,
But never spends much thought nor care that way.
It may look up, work up — the worse for those   140
It works on!   'Careth but for Setebos
The many-handed as a cuttle-fish,
Who, making Himself feared through what He does,
Looks up, first, and perceives he cannot soar
To what is quiet and hath happy life;   145
Next looks down here, and out of very spite
Makes this a bauble-world to ape yon real,

These good things to match those as hips do grapes.
'Tis solace making baubles, ay, and sport.
Himself peeped late, eyed Prosper at his books   150
Careless and lofty, lord now of the isle:
Vexed, 'stitched a book of broad leaves, arrow-shaped,
Wrote thereon, he knows what, prodigious words;
Has peeled a wand and called it by a name;
Weareth at whiles for an enchanter's robe   155
The eyed skin of a supple oncelot;
And hath an ounce sleeker than youngling mole,
A four-legged serpent he makes cower and couch,
Now snarl, now hold its breath and mind his eye,
And saith she is Miranda and my wife: 160
'Keeps for his Ariel a tall pouch-bill crane
He bids go wade for fish and straight disgorge;
Also a sea-beast, lumpish, which he snared,
Blinded the eyes of, and brought somewhat tame,
And split its toe-webs, and now pens the drudge   165
In a hole o' the rock and calls him Caliban;
A bitter heart that bides its time and bites.
'Plays thus at being Prosper in a way,
'Taketh his mirth with make-believes: so He.

His dam held that the Quiet made all things   170
Which Setebos vexed only: 'holds not so.
Who made them weak, meant weakness He might vex
Had He meant other, while His hand was in,
Why not make horny eyes no thorn could prick,
Or plate my scalp with bone against the snow,   175
Or overscale my flesh 'neath joint and joint,
Like an orc's armour?   Ay, — so spoil His sport!
He is the One now: only He doth all.

'Saith, He may like, perchance, what profits Him.
Ay, himself loves what does him good; but why?   180
'Gets good no otherwise.   This blinded beast
Loves whoso places flesh-meat on his nose,

But, had he eyes, would want no help, but hate
Or love, just as it liked him: He hath eyes.
Also it pleaseth Setebos to work,   **185**
Use all His hands, and exercise much craft,
By no means for the love of what is worked.
'Tasteth, himself, no finer good i' the world
When all goes right, in this safe summer-time,
And he wants little, hungers, aches not much,   **190**
Than trying what to do with wit and strength.
'Falls to make something: 'piled yon pile of turfs,
And squared and stuck there squares of soft white chalk,
And, with a fish-tooth, scratched a moon on each,
And set up endwise certain spikes of tree,   **195**
And crowned the whole with a sloth's skull a-top,
Found dead i' the woods, too hard for one to kill.
No use at all i' the work, for work's sole sake;
'Shall some day knock it down again: so He.

'Saith He is terrible: watch His feats in proof!   **200**
One hurricane will spoil six good months' hope.
He hath a spite against me, that I know,
Just as He favours Prosper, who knows why?
So it is, all the same, as well I find.
'Wove wattles half the winter, fenced them firm   **205**
With stone and stake to stop she-tortoises
Crawling to lay their eggs here: well, one wave,
Feeling the foot of Him upon its neck,
Gaped as a snake does, lolled out its large tongue,
And licked the whole labour flat: so much for spite.   **210**

'Saw a ball flame down late (yonder it lies)
Where, half an hour before, I slept i' the shade:
Often they scatter sparkles: there is force!
'Dug up a newt He may have envied once
And turned to stone, shut up inside a stone.   **215**
Please Him and hinder this? — What Prosper does?
Aha, if He would tell me how!   Not He!

There is the sport: discover how or die!
All need not die, for of the things o' the isle
Some flee afar, some dive, some run up trees;   220
Those at His mercy, — why, they please Him most
When . . . when . . . well, never try the same way twice!
Repeat what act has pleased, He may grow wroth.
You must not know His ways, and play Him off,
Sure of the issue.   'Doth the like himself: 225
'Spareth a squirrel that it nothing fears
But steals the nut from underneath my thumb,
And when I threat, bites stoutly in defence:
'Spareth an urchin that, contrariwise,
Curls up into a ball, pretending death   230
For fright at my approach: the two ways please.
But what would move my choler more than this,
That either creature counted on its life
To-morrow and next day and all days to come,
Saying, forsooth, in the inmost of its heart,   235
"Because he did so yesterday with me,
And otherwise with such another brute,
So must he do henceforth and always." — Ay?
Would teach the reasoning couple what "must" means!
'Doth as he likes, or wherefore Lord?   So He.   240

'Conceiveth all things will continue thus,
And we shall have to live in fear of Him
So long as He lives, keeps His strength: no change,
If He have done His best, make no new world
To please Him more, so leave off watching this, —   245
If He surprise not even the Quiet's self
Some strange day — or, suppose, grow into it
As grubs grow butterflies: else, here we are,
And there is He, and nowhere help at all.

'Believeth with the life, the pain shall stop.   250
His dam held different, that after death
He both plagued enemies and feasted friends:

Idly!   He doth His worst in this our life,
Giving just respite lest we die through pain,
Saving last pain for worst, — with which, an end.   253
Meanwhile, the best way to escape His ire
Is, not to seem too happy.   'Sees, himself,
Yonder two flies, with purple films and pink,
Bask on the pompion-bell above: kills both.
'Sees two black painful beetles roll their ball   260
On head and tail as if to save their lives:
Moves them the stick away they strive to clear.

Even so, 'would have Him misconceive, suppose
This Caliban strives hard and ails no less,
And always, above all else, envies Him;   265
Wherefore he mainly dances on dark nights,
Moans in the sun, gets under holes to laugh,
And never speaks his mind save housed as now:
Outside, 'groans, curses.   If He caught me here,
O'erheard this speech, and asked "What chucklest at?"   270
'Would, to appease Him, cut a finger off,
Or of my three kid yearlings burn the best,
Or let the toothsome apples rot on tree,
Or push my tame beast for the orc to taste:
While myself lit a fire, and made a song   275
And sung it, "*What I hate, be consecrate*
To celebrate Thee and Thy state, no mate
For Thee; what see for envy in poor me?"
Hoping the while, since evils sometimes mend,
Warts rub away and sores are cured with slime,   280
That some strange day, will either the Quiet catch
And conquer Setebos, or likelier He
Decrepit may doze, doze, as good as die.

————————————

[What, what?   A curtain o'er the world at once!
Crickets stop hissing; not a bird — or, yes,   285
There scuds His raven that has told Him all!
It was fool's play, this prattling!   Ha!   The wind

Shoulders the pillared dust, death's house o' the move,
And fast invading fires begin!   White blaze —
A tree's head snaps — and there, there, there, there, there, 290
His thunder follows!   Fool to gibe at Him!
Lo! 'Lieth flat and loveth Setebos!
'Maketh his teeth meet through his upper lip,
Will let those quails fly, will not eat this month
One little mess of whelks, so he may 'scape!]   295

CONFESSIONS

WHAT is he buzzing in my ears?
    "Now that I come to die,
Do I view the world as a vale of tears?"
    Ah, reverend sir, not I!

What I viewed there once, what I view again   5
    Where the physic bottles stand
On the table's edge, — is a suburb lane,
    With a wall to my bedside hand.

That lane sloped, much as the bottles do,
    From a house you could descry   10
O'er the garden-wall: is the curtain blue
    Or green to a healthy eye?

To mine, it serves for the old June weather
    Blue above lane and wall;
And that farthest bottle labelled "Ether"   15
    Is the house o'ertopping all.

At a terrace, somewhere near the stopper,
    There watched for me, one June,
A girl: I know, sir, it's improper,
    My poor mind's out of tune.   20

Only, there was a way . . . you crept
   Close by the side, to dodge
Eyes in the house, two eyes except:
   They styled their house "The Lodge."

What right had a lounger up their lane?   **25**
   But, by creeping very close,
With the good wall's help, — their eyes might **strain**
   And stretch themselves to Oes,

Yet never catch her and me together,
   As she left the attic, there,   **30**
By the rim of the bottle labelled "Ether,"
   And stole from stair to stair,

And stood by the rose-wreathed gate.   **Alas,**
   We loved, sir — used to meet:
How sad and bad and mad it was —   **35**
   But then, how it was sweet!

MAY AND DEATH

I wish that when you died last May,
   Charles, there had died along with you
Three parts of spring's delightful things;
   Ay, and, for me, the fourth part too.

A foolish thought, and worse, perhaps!   **5**
   There must be many a pair of friends
Who, arm in arm, deserve the warm
   Moon-births and the long evening-ends.

So, for their sake, be May still May!
   Let their new time, as mine of old,   **10**
Do all it did for me: I bid
   Sweet sights and sounds throng manifold.

Only, one little sight, one plant,
    Woods have in May, that starts up green
Save a sole streak which, so to speak,   · 15
    Is spring's blood, spilt its leaves between. —

That, they might spare; a certain wood
    Might miss the plant; their loss were small:
But I, — whene'er the leaf grows there,
    Its drop comes from my heart, that's all.   20

(look forward)

PROSPICE

Fear death? — to feel the fog in my throat,
    The mist in my face,
When the snows begin, and the blasts denote
    I am nearing the place,
The power of the night, the press of the storm,   5
    The post of the foe;
Where he stands, the Arch Fear in a visible form,
    Yet the strong man must go:
For the journey is done and the summit attained,
    And the barriers fall,   10
Though a battle's to fight ere the guerdon be gained,
    The reward of it all.
I was ever a fighter, so — one fight more,
    The best and the last!
I would hate that death bandaged my eyes, and forbore,   15
    And bade me creep past.
No! let me taste the whole of it, fare like my peers
    The heroes of old,
Bear the brunt, in a minute pay glad life's arrears
    Of pain, darkness and cold.   20
For sudden the worst turns the best to the brave,
    The black minute's at end,
And the elements' rage, the fiend-voices that rave,
    Shall dwindle, shall blend,

Shall change, shall become first a peace out of pain,   25
  Then a light, then thy breast,
O thou soul of my soul!   I shall clasp thee again,
  And with God be the rest!

EURYDICE TO ORPHEUS

A PICTURE BY LEIGHTON

BUT give them me, the mouth, the eyes, the brow!
Let them once more absorb me!   One look now
  Will lap me round for ever, not to pass
Out of its light, though darkness lie beyond:
Hold me but safe again within the bond   5
  Of one immortal look!   All woe that was,
Forgotten, and all terror that may be,
Defied, — no past is mine, no future: look at me!

YOUTH AND ART

IT once might have been, once only:
  We lodged in a street together,
You, a sparrow on the housetop lonely,
  I, a lone she-bird of his feather.

Your trade was with sticks and clay,   5
  You thumbed, thrust, patted and polished,
Then laughed "They will see some day
  Smith made, and Gibson demolished."

My business was song, song, song;
  I chirped, cheeped, trilled and twittered,   10
"Kate Brown's on the boards ere long,
  And Grisi's existence embittered!"

I earned no more by a warble
  Than you by a sketch in plaster;

You wanted a piece of marble,   15
   I needed a music-master.

We studied hard in our styles,
   Chipped each at a crust like Hindoos,
For air, looked out on the tiles,
   For fun, watched each other's windows.   20

You lounged, like a boy of the South,
   Cap and blouse — nay, a bit of beard too;
Or you got it, rubbing your mouth
   With fingers the clay adhered to.

And I — soon managed to find   25
   Weak points in the flower-fence facing,
Was forced to put up a blind
   And be safe in my corset-lacing.

No harm! It was not my fault
   If you never turned your eye's tail up,   30
As I shook upon E *in alt.*,
   Or ran the chromatic scale up:

For spring bade the sparrows pair,
   And the boys and girls gave guesses,
And stalls in our street looked rare   35
   With bulrush and watercresses.

Why did not you pinch a flower
   In a pellet of clay and fling it?
Why did not I put a power
   Of thanks in a look, or sing it?   40

I did look, sharp as a lynx,
   (And yet the memory rankles),
When models arrived, some minx
   Tripped upstairs, she and her ankles.

But I think I gave you as good!   45
   "That foreign fellow, — who can know
How she pays, in a playful mood,
   For his tuning her that piano?"

Could you say so, and never say,
   "Suppose we join hands and fortunes,   50
And I fetch her from over the way,
   Her, piano, and long tunes and short tunes"?

No, no: you would not be rash,
   Nor I rasher and something over:
You've to settle yet Gibson's hash,   55
   And Grisi yet lives in clover.

But you meet the Prince at the Board,
   I'm queen myself at *bals-parés*,
I've married a rich old lord,
   And you're dubbed knight and an R.A   60

Each life unfulfilled, you see;
   It hangs still, patchy and scrappy:
We have not sighed deep, laughed free,
   Starved, feasted, despaired, — been happy,

And nobody calls you a dunce,   65
   And people suppose me clever:
This could but have happened once,
   And we missed it, lost it for ever.

A LIKENESS

Some people hang portraits up
In a room where they dine or sup:
   And the wife clinks tea-things under,

And her cousin, he stirs his cup,
 Asks, "Who was the lady, I wonder?" 5
"'Tis a daub John bought at a sale,"
 Quoth the wife, — looks black as thunder:
"What a shade beneath her nose!
Snuff-taking, I suppose, — "
Adds the cousin, while John's corns ail. 10

Or else, there's no wife in the case,
But the portrait's queen of the place,
Alone 'mid the other spoils
Of youth — masks, gloves and foils,
And pipe-sticks, rose, cherry-tree, jasmine, 15
 And the long whip, the tandem-lasher,
And the cast from a fist ("not, alas! mine,
 But my master's, the Tipton Slasher"),
And the cards where pistol-balls mark ace,
And a satin shoe used for cigar-case, 20
And the chamois-horns ("shot in the Chablais"),
 And prints — Rarey drumming on Cruiser,
 And Sayers, our champion, the bruiser,
And the little edition of Rabelais:
Where a friend, with both hands in his pockets, 25
 May saunter up close to examine it,
 And remark a good deal of Jane Lamb in it,
"But the eyes are half out of their sockets;
That hair's not so bad, where the gloss is,
But they've made the girl's nose a proboscis: 30
Jane Lamb, that we danced with at Vichy!
What, is not she Jane? Then, who is she?"

All that I own is a print,
An etching, a mezzotint;
'Tis a study, a fancy, a fiction, 35
Yet a fact (take my conviction)
Because it has more than a hint
 Of a certain face, I never

Saw elsewhere touch or trace of
In women I've seen the face of: 40
  Just an etching, and, so far, clever.

I keep my prints, an imbroglio,
Fifty in one portfolio.
When somebody tries my claret,
We turn round chairs to the fire,   45
Chirp over days in a garret,
  Chuckle o'er increase of salary,
Taste the good fruits of our leisure,
Talk about pencil and lyre,
  And the National Portrait Gallery: 50
Then I exhibit my treasure.
After we've turned over twenty,
  And the debt of wonder my crony owes
  Is paid to my Marc Antonios,
He stops me — "*Festina lentè!*   55
What's that sweet thing there, the etching?"
How my waistcoat-strings want stretching,
  How my cheeks grow red as tomatoes,
How my heart leaps!   But hearts, after leaps, ache.

"By the by, you must take, for a keepsake,   60
  That other, you praised, of Volpato's."
The fool!   Would he try a flight further and say —
He never saw, never before to-day,
What was able to take his breath away,
A face to lose youth for, to occupy age   65
With the dream of, meet death with, — why, I'll not engage
But that, half in a rapture and half in a rage,
I should toss him the thing's self — "'Tis only a duplicate,
A thing of no value!   Take it, I supplicate!"

APPARENT FAILURE

" We shall soon lose a celebrated building."
Paris Newspaper

No, for I'll save it!   Seven years since,
   I passed through Paris, stopped a day
To see the baptism of your Prince;
   Saw, made my bow, and went my way:
Walking the heat and headache off,   5
   I took the Seine-side, you surmise,
Thought of the Congress, Gortschakoff,
   Cavour's appeal and Buol's replies,
So sauntered till — what met my eyes?

Only the Doric little Morgue!   10
   The dead-house where you show your drowned:
Petrarch's Vaucluse makes proud the Sorgue,
   Your Morgue has made the Seine renowned.
One pays one's debt in such a case;
   I plucked up heart and entered — stalked,   15
Keeping a tolerable face
   Compared with some whose cheeks were chalked:
Let them!   No Briton's to be balked'

First came the silent gazers; next,
   A screen of glass, we're thankful for;   20
Last, the sight's self, the sermon's text,
   The three men who did most abhor
Their life in Paris yesterday,
   So killed themselves: and now, enthroned
Each on his copper couch, they lay   25
   Fronting me, waiting to be owned.
I thought, and think, their sin's atoned.

Poor men, God made, and all for that!
   The reverence struck me; o'er each head
Religiously was hung its hat,   30
   Each coat dripped by the owner's bed,

Sacred from touch: each had his berth,
  His bounds, his proper place of rest,
Who last night tenanted on earth
  Some arch, where twelve such slept abreast, —   35
Unless the plain asphalt seemed best.

How did it happen, my poor boy?
  You wanted to be Buonaparte
And have the Tuileries for toy,
  And could not, so it broke your heart?   40
You, old one by his side, I judge,
  Were, red as blood, a socialist,
A leveller! Does the Empire grudge
  You've gained what no Republic missed?
Be quiet, and unclench your fist!   45

And this — why, he was red in vain,
  Or black, — poor fellow that is blue!
What fancy was it turned your brain?
  Oh, women were the prize for you!
Money gets women, cards and dice   50
  Get money, and ill-luck gets just
The copper couch and one clear nice
  Cool squirt of water o'er your bust,
The right thing to extinguish lust!

It's wiser being good than bad;   55
  It's safer being meek than fierce:
It's fitter being sane than mad.
  My own hope is, a sun will pierce
The thickest cloud earth ever stretched;
  That, after Last, returns the First,   60
Though a wide compass round be fetched;
  That what began best, can't end worst,
Nor what God blessed once, prove accurst.

HOUSE

Shall I sonnet-sing you about myself?
   Do I live in a house you would like to see?
Is it scant of gear, has it store of pelf?
   "Unlock my heart with a sonnet-key?"

Invite the world, as my betters have done?   5
   "Take notice: this building remains on view,
Its suites of reception every one,
   Its private apartment and bedroom too;

"For a ticket, apply to the Publisher."
   No: thanking the public, I must decline.   10
A peep through my window, if folk prefer;
   But, please you, no foot over threshold of mine!

I have mixed with a crowd and heard free talk
   In a foreign land where an earthquake chanced,
And a house stood gaping, naught to balk   15
   Man's eye wherever he gazed or glanced.

The whole of the frontage shaven sheer,
   The inside gaped: exposed to day,
Right and wrong and common and queer,
   Bare, as the palm of your hand, it lay.   20

The owner?   Oh, he had been crushed, no doubt!
   "Odd tables and chairs for a man of wealth!
What a parcel of musty old books about!
   He smoked, — no wonder he lost his health!

"I doubt if he bathed before he dressed.   25
   A brasier? — the pagan, he burned perfumes!
You see it is proved, what the neighbours guessed:
   His wife and himself had separate rooms."

Friends, the goodman of the house at least
    Kept house to himself till an earthquake came: **30**
'Tis the fall of its frontage permits you feast
    On the inside arrangement you praise or blame.

Outside should suffice for evidence:
    And whoso desires to penetrate
Deeper, must dive by the spirit-sense —   **35**
    No optics like yours, at any rate!

"Hoity-toity!   A street to explore,
    Your house the exception!   '*With this same key
Shakespeare unlocked his heart,*' once more!"
    Did Shakespeare?   If so, the less Shakespeare **he**!   **40**

HERVÉ RIEL

I

On the sea and at the Hogue, sixteen hundred ninety-two,
    Did the English fight the French, — woe to France!
And, the thirty-first of May, helter-skelter through the blue,
Like a crowd of frightened porpoises a shoal of sharks pursue,
    Came crowding ship on ship to Saint-Malo on the Rance, 5
With the English fleet in view.

II

'Twas the squadron that escaped, with the victor in full
    chase;
    First and foremost of the drove, in his great ship, Dam-
    freville;
      Close on him fled, great and small,
      Twenty-two good ships in all;   **10**
And they signalled to the place
" Help the winners of a race!
    Get us guidance, give us harbour, take us quick — or,
    quicker still,
    Here's the English can and will!"

III

Then the pilots of the place put out brisk and leapt on
    board; 15
  "Why, what hope or chance have ships like these to pass?"
    laughed they:
"Rocks to starboard, rocks to port, all the passage scarred
    and scored, —
Shall the 'Formidable' here, with her twelve and eighty guns,
  Think to make the river-mouth by the single narrow way,
Trust to enter — where 'tis ticklish for a craft of twenty
    tons, 20
    And with flow at full beside?
    Now, 'tis slackest ebb of tide.
  Reach the mooring?   Rather say,
While rock stands or water runs,
    Not a ship will leave the bay!" 25

IV

Then was called a council straight.
Brief and bitter the debate:
"Here's the English at our heels; would you have them take
    in tow
All that's left us of the fleet, linked together stern and bow,
For a prize to Plymouth Sound? 30
Better run the ships aground!"
  (Ended Damfreville his speech.)
" Not a minute more to wait!
  Let the Captains all and each
    Shove ashore, then blow up, burn the vessels on the
    beach! 35
France must undergo her fate.

V

"Give the word!"   But no such word
Was ever spoke or heard;
  For up stood, for out stepped, for in struck amid all these

— A Captain?   A Lieutenant?   A Mate — first, second,
     third?   40
     No such man of mark, and meet
     With his betters to compete!
     But a simple Breton sailor pressed by Tourville for the
       fleet,
A poor coasting-pilot he, Hervé Riel the Croisickese.

VI

And "What mockery or malice have we here?" cries Hervé
     Riel: 45
     "Are you mad, you Malouins?   Are you cowards, fools,
       or rogues?
Talk to me of rocks and shoals, me who took the soundings,
     tell
On my fingers every bank, every shallow, every swell
     'Twixt the offing here and Grève where the river disem-
       bogues?
Are you bought by English gold?   Is it love the lying's
     for?   50
     Morn and eve, night and day,
     Have I piloted your bay,
Entered free and anchored fast at the foot of Solidor.
     Burn the fleet and ruin France?   That were worse than
       fifty Hogues!
     Sirs, they know I speak the truth!   Sirs, believe me
       there's a way!   55
Only let me lead the line,
     Have the biggest ship to steer,
     Get this 'Formidable' clear,
Make the others follow mine,
And I lead them, most and least, by a passage I know well, 60
     Right to Solidor past Grève,
     And there lay them safe and sound;
     And if one ship misbehave,
     — Keel so much as grate the ground,
Why, I've nothing but my life, — here's my head!" cries
     Hervé Riel.   65

VII

Not a minute more to wait.
"Steer us in, then, small and great!
  Take the helm, lead the line, save the squadron!" cried its
    chief.
Captains, give the sailor place!
  He is Admiral, in brief.   70
Still the north-wind, by God's grace!
See the noble fellow's face
As the big ship, with a bound,
Clears the entry like a hound,
Keeps the passage, as its inch of way were the wide sea's
    profound!   75
  See, safe through shoal and rock,
  How they follow in a flock,
Not a ship that misbehaves, not a keel that grates the
    ground,
  Not a spar that comes to grief!
The peril, see, is past.   80
All are harboured to the last,
And just as Hervé Riel hollas "Anchor!" — sure as fate,
Up the English come, — too late!

VIII

So, the storm subsides to calm:
  They see the green trees wave   85
  On the heights o'erlooking Grève.
Hearts that bled are stanched with balm.
"Just our rapture to enhance,
  Let the English rake the bay,
Gnash their teeth and glare askance   90
  As they cannonade away!
'Neath rampired Solidor pleasant riding on the Rance!"
How hope succeeds despair on each Captain's countenance!
Out burst all with one accord,
  "This is Paradise for Hell!   95

Let France, let France's King
    Thank the man that did the thing!"
What a shout, and all one word,
    "Hervé Riel!"
As he stepped in front once more.   100
    Not a symptom of surprise
    In the frank blue Breton eyes,
Just the same man as before.

                            IX

Then said Damfreville, "My friend,
I must speak out at the end,   105
    Though I find the speaking hard.
Praise is deeper than the lips:
You have saved the King his ships,
    You must name your own reward.
'Faith, our sun was near eclipse!   110
Demand whate'er you will,
France remains your debtor still.
Ask to heart's content and have! or my name's not Dam-
        freville."

                            X

Then a beam of fun outbroke
On the bearded mouth that spoke,   115
As the honest heart laughed through
Those frank eyes of Breton blue:
"Since I needs must say my say,
    Since on board the duty's done,
    And from Malo Roads to Croisic Point, what is it but a
        run? —   120
Since 'tis ask and have, I may —
    Since the others go ashore —
Come!   A good whole holiday!
    Leave to go and see my wife, whom I call the Belle
        Aurore!"
    That he asked and that he got, — nothing more.   125

XI

Name and deed alike are lost:
Not a pillar nor a post
   In his Croisic keeps alive the feat as it befell;
Not a head in white and black
On a single fishing-smack,   130
In memory of the man but for whom had gone to wrack
   All that France saved from the fight whence England bore
      the bell.
Go to Paris: rank on rank
   Search the heroes flung pell-mell
On the Louvre, face and flank!   135
   You shall look long enough ere you come to Hervé Riel.
So, for better and for worse,
Hervé Riel, accept my verse!
In my verse, Hervé Riel, do thou once more
Save the squadron, honour France, love thy wife the Belle
      Aurore!   140

PHEIDIPPIDES

λαίρετε, νικῶμεν

FIRST I salute this soil of the blessed, river and rock!
Gods of my birthplace, dæmons and heroes, honour to all!
Then I name thee, claim thee for our patron, co-equal in
    praise
— Ay, with Zeus the Defender, with Her of the ægis and
    spear!
Also, ye of the bow and the buskin, praised be your peer, 5
Now, henceforth and for ever, — O latest to whom I upraise
Hand and heart and voice!   For Athens, leave pasture and
    flock!
Present to help, potent to save, Pan — patron I call!

Archons of Athens, topped by the tettix, see, I return!
See, 'tis myself here standing alive, no spectre that speaks! 10

Crowned with the myrtle, did you command me, Athens and
     you,
"Run, Pheidippides, run and race, reach Sparta for aid!
Persia has come, we are here, where is She?" Your com-
     mand I obeyed,
Ran and raced: like stubble, some field which a fire runs
     through,
Was the space between city and city: two days, two nights
     did I burn   15
Over the hills, under the dales, down pits and up peaks.

Into their midst I broke: breath served but for "Persia has
     come!
Persia bids Athens proffer slaves'-tribute, water and earth;
Razed to the ground is Eretria — but Athens, shall Athens
     sink,
Drop into dust and die — the flower of Hellas utterly die,
Die, with the wide world spitting at Sparta, the stupid, the
     stander-by?   21
Answer me quick, what help, what hand do you stretch o'er
     destruction's brink?
How, — when? No care for my limbs! — there's lightning
     in all and some —
Fresh and fit your message to bear, once lips give it birth!"

O my Athens — Sparta love thee? Did Sparta respond?
Every face of her leered in a furrow of envy, mistrust,   26
Malice, — each eye of her gave me its glitter of gratified
     hate!
Gravely they turned to take counsel, to cast for excuses. I
     stood
Quivering, — the limbs of me fretting as fire frets, an inch
     from dry wood: 29
"Persia has come, Athens asks aid, and still they debate?
Thunder, thou Zeus! Athené, are Spartans a quarry beyond
Swing of thy spear? Phoibos and Artemis, clang them 'Ye
     must'!"

No bolt launched from Olumpos! Lo, their answer at last!

"Has Persia come, — does Athens ask aid, — may Sparta
    befriend?

Nowise precipitate judgement — too weighty the issue at
    stake!   35

Count we no time lost time which lags through respect to the
    Gods!

Ponder that precept of old, 'No warfare, whatever the odds

In your favour, so long as the moon, half-orbed, is unable to
    take

Full-circle her state in the sky!' Already she rounds to it
    fast:

Athens must wait, patient as we — who judgement suspend."

Athens, — except for that sparkle, — thy name, I had
    mouldered to ash!   41

That sent a blaze through my blood; off, off and away was I
    back,

— Not one word to waste, one look to lose on the false and
    the vile!

Yet "O Gods of my land!" I cried, as each hillock and
    plain,

Wood and stream, I knew, I named, rushing past them
    again,

"Have ye kept faith, proved mindful of honours we paid you
    erewhile?   46

Vain was the filleted victim, the fulsome libation! Too rash

Love in its choice, paid you so largely service so slack!

"Oak and olive and bay, — I bid you cease to enwreathe

Brows made bold by your leaf! Fade at the Persian's foot,

You that, our patrons were pledged, should never adorn a
    slave!   51

Rather I hail thee, Parnes, — trust to thy wild waste tract!

Treeless, herbless, lifeless mountain! What matter if
    slacked

My speed may hardly be, for homage to crag and to cave

No deity deigns to drape with verdure? at least I can
    breathe,   55
Fear in thee no fraud from the blind, no lie from the mute!"

Such my cry as, rapid, I ran over Parnes' ridge;
Gully and gap I clambered and cleared till, sudden, a bar
Jutted, a stoppage of stone against me, blocking the way.
Right! for I minded the hollow to traverse, the fissure
    across: 60
"Where I could enter, there I depart by! Night in the
    fosse?
Athens to aid?   Though the dive were through Erebos, thus
    I obey —
Out of the day dive, into the day as bravely arise! No
    bridge
Better!" — when — ha! what was it I came on, of wonders
    that are?

There, in the cool of a cleft, sat he — majestical Pan!   65
Ivy drooped wanton, kissed his head, moss cushioned his
    hoof:
All the great God was good in the eyes grave-kindly — the
    curl
Carved on the bearded cheek, amused at a mortal's awe,
As, under the human trunk, the goat-thighs grand I saw.
"Halt, Pheidippides!" — halt I did, my brain of a whirl:
"Hither to me! Why pale in my presence?" he gracious
    began: 71
"How is it, — Athens, only in Hellas, holds me aloof?

"Athens, she only, rears me no fane, makes me no feast!
Wherefore?   Than I what godship to Athens more helpful
    of old?
Ay, and still, and for ever her friend! Test Pan, trust me! 75
Go, bid Athens take heart, laugh Persia to scorn, have faith
In the temples and tombs!   Go, say to Athens, 'The Goat-
    God saith:

When Persia — so much as strews not the soil — is cast in
    the sea.
Then praise Pan who fought in the ranks with your most and
    least,
Goat-thigh to greaved-thigh, made one cause with the free
    and the bold!'   80

"Say Pan saith: 'Let this, foreshowing the place, be the
    pledge!'"
(Gay, the liberal hand held out this herbage I bear
— Fennel — I grasped it a-tremble with dew — whatever it
    bode.)
"While, as for thee ..." But enough! He was gone. If I
    ran hitherto —
Be sure that, the rest of my journey, I ran no longer, but
    flew.   85
Parnes to Athens — earth no more, the air was my road:
Here am I back. Praise Pan, we stand no more on the
    razor's edge!
Pan for Athens, Pan for me! I too have a guerdon rare!

———

Then spoke Miltiades. "And thee, best runner of Greece,
Whose limbs did duty indeed, — what gift is promised thy-
    self?   90
Tell it us straightway, — Athens the mother demands of her
    son!"
Rosily blushed the youth: he paused: but, lifting at length
His eyes from the ground, it seemed as he gathered the rest
    of his strength
Into the utterance — "Pan spoke thus: 'For what thou hast
    done
Count on a worthy reward! Henceforth be allowed thee
    release   95
From the racer's toil, no vulgar reward in praise or in pelf!'

"I am bold to believe, Pan means reward the most to my
    mind!

Fight I shall, with our foremost, wherever this fennel may
  grow, —
Pound — Pan helping us — Persia to dust, and, under the
  deep,   99
Whelm her away for ever; and then — no Athens to save —
Marry a certain maid, I know keeps faith to the brave, —
Hie to my house and home: and, when my children shall
  creep
Close to my knees, — recount how the God was awful yet
  kind,
Promised their sire reward to the full — rewarding him —
  so!"

Unforeseeing one! Yes, he fought on the Marathon day:
So, when Persia was dust, all cried "To Akropolis!   106
Run, Pheidippides, one race more! the meed is thy due!
'Athens is saved, thank Pan,' go shout!" He flung down
  his shield,
Ran like fire once more: and the space 'twixt the Fennel-field
And Athens was stubble again, a field which a fire runs
  through,   110
Till in he broke: "Rejoice, we conquer!" Like wine through
  clay,
Joy in his blood bursting his heart, he died — the bliss!

So, to this day, when friend meets friend, the word of salute
Is still "Rejoice!" — his word which brought rejoicing in-
  deed.
So is Pheidippides happy for ever, — the noble strong man
Who could race like a God, bear the face of a God, whom
  a God loved so well;   116
He saw the land saved he had helped to save, and was suf-
  fered to tell
Such tidings, yet never decline, but, gloriously as he began,
So to end gloriously — once to shout, thereafter be mute:
"Athens is saved!" — Pheidippides dies in the shout for his
  meed.   120

HALBERT AND HOB

HERE is a thing that happened.   Like wild beasts whelped, for den,

In a wild part of North England, there lived once two wild men

Inhabiting one homestead, neither a hovel nor hut,

Time out of mind their birthright: father and son, these — but —

Such a son, such a father!   Most wildness by degrees   5

Softens away: yet, last of their line, the wildest and worst were these.

Criminals, then?   Why, no: they did not murder and rob;

But, give them a word, they returned a blow — old Halbert as young Hob:

Harsh and fierce of word, rough and savage of deed,

Hated or feared the more — who knows? — the genuine wild-beast breed.   10

Thus were they found by the few sparse folk of the country-side;

But how fared each with other?   E'en beasts couch, hide by hide,

In a growling, grudged agreement: so, father and son aye curled

The closelier up in their den because the last of their kind in the world.

Still, beast irks beast on occasion.   One Christmas night of snow,   15

Came father and son to words — such words! more cruel because the blow

To crown each word was wanting, while taunt matched gibe, and curse

Competed with oath in wager, like pastime in hell, — nay, worse:

For pastime turned to earnest, as up there sprang at last
The son at the throat of the father, seized him and held him
      fast.   20

"Out of this house you go!" (there followed a hideous
      oath) —
"This oven where now we bake, too hot to hold us both!
If there's snow outside, there's coolness: out with you, bide
      a spell
In the drift and save the sexton the charge of a parish shell!"

Now, the old trunk was tough, was solid as stump of oak   25
Untouched at the core by a thousand years: much less had
      its seventy broke
One whipcord nerve in the muscly mass from neck to
      shoulder-blade
Of the mountainous man, whereon his child's rash hand like
      a feather weighed.

Nevertheless at once did the mammoth shut his eyes,
Drop chin to breast, drop hands to sides, stand stiffened –
      arms and thighs   30
All of a piece — struck mute, much as a sentry stands,
Patient to take the enemy's fire: his captain so commands.

Whereat the son's wrath flew to fury at such sheer scorn
Of his puny strength by the giant eld thus acting the babe
      new-born:
And "Neither will this turn serve!" yelled he. "Out with
      you! Trundle, log!   35
If you cannot tramp and trudge like a man, try all-fours like
      a dog!"

Still the old man stood mute. So, logwise — down to floor
Pulled from his fireside place, dragged on from hearth to
      door —
Was he pushed, a very log, staircase along, until

A certain turn in the steps was reached, a yard from the
house-door-sill.   40

Then the father opened eyes — each spark of their rage
extinct, —
Temples, late black, dead-blanched — right-hand with left-
hand linked, —
He faced his son submissive; when slow the accents came,
They were strangely mild though his son's rash hand on his
neck lay all the same.

"Hob, on just such a night of a Christmas long ago,   45
For such a cause, with such a gesture, did I drag — so —
My father down thus far: but, softening here, I heard
A voice in my heart, and stopped: you wait for an outer word.

"For your own sake, not mine, soften you too!   Untrod
Leave this last step we reach, nor brave the finger of God! 50
I dared not pass its lifting: I did well.   I nor blame
Nor praise you. I stopped here: and, Hob, do you the
same!"

Straightway the son relaxed his hold of the father's throat.
They mounted, side by side, to the room again: no note
Took either of each, no sign made each to either: last   55
As first, in absolute silence, their Christmas-night they
passed.

At dawn, the father sate on, dead, in the self-same place,
With an outburst blackening still the old bad fighting-face:
But the son crouched all a-tremble like any lamb new-
yeaned.

When he went to the burial, some one's staff he borrowed —
tottered and leaned.   60
But his lips were loose, not locked, — kept muttering,
mumbling. "There!

At his cursing and swearing!" the youngsters cried: but the
    elders thought "In prayer."
A boy threw stones: he picked them up and stored them in
    his vest.

So tottered, muttered, mumbled he, till he died, perhaps
    found rest.
"Is there a reason in nature for these hard hearts?" O
    Lear,   65
That a reason out of nature must turn them soft, seems clear!

ECHETLOS

HERE is a story, shall stir you!   Stand up, Greeks dead and
    gone,
Who breasted, beat Barbarians, stemmed Persia rolling on,
Did the deed and saved the world, for the day was Marathon!

No man but did his manliest, kept rank and fought away
In his tribe and file: up, back, out, down — was the spear-
    arm play: 5
Like a wind-whipt branchy wood, all spear-arms a-swing
    that day!

But one man kept no rank, and his sole arm plied no spear,
As a flashing came and went, and a form i' the van, the rear,
Brightened the battle up, for he blazed now there, now here.

Nor helmed nor shielded, he! but, a goat-skin all his wear, 10
Like a tiller of the soil, with a clown's limbs broad and bare,
Went he ploughing on and on: he pushed with a ploughman's
    share.

Did the weak mid-line give way, as tunnies on whom the
    shark
Precipitates his bulk?   Did the right-wing halt when, stark
On his heap of slain lay stretched Kallimachos Polemarch? 15

Did the steady phalanx falter? To the rescue, at the need,
The clown was ploughing Persia, clearing Greek earth of
    weed,
As he routed through the Sakian and rooted up the Mede.

But the deed done, battle won, — nowhere to be descried
On the meadow, by the stream, at the marsh, — look far and
    wide   20
From the foot of the mountain, no, to the last blood-plashed
    seaside, —

Not anywhere on view blazed the large limbs thronged and
    brown,
Shearing and clearing still with the share before which —
    down
To the dust went Persia's pomp, as he ploughed for Greece,
    that clown!

How spake the Oracle? "Care for no name at all!   25
Say but just this: 'We praise one helpful whom we call
The Holder of the Ploughshare.' The great deed ne'er
    grows small."

Not the great name! Sing — woe for the great name
    Míltiadés
And its end at Paros isle! Woe for Themistokles   29
— Satrap in Sardis court! Name not the clown like these!

"WANTING IS — WHAT?"

    WANTING is — what?
    Summer redundant,
    Blueness abundant,
      — Where is the blot?
Beamy the world, yet a blank all the same,   5
    — Framework which waits for a picture to frame:

What of the leafage, what of the flower?
Roses embowering with naught they embower!
Come then, complete incompletion, O comer,
Pant through the blueness, perfect the summer!   10
     Breathe but one breath
     Rose-beauty above,
     And all that was death
     Grows life, grows love,
       Grows love!   15

DONALD

"WILL you hear my story also,
    — Huge Sport, brave adventure in plenty?"
The boys were a band from Oxford,
    The oldest of whom was twenty.

The bothy we held carouse in   5
    Was bright with fire and candle;
Tale followed tale like a merry-go-round
    Whereof Sport turned the handle.

In our eyes and noses — turf-smoke:
    In our ears a tune from the trivet,   10
Whence "Boiling, boiling," the kettle sang,
    "And ready for fresh Glenlivet."

So, feat capped feat, with a vengeance:
    Truths, though, — the lads were loyal:
"Grouse, five-score brace to the bag!   15
    Deer, ten hours' stalk of the Royal!"

Of boasting, not one bit, boys!
    Only there seemed to settle
Somehow above your curly heads,
    — Plain through the singing kettle,   20

Palpable through the cloud,
   As each new-puffed Havana
Rewarded the teller's well-told tale, —
   This vaunt "To Sport — Hosanna!

"Hunt, fish, shoot,   25
   Would a man fulfil life's duty!
Not to the bodily frame alone
   Does Sport give strength and beauty,

"But character gains in — courage?
   Ay, Sir, and much beside it!   30
You don't sport, more's the pity:
   You soon would find, if you tried it,

"Good sportsman means good fellow,
   Sound-hearted he, to the centre;
Your mealy-mouthed mild milksops   35
   — There's where the rot can enter!

"There's where the dirt will breed,
   The shabbiness Sport would banish!
Oh no, Sir, no! In your honoured case
   All such objections vanish.   40

"'Tis known how hard you studied:
   A Double-First — what, the jigger!
Give me but half your Latin and Greek,
   I'll never again touch trigger!

"Still, tastes are tastes, allow me!   45
   Allow, too, where there's keenness
For Sport, there's little likelihood
   Of a man's displaying meanness!"

So, put on my mettle, I interposed.
   "Will you hear my story?" quoth I.   50

"Never mind how long since it happed,
    I sat, as we sit, in a bothy;

"With as merry a band of mates, too,
    Undergrads all on a level:
(One's a Bishop, one's gone to the Bench,   55
    And one's gone — well, to the Devil.)

"When, lo, a scratching and tapping!
    In hobbled a ghastly visitor.
Listen to just what he told us himself
    — No need of our playing inquisitor!"   60

————————

Do you happen to know in Ross-shire
    Mount . . . Ben . . . but the name scarce matters:
Of the naked fact I am sure enough,
    Though I clothe it in rags and tatters.

You may recognize Ben by description;   65
    Behind him — a moor's immenseness:
Up goes the middle mount of a range,
    Fringed with its firs in denseness.

Rimming the edge, its fir-fringe, mind!
    For an edge there is, though narrow;   70
From end to end of the range, a strip
    Of path runs straight as an arrow.

And the mountaineer who takes that path
    Saves himself miles of journey
He has to plod if he crosses the moor   75
    Through heather, peat and burnie.

But a mountaineer he needs must be,
    For, look you, right in the middle
Projects bluff Ben — with an end in *ich* —
    Why planted there, is a riddle: 80

Since all Ben's brothers little and big
   Keep rank, set shoulder to shoulder,
And only this burliest out must bulge
   Till it seems — to the beholder

From down in the gully — as if Ben's breast,   85
   To a sudden spike diminished,
Would signify to the boldest foot
   "All further passage finished!'

Yet the mountaineer who sidles on
   And on to the very bending,   90
Discovers, if heart and brain be proof,
   No necessary ending.

Foot up, foot down, to the turn abrupt
   Having trod, he, there arriving,
Finds — what he took for a point was breadth,   95
   A mercy of Nature's contriving.

So, he rounds what, when 'tis reached, proves straight,
   From one side gains the other:
The wee path widens — resume the march,
   And he foils you, Ben my brother!   100

But Donald — (that name, I hope, will do) —
   I wrong him if I call "foiling"
The tramp of the callant, whistling the while
   As blithe as our kettle's boiling.

He had dared the danger from boyhood up,   105
   And now — when perchance was waiting
A lass at the brig below — 'twixt mount
   And moor would he stand debating?

Moreover this Donald was twenty-five,
   A glory of bone and muscle: 110

Did a fiend dispute the right of way.
    Donald would try a tussle.

Lightsomely marched he out of the broad
    On to the narrow and narrow;
A step more, rounding the angular rock,   115
    Reached the front straight as an arrow.

He stepped it, safe on the ledge he stood,
    When — whom found he full-facing?
What fellow in courage and wariness too,
    Had scouted ignoble pacing,   120

And left low safety to timid mates,
    And made for the dread dear danger,
And gained the height where — who could guess
    He would meet with a rival ranger?

'Twas a gold-red stag that stood and stared,   125
    Gigantic and magnific,
By the wonder — ay, and the peril — struck
    Intelligent and pacific:

For a red deer is no fallow deer
    Grown cowardly through park-feeding;   130
He batters you like a thunderbolt
    If you brave his haunts unheeding.

I doubt he could hardly perform *volte-face*
    Had valour advised discretion:
You may walk on a rope, but to turn on a rope 135
    No Blondin makes profession.

Yet Donald must turn, would pride permit,
    Though pride ill brooks retiring:
Each eyed each — mute man, motionless beast —
    Less fearing than admiring.   140

These are the moments when quite new sense,
  To meet some need as novel,
Springs up in the brain: it inspired resource:
  — "Nor advance nor retreat but — grovel!"

And slowly, surely, never a whit   145
  Relaxing the steady tension
Of eye-stare which binds man to beast, —
  By an inch and inch declension,

Sank Donald sidewise down and down:
  Till flat, breast upwards, lying   150
At his six-foot length, no corpse more still,
  — "If he cross me! The trick's worth trying."

Minutes were an eternity;
  But a new sense was created
In the stag's brain too; he resolves! Slow, sure,   155
  With eye-stare unabated,

Feelingly he extends a foot
  Which tastes the way ere it touches
Earth's solid and just escapes man's soft,
  Nor hold of the same unclutches   160

Till its fellow foot, light as a feather whisk,
  Lands itself no less finely:
So a mother removes a fly from the face
  Of her babe asleep supinely

And now 'tis the haunch and hind-foot's turn   165
  — That's hard: can the beast quite raise it?
Yes, traversing half the prostrate length,
  His hoof-tip does not graze it.

Just one more lift! But Donald, you see,
  Was sportsman first, man after: 170

A fancy lightened his caution through,
  — He well-nigh broke into laughter:

"It were nothing short of a miracle!
  Unrivalled, unexampled —
All sporting feats with this feat matched   175
  Were down and dead and trampled!"

The last of the legs as tenderly
  Follows the rest: or never
Or now is the time! His knife in reach,
  And his right-hand loose — how clever!   180

For this can stab up the stomach's soft,
  While the left-hand grasps the pastern.
A rise on the elbow, and — now's the time
  Or never: this turn's the last turn!

I shall dare to place myself by God   185
  Who scanned — for He does — each feature
Of the face thrown up in appeal to Him
  By the agonizing creature.

Nay, I hear plain words: "Thy gift brings this!"
  Up he sprang, back he staggered,   190
Over he fell, and with him our frienc
  — At following game no laggard.

Yet he was not dead when they picked next day
  From the gully's depth the wreck of him;
His fall had been stayed by the stag beneath   195
  Who cushioned and saved the neck of him.

But the rest of his body — why, doctors said,
  Whatever could break was broken;
Legs, arms, ribs, all of him looked like a toast
  In a tumbler of port-wine soaken.   200

"That your life is left you, thank the stag!"
  Said they when — the slow cure ended —
They opened the hospital-door, and thence
  — Strapped, spliced, main fractures mended,

And minor damage left wisely alone, —   205
  Like an old shoe clouted and cobbled,
Out — what went in a Goliath well-nigh —
  Some half of a David hobbled.

"You must ask an alms from house to house:
  Sell the stag's head for a bracket,   210
With its grand twelve tines — I'd buy it myself —
  And use the skin for a jacket!"

He was wiser, made both head and hide
  His win-penny: hands and knees on,
Would manage to crawl — poor crab — by the roads 215
  In the misty stalking-season.

And if he discovered a bothy like this,
  Why, harvest was sure: folk listened.
He told his tale to the lovers of Sport:
  Lips twitched, cheeks glowed, eyes glistened.   220

And when he had come to the close, and spread
  His spoils for the gazers' wonder,
With "Gentlemen, here's the skull of the stag
  I was over, thank God, not under!" —

The company broke out in applause;   225
  "By Jingo, a lucky cripple!
Have a munch of grouse and a hunk of bread,
  And a tug, besides, at our tipple!"

And "There's my pay for your pluck!" cried This,
  "And mine for your jolly story!"   230

Cried That, while T'other — but he was drunk —
  Hiccupped "A trump, a Tory!"

I hope I gave twice as much as the rest;
  For, as Homer would say, "within grate
Though teeth kept tongue," my whole soul growled.   235
  "Rightly rewarded, — Ingrate!"

"NEVER THE TIME AND THE PLACE"

Never the time and the place
  And the loved one all together!
This path — how soft to pace!
  This May — what magic weather!
Where is the loved one's face?   5
In a dream that loved one's face meets mine,
  But the house is narrow, the place is bleak
Where, outside, rain and wind combine
  With a furtive ear, if I strive to speak,
With a hostile eye at my flushing cheek,   10
With a malice that marks each word, each sign!
O enemy sly and serpentine,
  Uncoil thee from the waking man!
    Do I hold the Past
    Thus firm and fast   15
Yet doubt if the Future hold I can?
This path so soft to pace shall lead
Through the magic of May to herself indeed!
Or narrow if needs the house must be,
Outside are the storms and strangers: we —   20
Oh, close, safe, warm sleep I and she,
  — I and she!

HUMILITY

What girl but, having gathered flowers,
Stript the beds and spoilt the bowers,

From the lapful light she carries
Drops a careless bud? — nor tarries
To regain the waif and stray: 5
"Store enough for home" — she'll say.

So say I too: give your lover
Heaps of loving — under, over,
Whelm him — make the one the wealthy!
Am I all so poor who — stealthy   10
Work it was! — picked up what fell:
Not the worst bud — who can tell?

POETICS

"So say the foolish!"   Say the foolish so, Love?
  "Flower she is, my rose" — or else, "My very swan is
    she" —
Or perhaps, "Yon maid-moon, blessing earth below, Love,
    That art thou!" — to them, belike: no such vain words
    from me.

"Hush, rose, blush! no balm like breath," I chide it: 5
  "Bend thy neck its best, swan, — hers the whiter curve!"
Be the moon the moon: my Love I place beside it:
    What is she?   Her human self, — no lower word will serve.

SUMMUM BONUM

ALL the breath and the bloom of the year in the bag of one
    bee:
  All the wonder and wealth of the mine in the heart of one
    gem:
In the core of one pearl all the shade and the shine of the sea:
    Breath and bloom, shade and shine, — wonder, wealth,
    and — how far above them —

Truth, that's brighter than gem,   5
  Trust, that's purer than pearl, —
Brightest truth, purest trust in the universe — all were for
    me
      In the kiss of one girl.

WHICH?

So, the three Court-ladies began
  Their trial of who judged best
In esteeming the love of a man:
Who preferred with most reason was thereby confessed
Boy-Cupid's exemplary catcher and cager;   5
An Abbé crossed legs to decide on the wager.

First the Duchesse: "Mine for me —
  Who were it but God's for Him,
  And the King's for — who but he?
Both faithful and loyal, one grace more shall brim   10
His cup with perfection: a lady's true lover,
He holds — save his God and his king — none above her."

"I require" — outspoke the Marquise —
  "Pure thoughts, ay, but also fine deeds:
  Play the paladin must he, to please   15
My whim, and — to prove my knight's service exceeds
Your saint's and your loyalist's praying and kneeling —
Show wounds, each wide mouth to my mercy appealing."

Then the Comtesse: "My choice be a wretch,
  Mere losel in body and soul,   20
  Thrice accurst! What care I, so he stretch
Arms to me his sole saviour, love's ultimate goal,
Out of earth and men's noise — names of 'infidel,' 'traitor,'
Cast up at him? Crown me, crown's adjudicator!"

And the Abbé uncrossed his legs,   25
  Took snuff, a reflective pinch,
  Broke silence: "The question begs
Much pondering ere I pronounce.   Shall I flinch?
The love which to one and one only has reference
Seems terribly like what perhaps gains God's preference."   30

"IMPERANTE AUGUSTO NATUS EST—"

WHAT it was struck the terror into me?
This, Publius: closer! while we wait our turn
I'll tell you.   Water's warm (they ring inside)
At the eighth hour, till when no use to bathe.

Here in the vestibule where now we sit,   5
One scarce stood yesterday, the throng was such
Of loyal gapers, folk all eye and ear
While Lucius Varius Rufus in their midst
Read out that long-planned late-completed piece,
His Panegyric on the Emperor.   10
"Nobody like him," little Flaccus laughed,
"At leading forth an Epos with due pomp!
Only, when godlike Cæsar swells the theme,
How should mere mortals hope to praise aright?
Tell me, thou offshoot of Etruscan kings!"   15
Whereat Mæcenas smiling sighed assent.

I paid my quadrans, left the Thermæ's roar
Of rapture as the poet asked, "What place
Among the godships Jove, for Cæsar's sake,
Would bid its actual occupant vacate   20
In favour of the new divinity?"
And got the expected answer, "Yield thine own!" —
Jove thus dethroned, I somehow wanted air,
And found myself a-pacing street and street,
Letting the sunset, rosy over Rome,   25
Clear my head dizzy with the hubbub — say,

As if thought's dance therein had kicked up dust
By trampling on all else: the world lay prone,
As — poet-propped, in brave hexameters —
Their subject triumphed up from man to God.   30
Caius Octavius Cæsar the August —
Where was escape from his prepotency?
I judge I may have passed — how many piles
Of structure dropt like doles from his free hand
To Rome on every side?   Why, right and left,   35
For temples you've the Thundering Jupiter,
Avenging Mars, Apollo Palatine:
How count Piazza, Forum — there's a third
All but completed.   You've the Theatre
Named of Marcellus — all his work, such work! —   40
One thought still ending, dominating all —
With warrant Varius sang, "Be Cæsar God!"
By what a hold arrests he Fortune's wheel,
Obtaining and retaining heaven and earth
Through Fortune, if you like, but favour — no!   45
For the great deeds flashed by me, fast and thick
As stars which storm the sky on autumn nights —
Those conquests! but peace crowned them, — so, of peace
Count up his titles only — these, in few —
Ten years Triumvir, Consul thirteen times,   50
Emperor, nay — the glory topping all —
Hailed Father of his Country, last and best
Of titles, by himself accepted so:
And why not?   See but feats achieved in Rome —
Not to say, Italy — he planted there   55
Some thirty colonies — but Rome itself
All new-built, "marble now, brick once," he boasts:
This Portico, that Circus.   Would you sail?
He has drained Tiber for you: would you walk?
He straightened out the long Flaminian Way.   60
Poor?   Profit by his score of donatives!
Rich — that is, mirthful?   Half-a-hundred games
Challenge your choice!   There's Rome — for you and me

Only?   The centre of the world besides!
For, look the wide world over, where ends Rome?   65
To sunrise?   There's Euphrates — all between!
To sunset?   Ocean and immensity:
North, stare till Danube stops you: South, see Nile,
The Desert and the earth-upholding Mount.
Well may the poet-people each with each   70
Vie in his praise, our company of swans,
Virgil and Horace, singers — in their way —
Nearly as good as Varius, though less famed:
Well may they cry, "No mortal, plainly God!"

Thus to myself myself said, while I walked: 75
Or would have said, could thought attain to speech,
Clean baffled by enormity of bliss
The while I strove to scale its heights and sound
Its depths — this masterdom o'er all the world
Of one who was but born — like you, like me,   80
Like all the world he owns — of flesh and blood.
But he — how grasp, how gauge his own conceit
Of bliss to me near inconceivable?
Or — since such flight too much makes reel the brain —
Let's sink — and so take refuge, as it were,   85
From life's excessive altitude — to life's
Breathable wayside shelter at its base!
If looms thus large this Cæsar to myself
— Of senatorial rank and somebody —
How must he strike the vulgar nameless crowd,   90
Innumerous swarm that's nobody at all?
Why — for an instance — much as yon gold shape
Crowned, sceptred, on the temple opposite —
Fulgurant Jupiter — must daze the sense
Of — say, yon outcast begging from its step!   95
"What, Anti-Cæsar, monarch in the mud,
As he is pinnacled above thy pate?
Ay, beg away! thy lot contrasts full well
With his whose bounty yields thee this support —

Our Holy and Inviolable One,   100
Cæsar, whose bounty built the fane above!
Dost read my thought?   Thy garb, alack, displays
Sore usage truly in each rent and stain —
Faugh!   Wash though in Suburra!   'Ware the dogs
Who may not so disdain a meal on thee!   105
What, stretchest forth a palm to catch my alms?
Aha, why yes: I must appear — who knows? —
I, in my toga, to thy rags and thee —
Quæstor — nay, Ædile, Censor — Pol! perhaps
The very City-Prætor's noble self!   110
As to me Cæsar, so to thee am I?
Good: nor in vain shall prove thy quest, poor rogue!
Hither — hold palm out — take this quarter-as!"

And who did take it?   As he raised his head,
(My gesture was a trifle — well, abrupt),   115
Back fell the broad flap of the peasant's-hat,
The homespun cloak that muffled half his cheek
Dropped somewhat, and I had a glimpse — just one!
One was enough.   Whose — whose might be the face?
That unkempt careless hair — brown, yellowish —   120
Those sparkling eyes beneath their eyebrows' ridge
(Each meets each, and the hawk-nose rules between)
— That was enough, no glimpse was needed more!
And terrifyingly into my mind
Came that quick-hushed report was whispered us,   125
"They do say, once a year in sordid garb
He plays the mendicant, sits all day long,
Asking and taking alms of who may pass,
And so averting, if submission help,
Fate's envy, the dread chance and change of things   130
When Fortune — for a word, a look, a naught —
Turns spiteful and — the petted lioness —
Strikes with her sudden paw, and prone falls each
Who patted late her neck superiorly,
Or trifled with those claw-tips velvet-sheathed."   135

"He's God!" shouts Lucius Varius Rufus: "Man
And worms'-meat any moment!" mutters low
Some Power, admonishing the mortal-born.

Ay, do you mind?   There's meaning in the fact
That whoso conquers, triumphs, enters Rome,   140
Climbing the Capitolian, soaring thus
To glory's summit — Publius, do you mark —
Ever the same attendant who, behind,
Above the Conqueror's head supports the crown
All-too-demonstrative for human wear,   145
— One hand's employment — all the while reserves
Its fellow, backward flung, to point how, close
Appended from the car, beneath the foot
Of the up-borne exulting Conqueror,
Frown — half-descried — the instruments of shame,   150
The malefactor's due.   Crown, now — Cross, when?

Who stands secure?   Are even Gods so safe?
Jupiter that just now is dominant —
Are not there ancient dismal tales how once
A predecessor reigned ere Saturn came,   155
And who can say if Jupiter be last?
Was it for nothing the grey Sibyl wrote
"Cæsar Augustus regnant, shall be born
In blind Judæa" — one to master him,
Him and the universe?   An old-wife's tale?   160

Bath-drudge! Here, slave! No cheating! Our turn next.
No loitering, or be sure you taste the lash!
Two strigils, two oil-drippers, each a sponge!

DEVELOPMENT

My Father was a scholar and knew Greek.
When I was five years old, I asked him once

"What do you read about?"
                                    "The siege of Troy."
"What is a siege, and what is Troy?"
                                                      Whereat
.He piled up chairs and tables for a town,   5
Set me a-top for Priam, called our cat
— Helen, enticed away from home (he said)
By wicked Paris, who couched somewhere close
Under the footstool, being cowardly,
But whom — since she was worth the pains, poor puss —   10
Towzer and Tray — our dogs, the Atreidai — sought
By taking Troy to get possession of
— Always when great Achilles ceased to sulk,
(My pony in the stable) — forth would prance
And put to flight Hector — our page-boy's self.   15
This taught me who was who and what was what:
So far I rightly understood the case
At five years old; a huge delight it proved
And still proves — thanks to that instructor sage
My Father, who knew better than turn straight   20
Learning's full flare on weak-eyed ignorance,
Or, worse yet, leave weak eyes to grow sand-blind,
Content with darkness and vacuity.

It happened, two or three years afterward,
That — I and playmates playing at Troy's Siege —   25
My Father came upon our make-believe.
"How would you like to read yourself the tale
Properly told, of which I gave you first
Merely such notion as a boy could bear?
Pope, now, would give you the precise account   30
Of what, some day, by dint of scholarship,
You'll hear — who knows? — from Homer's very mouth.
Learn Greek by all means, read the 'Blind Old Man,
Sweetest of Singers' — *tuphlos* which means 'blind,'
Hedistos which means 'sweetest.'   Time enough!   35
Try, anyhow, to master him some day;

Until when, take what serves for substitute,
Read Pope, by all means!"
                              So I ran through Pope,
Enjoyed the tale — what history so true?
Also attacked my Primer, duly drudged,   40
Grew fitter thus for what was promised next —
The very thing itself, the actual words,
When I could turn — say, Buttmann to account.

Time passed, I ripened somewhat: one fine day,
"Quite ready for the Iliad, nothing less?   45
There's Heine, where the big books block the shelf:
Don't skip a word, thumb well the Lexicon!"

I thumbed well and skipped nowise till I learned
Who was who, what was what, from Homer's tongue,
And there an end of learning. Had you asked   50
The all-accomplished scholar, twelve years old,
"Who was it wrote the Iliad?" — what a laugh!
"Why, Homer, all the world knows: of his life
Doubtless some facts exist: it's everywhere:
We have not settled, though, his place of birth: 55
He begged, for certain, and was blind beside:
Seven cities claimed him — Scio, with best right,
Thinks Byron. What he wrote? Those Hymns we have.
Then there's the 'Battle of the Frogs and Mice,'
That's all — unless they dig 'Margites' up   60
(I'd like that) nothing more remains to know."

Thus did youth spend a comfortable time;
Until — "What's this the Germans say is fact
That Wolf found out first? It's unpleasant work
Their chop and change, unsettling one's belief: 65
All the same, while we live, we learn, that's sure."
So, I bent brow o'er *Prolegomena*.
And after Wolf, a dozen of his like
Proved there was never any Troy at all.

Neither Besiegers nor Besieged, — nay, worse, —   70
No actual Homer, no authentic text,
No warrant for the fiction I, as fact,
Had treasured in my heart and soul so long —
Ay, mark you! and as fact held still, still hold,
Spite of new knowledge, in my heart of hearts   75
And soul of souls, fact's essence freed and fixed
From accidental fancy's guardian sheath.
Assuredly thenceforward — thank my stars! —
However it got there, deprive who could —
Wring from the shrine my precious tenantry,   80
Helen, Ulysses, Hector and his Spouse,
Achilles and his Friend? — though Wolf — ah, Wolf!
Why must he needs come doubting, spoil a dream?

But then "No dream's worth waking" — Browning says:
And here's the reason why I tell thus much: 85
I, now mature man, you anticipate,
May blame my Father justifiably
For letting me dream out my nonage thus,
And only by such slow and sure degrees
Permitting me to sift the grain from chaff,   90
Get truth and falsehood known and named as such.
Why did he ever let me dream at all,
Not bid me taste the story in its strength?
Suppose my childhood was scarce qualified
To rightly understand mythology,   95
Silence at least was in his power to keep:
I might have — somehow — correspondingly —
Well, who knows by what method, gained my gains,
Been taught, by forthrights not meanderings,
My aim should be to loathe, like Peleus' son,   100
A lie as Hell's Gate, love my wedded wife,
Like Hector, and so on with all the rest.
Could not I have excogitated this
Without believing such man really were?
That is — he might have put into my hand   105

The "Ethics"? In translation, if you please,
Exact, no pretty lying that improves,
To suit the modern taste: no more, no less —
The "Ethics": 'tis a treatise I find hard
To read aright now that my hair is grey,   110
And I can manage the original.
At five years old — how ill had fared its **leaves**!
Now, growing double o'er the Stagirite,
At least I soil no page with bread and milk,
Nor crumple, dogsear and deface — boys' **way**.   115

EPILOGUE TO *ASOLANDO*

A<small>T</small> the midnight in the silence of the sleep-time,
    When you set your fancies free,
Will they pass to where — by death, fools think, imprisoned —
Low he lies who once so loved you, whom you loved so,
    — Pity me?   5

Oh to love so, be so loved, yet so mistaken!
    What had I on earth to do
With the slothful, with the mawkish, the unmanly?
Like the aimless, helpless, hopeless, did I drivel
    — Being — who?   10

One who never turned his back but marched breast forward,
    Never doubted clouds would break,
Never dreamed, though right were worsted, wrong would
      triumph,
Held we fall to rise, are baffled to fight better,
    Sleep to wake.   15

No, at noonday in the bustle of man's work-time
    Greet the unseen with a cheer!
Bid him forward, breast and back as either should be.
"Strive and thrive!" cry, "Speed, — fight on, fare ever
      There as here!"   20

NOTES[1]

"EYES, CALM BESIDE THEE"

This poem and the five following represent the degree of Browning's interest and skill in the sonnet. Like Shelley, he rather faltered as a sonneteer, although for somewhat different reasons, Browning's dramatic instinct finding the form 'cribb'd, cabined and confined.' The present rhyme-scheme is *ababccabdeadea*, an extraordinarily irregular variation. This youthful sonnet (written August 17, 1834) is copied from Fox's *Monthly Repository* for the same month by Edmund Gosse in his *Personalia*. *Cf.* Byron: *Childe Harold's Pilgrimage*, II, 32.

HELEN'S TOWER

This, easily Browning's best sonnet, was written April 26, 1870, at the request of the young Earl of Dufferin and Clandeboye, as a dedication of the tower the Earl had built to the memory of his mother, Helen, Countess of Gifford, on a rock at Clandeboye, near Belfast, Ireland. It appeared in the *Pall Mall Gazette*, December 28, 1883. Italian in form. *Cf.* Tennyson's lyric under the same title in *Tiresias, and Other Poems*.

GOLDONI

The poet contributed this sonnet to the album (edited by Cavaliere Molmenti) of the Committee of the Goldoni monument, erected at Venice in 1883. Italian in form. Written November 27, 1883. Published in the *Pall Mall Gazette*, December 8, 1883. Carlo Goldoni (1707–93) was indeed a 'king' of Italian comedy, producing some hundred and twenty comedies, among the best being *Ventaglio* and *La Locandiera*. He was born in Venice in 1707 and died in 1793.

RAWDON BROWN

Rawdon Brown, an Englishman, after visiting Venice for the first time, decided to make the city his home. He lived there for forty years, dying in 1883. The story told in the sonnet may or may not be precisely true to fact, but it is true to the spirit of Brown. The sonnet was written November 28, 1883, and appeared in the *Century Magazine* for February, 1884. The Venetian saying means: 'Every one follows his own taste, and I follow mine.' The sonnet is Italian in form, with a slight variation in the second tercet. Toni was Brown's gondolier and man-servant.

[1] In the notes to each poem reference is made (usually at first) to the place and date of its original publication.
References to *The Ring and the Book* are based on the line-numbering used by Charles W. Hodell in the Everyman edition.

The Names (*To Shakespeare*)

This sonnet was contributed by Browning, at Dr. F. J. Furnivall's request, to the *Shakespearean Show-Book* of the "Shakespearean Show" held at the Albert Hall, London, in May, 1884. He wrote it on March 12 of that year. It, too, follows the Italian form, but employs the irregular scheme *cdcddc* for the sestet. Indeed, in *The Founder of the Feast*, he even adds a line to the sestet. The student should consider also Browning's sonnet-sequence of three members following *Jochanan Hakkadosh.*

5–8. *Cf. Abt Vogler*, l. 7; *The Ring and the Book*, VI, ll. 280–89.

Why I am a Liberal

Browning contributed this sonnet to a book edited by Andrew Reid (1885) in which various thinkers explained their Liberalism. Italian in form. The poet was a thorough-going Liberal (although not a partisan one), believing strongly in individual freedom and opportunity. *Cf. The Lost Leader, Colombe's Birthday*, and *Luria.*

Cavalier Tunes

Bells and Pomegranates, III (*Dramatic Lyrics*), 1842. These songs stirringly suggest the spirit of the King's men as against that of the Parliamentary party. The student should consult *Strafford* for a dramatic treatment of that historic conflict. The songs have been set to music by Sir C. Villiers Stanford. The first is a marching song, the second a drinking song, and the third a riding song.

I. *Marching Along*

2. The Puritan Parliament of 1640 is referred to. The Puritans habitually wore cropped hair.

7. John Pym (1584–1643) was a great parliamentary leader. He and John Hampden (1594–1643) and their fellows, whose names are mentioned in ll. 14 and 15, are treated dramatically in *Strafford.* 'Carles' means churls.

8. 'Parles.' Parleyings or speeches.

15. 'Young Harry' is Sir Henry Vane (1612–62), who, despite the fact that he was a son of Charles/I's Secretary of State, supported the Puritans. He was Governor of Massachusetts in 1636–37. After the Restoration he was executed for treason. See Milton's sonnet addressed to him.

16. Rupert, Prince of Bavaria (1619–82), was the King's nephew, and was a dashing leader of cavalry during the Civil War.

23. The Royalists made their first stand at Nottingham.

II. *Give a Rouse*

16. 'Noll' is a contemptuous nickname for Oliver Cromwell.

III. *Boot and Saddle.*

This fine riding song should be compared in its swinging rhythm with *How they Brought the Good News from Ghent to Aix*, with *Through the Metidja to Abd-el-Kadr*, and with *Muléykeh.*

13. 'My wife Gertrude,' after whom this song was originally

named, held Castle Brancepeth, near Durham, against the Round-heads.

THE LOST LEADER

Bells and Pomegranates, VII (*Dramatic Romances and Lyrics*), 1845. Browning once told Walter Thornbury and Jonathan Bouchier that the poem refers to Wordsworth, but that the portrait it presents is "purposely disguised a little, used in short as an artist uses a model, retailing certain characteristic traits, and discarding the others." In a letter to the Rev. A. B. Grosart, dated February 24, 1875, he reaffirms this, but emphasizes his intention to use Wordsworth as a type only, without in any sense "portraying the entire man." He insists that "handfuls of silver and bits of ribbon" could never have influenced "the change of politics in the great poet, whose defection, nevertheless, . . . was to my juvenile apprehension, and even mature consideration, an event to deplore." As Mr. Furnivall puts it, the poem represents the feelings of those Liberals who were left behind when Wordsworth and others deserted the companions of their youth. Shelley's sonnet to Wordsworth strikes much the same note. The poem is applicable, as Arthur Symons says, "to any popular apostasy. This is one of those songs that do the work of swords." Compare Browning's treatment of the politics of Strafford.

20. The "whom" refers to the people generally. Consider the poet's attitude toward popular aspirations as expressed in his sonnet, *Why I am a Liberal*.

"HOW THEY BROUGHT THE GOOD NEWS FROM GHENT TO AIX"

Bells and Pomegranates, VII (*Dramatic Romances and Lyrics*), 1845. Set to music by Miss Helen J. Ormerod. Browning himself said that there was no sort of historical foundation for this poem. "I wrote it under the bulwark of a vessel, off the African coast, after I had been at sea long enough to appreciate even the fancy of a gallop on the back of a certain good horse 'York,' then in my stable at home." Nevertheless, such a ride as is here described might have occurred at the time of the "Pacification of Ghent" in 1576, when Holland, Zealand, and the southern Netherlands united under William of Orange to resist Philip II of Spain. See Kenyon: *New Poems of Robert Browning and Elizabeth Barrett Browning*, pp. 154–55.

6. This line, wrote Miss Barrett in a letter to Browning, November 11, 1845, "drew us out into the night as witnesses."

10. Pique. The pommel of the saddle.

14. Lokeren. Twelve miles to the northeast of Ghent.

15. Boom. Sixteen miles farther east.

16. Düffeld. Twelve miles east of Boom.

17. Mecheln. Flemish for Mechlin.

19. Aershot. Fifteen miles from Düffeld.

31. Hasselt. Some eighty miles from Ghent. At this point Dirck's horse fails.

38. Looz. Eight miles south of Hasselt. Both Looz and Tongres mark an unexplained détour from the direct route.

41. The dome-spire is probably that of the Cathedral. Here, near Dalhem, the second horse is spent.

46. Aix-la-Chapelle would take heart at the news of the making of the treaty, the Pacification of Ghent. See also line 60.

56–58. Miss Barrett comments on the fineness of this touch, as it "acts back upon the energy and resolution and exalts both. . . ." (Letter of November 15, 1845.)

The galloping motion of the horses is finely suggested by the metre, and the particulars of place and time add much to the verisimilitude of the whole narrative. The total distance covered by Roland and his rider is well over ninety miles.

THROUGH THE METIDJA TO ABD-EL-KADR

Bells and Pomegranates, III (*Dramatic Lyrics*), 1842. The Abd-el-Kadr of the title (the name means "Servant of God"), was born in Algeria in 1807, and in 1831 became Emir of Mascara. He resisted several French invasions, and through his masterful qualities united the Arab tribes; but the French finally overcame and imprisoned him. They released him in 1852, but forbade his return to Algeria. He died in the Near East in 1883. The poem suggests in its rapid anapæsts the crowding thoughts and eager riding of an Arab insurg nt as he dashes through the desert to rejoin his chieftain. The Duc d'Aumale raided Abd-el-Kadr's camp in 1842, and the scattered Arabs are seeking to rejoin their leader at the moment of the poem. Browning was very fond of conquering difficulties in the use of rhyme, as the present verses illustrate, since they constitute a monorhyme, having thirty-six variations. The poem might be usefully compared in this respect with Thomas Hardy's *The Resp cta ble Burgher* and *The Mother Mourns*. The Metidja is the great plain southwest of Algiers.

38. The Prophet and the Bride. A reference to Mahomet and Ayesha, preferred among his wives.

SOLILOQUY OF THE SPANISH CLOISTER

Bells and Pomegranates, III (*Dramatic Lyrics*), 1842. It was the second of two poems (the first being *Incident of the French Camp*), printed under the same general title, *Camp and Cloister*. While the poem has no historical foundation, Browning's wide reading in the mediæval field made him see such a situation vividly as probable enough. The speaker is a jealous Spanish monk, whose idea of religion is one of form and ritual. He suspects hypocrisy to be the only rational explanation of the apparent character of a simple-minded and good-hearted brother monk, who is devoted to gardening, but who fails to conform satisfactorily to the speaker's ritualistic ideas.

10. '*Salve tibi!*' Hail to thee!

39. Arius (whose heresy is termed Arian) was a fourth-century presbyter who said that Christ, while the noblest of God's creatures, was nevertheless not equal to God in being and dignity.

49. "A great text in Galatians." Edward Berdoe thinks that this is the tenth verse of the third chapter, as pointing to Deuteronomy

xVIII : 15–68.   George W. Cooke, however, takes it to be Galatians v : 19–21, and explains the reference to the seventeen "works
of the flesh" as satisfying the idea of twenty-nine distinct damnations, by reminding the reader that the French mean by *trente-six*
any fairly large number, Browning using twenty-nine in a similar
way. *Cf. Twelfth Night*, III, ii, 37: "Hurt him in eleven places."

56. Manichee.   The Manicheans tried to synthesize Oriental
philosophy with Christianity, and were regarded as dangerous
heretics.

71–72. 'Hail, virgin, full of grace!'   A form of prayer required
at the sound of the vesper bell.

THE LABORATORY

First published in *Hood's Magazine*, June, 1844, and afterwards in
Dramatic Romances and Lyrics, in the seventh number of *Bells and
Pomegranates*.   The speaker here is a passionate woman, determined ruthlessly to slay her rival by the use of poison (arsenic, apparently, for the most part), to secure which she has gone to the
laboratory of an old alchemist.   The situation is not historical.
D. G. Rossetti's first water-colour painting is based upon this poem.
Arthur Symons calls it "one of the very finest examples of Browning's unique power of compressing and concentrating intense emotion into a few pregnant words, each of which has its own visible
gesture and audible intonation."   In her letter of July 21, 1845, to
Browning, Miss Barrett objects to the opening lines, thinking them
unduly difficult because of their "uncertainty of rhythm."   The
second stanza is especially striking in its use of antitheses.   See also,
for specific changes suggested by Miss Barrett, Kenyon: *New Poems
by Robert Browning and Elizabeth Barrett Browning*, p. 46.

CRISTINA

Bells and Pomegranates, III (*Dramatic Lyrics*), 1842.   Christina
Maria was the daughter of Francis I, King of the Two Sicilies.   She
was born in 1806, became the fourth wife of Ferdinand VII of Spain
in 1829, and was made Regent after his death, in 1833.   Her daughter became Queen Isabelle II in 1843.   Lord Malmesbury describes
her as a royal coquette, and she earned a reputation also as a political
intriguer.   The speaker in the poem is a man with whom she has
played the heartless flirt.   As stated in the Introduction, Browning
has written many short love poems from the point of view of the unsuccessful lover.   In this instance the poem seems penetrated by
Platonic influence, especially in the fifth and sixth stanzas.   *Cf.*
from *La Morte Amoureuse*, by Théophile Gautier: "This love, thus
born in an hour, had struck root too deep for me to dream of casting
it from my heart.   This woman had made me utterly her own, a
glance had been enough to change me, her will had passed upon me;
I lived not for myself, but in her and for her."   *Cf.* also from *On the
Branch*, by Pierre de Coulevaine: "I even believe that for creatures
to be attracted by each other like this, they must have been in relation with each other previously, elsewhere."

MEETING AT NIGHT
PARTING AT MORNING

This and the companion poem first appeared as *Night* and *Morning* in *Bells and Pomegranates*, VII (*Dramatic Romances and Lyrics*), 1845. In both cases the speaker is the man (although some students of Browning have strangely supposed that in the second case the woman speaks). In the first poem the man is eagerly approaching the home of his beloved to seek there the joy and rapture that love offers, but in the second poem he realizes that a merely personal and selfish love is insufficient, and that he must vindicate and exalt his love by loyalty to his task in life. Browning himself definitely settled the problem (if there be one) in his reply to a letter of the Reverend Sackville A. Berkeley. See Kenyon: *New Poems by Robert Browning and Elizabeth Barrett Browning*, p. 179.

1–6. These lines are intended to suggest by both their style and their content the movement of a small boat across a bay.

7–8. Movement across beach and farmland is suggested.

9–10. These lines provide three fine examples of onomatopœia. *Cf.* with *Parting at Morning* ll. 13–18 of *A Forgiveness:*

> . . . since beneath my roof
> Housed she who made home heaven, in heaven's behoof
> I went forth every day, and all day long
> Worked for the world. Look, how the labourer's song
> Cheers him! Thus sang my soul, at each sharp throe
> Of labouring flesh and blood — "She loves me so!"

See also the closing lines of Sidney Lanier's *Sunrise.*

A WOMAN'S LAST WORD

Men and Women, 1855. It has been set to music by Leslie Johnson. Arthur Symons calls it "an exquisite little lyric which sings itself to its own music of delicate gravity and gentle pathos."

EVELYN HOPE

Men and Women, 1855. Like *Cristina*, although in a very different way, this poem illustrates the spiritual beauty and power of a true love. In his *Philosophy of Composition*, Edgar Allan Poe expresses the opinion that "the death of a beautiful woman is unquestionably the most poetical topic in the world, and equally is it beyond doubt that the lips best suited for such topic are those of a bereaved lover." While the first superlative is unfortunate, there can be no doubt of the unusual poetic value of this theme, as suggesting the antithesis between the hope and anticipation of a beautiful young woman and the dark silence and vacancy of death. Poe himself has written several poems so inspired, and the student will find other examples in Wordsworth's *Three Years She Grew;* Matthew Arnold's *Requiescat;* Landor's *Rose Aylmer;* Walter de la Mare's *An Epitaph;* and Rossetti's *Blessed Damozel.* The character of the dead girl is finely suggested by her love of flowers (see ll. 4, 38, and 53). Compare for similar woman-flower relationships in Browning, *The Flower's Name; Women and Roses;* Pippa's heartsease and martagon lily in *Pippa Passes;* and the likening of Pompilia to a lily in *The Ring and the Book.*

27. Compare *Colombe's Birthday*, Act V, ll. 183–84.

LOVE AMONG THE RUINS

Men and Women, 1855. This is one of the loveliest of Browning's studies in romantic affection. The lovers have chosen as a trysting place a "single little turret" among ancient Roman ruins, and the importance of their experience as against the present unimportance of the ancient civilization represented by the ruins is emphasized. The man speaking "delays his rapture," says Edward Dowden, "to make its arrival more entirely rapturous; he uses his imagination to check and to enhance his passion." The "metre of this poem," as Professor Padelford remarks, "is indeed a triumph, capable one moment of giving these liquid effects and the next of depicting the abrupt and breathless staccato movements of the lovers."

84. "Love is best." Compare *The Flight of the Duchess*, l. 615; *In a Balcony*, ll. 374–76; *Colombe's Birthday*, Act V, ll. 304–08; *A Death in the Desert*, ll. 244–47; and *Epilogue to Fifine at the Fair*, l. 32.

UP AT A VILLA — DOWN IN THE CITY (AS DISTINGUISHED BY AN ITALIAN PERSON OF QUALITY).

Men and Women, 1855. "Cities give us collision," says Emerson, and so thinks this rather rueful Italian gentleman, in his dull villa, longing for the sights and sounds of city life, of which he would gladly be a permanent part could he afford it. The poet has developed with admirable skill and humour the self-portraiture of this "person of quality," with his naïve simple taste for urban pleasures — scandals, religious processions, shops, proclamations, and street-shows — and his wry contempt for rural life.

42. Strolling players would sound a trumpet to announce the advent of Pulcinello, a popular clown-character in puppet-shows.

52. The seven swords symbolize the Seven Sorrows of Our Lady. The speaker approves equally the "pink gauze gown all spangles" and the "seven swords," and recognizes no incongruity.

56–58. Italy taxes salt, and the *octroi* (town-dues) to be paid on incoming provisions are often a petty annoyance.

A TOCCATA OF GALUPPI'S

Men and Women, 1855. Baldassare Galuppi (Il Buranello) was born on the Island of Burano, near Venice, October 15, 1706. Although of humble origin, he secured a musical education and became a pupil of Lotti. In 1729 he scored a success with his comic opera *Dorinda*. In 1762 he was made organist of St. Mark's and director of the Conservatorio degl' Incurabili. He visited England, where he had a great vogue, from 1741 to 1744, and Russia from 1766 to 1768. Most of his sixty or more operas are comic, the best being *Il Mondo della Luna*. He died at Venice January 3, 1785. Ritter (*History of Music*) finds the chief features of his operas "melodic elegance and lively and spirited comic forms; but they are rather thin and weak in execution." *Toccata* means touch-piece, an overture illustrating technique. Browning himself was fond of playing Galuppi. He imagines here a thoughtful Englishman of scientific bent, never out of England, listening to a toccata which seems to him to evoke the very soul of eighteenth-century Venice, "where the

merchants were the kings," and where youth spent its life gladly and
gracefully, with yet a moment for "those suspensions, those solutions" in the music, "good alike at grave and gay," of Master
Galuppi. 'Was the careless life of the youth of Venice of so much
less worth, so much more mortal, than my careful one?' asks the
speaker. The music seems to challenge an answer. Its end is ar-
tistically melancholy, not artfully moral. This poem should be
compared with Browning's other poems on music and musicians,
such as *Abt Vogler, Master Hugues of Saxe-Gotha,* and *Flute-Music,
with an Accompaniment.*

6. Saint Mark's is the great Venetian cathedral. See Ruskin's
description of it in his *Stones of Venice.* Pope Alexander III insti-
tuted in 1177 the custom of "wedding the Adriatic." After the
victory of the Venetian galleys at Istria over Frederick Barbarossa
the Pope gave the Doge Ziani a gold ring, commanding him to wed
the Adriatic with it each Ascension Day, that the sea might thus
acknowledge Venice as her lord and master. See Shelley's *Lines
Written among the Euganean Hills,* l. 116.

8. The Rialto is, of course, "Shylock's Bridge."

18. A clavichord was a keyed and stringed instrument, preceding
the pianoforte.

19-25. Miss Helen J. Ormerod, in the *Browning Society Papers,*
where she deals with Browning's poems about music, points out that
the lesser 'plaintive' third shows the key to be minor. "Pauer
tells that 'the minor third gives the idea of tenderness, grief and
romantic feeling.' Next come the 'diminished sixths': these are
sixths possessing a semitone less than a minor sixth, for instance
from C sharp to A flat; this interval in a different key would stand
as a perfect fifth. . . . A suspension is the stoppage of one or more
parts for a moment, while the others move on; this produces a dis-
sonance, which is only resolved by the parts which produced it moving on to the position which would have been theirs had the parts
moved simultaneously. . . . Of all dissonances none is so pleasing to
the ear or so attractive to musicians as that of minor and diminished
sevenths . . . in fact, the minor seventh is so charming in its discord
as to suggest concord . . . After all this, the love-making begins
again, but kisses are interrupted by the 'dominant's persistence
[the dominant is the fifth, the most characteristic note of the scale]
till it must be answered to'; this seems to indicate the close of the
piece, the dominant being answered by an octave which suggests
the perfect authentic cadence, in which the chord of the dominant
is followed by that of the tonic." Quoted by George W. Cooke in
the *Browning Guide-Book.* See also *Poet-Lore* for October, 1890,
p. 546.

OLD PICTURES IN FLORENCE

Men and Women, 1855. Here, as in *Pictor Ignotus, Andrea del
Sarto,* and *Fra Lippo Lippi,* Browning develops his ideas about the
art of painting. In his essay on Shelley he tells us that it is possible
to fail in art, "only to succeed in highest art," meaning obviously
that artistic technique or artifice, important as it is, is far less im-

portant than the spiritual quality with which all true art must be penetrated. So, in the present poem, he defends the 'rough-hewn' art of some of the (so-called) lesser Florentine masters, as against the 'polished' perfection of the Greeks, insisting that growth is the secret of both life and art. *Cf. Andrea del Sarto*, ll. 97-98; 112-17; 194-97. See Herman Grimm: *Life of Michael Angelo*, Chapters I and II.

15. Giotto di Bondone, pupil of Cimabue and friend of Dante, was born in 1276, and died in 1337. He was the greatest of the early Florentine painters. Frescos of his are in the Church of S. Francesco d'Assisi; the Capella dell' Arena at Padua; and in Santa Croce and the Bargello at Florence. The bell-tower or campanile is that of the Duomo (Santa Maria del Fiore) in Florence. It is a structure of exquisite beauty in point of proportion and dignity, although Giotto was unable to complete it. It was to have had a spire of one hundred feet. See ll. 273-88.

44. "One" is the antecedent of "lion" and of "the wronged great soul of an ancient master."

64. Leonardo da Vinci, the famous mediæval painter, musician, and engineer, was born in 1452 and died in 1519. Dello, or Dello di Niccolo Delli, was both painter and sculptor. The thought here is that of the unity and continuity of art.

69. Stefano was a pupil of Giotto's called *"sciama della Natura"* (Nature's ape) on account of his marked realism.

72. Giorgio Vasari (1511-74) was the author of *Lives of the Most Excellent Italian Architects, Painters, and Sculptors* (1550 and 1568), much consulted by Browning.

81. This line represents the conventional critical attitude.

82. This line lacks a foot.

89-169. These eighty lines contain the core of the argument.

98. Theseus is the subject of a statue from the eastern pediment of the Parthenon, now in the British Museum.

99. The Son of Priam is Paris.

101. The reference is to the 15th book of the *Iliad*.

102-04. The Niobe group and the dying Alexander are in the Uffizi Gallery at Florence. The Racers' frieze of the Parthenon is meant.

112. *Cf. A Death in the Desert*, ll. 424-52.

133-35. Pope Boniface VIII having asked for proof of Giotto's skill, the painter drew a complete circle "done at a stroke." He was accordingly engaged to adorn the papal palace at Avignon.

136. See line 15.

145-60. The argument summarized.

179. Nicolo the Pisan was a famous sculptor and architect of the thirteenth century.

180. Giovanni Cimabue was born in 1240 and died about 1302. Although touched by the long Byzantine influence, he initiated through his beautiful Madonnas (especially that in Santa Maria Novella) the long succession of Florentine Renaissance painters. It is his spirit especially that shines through "Art's spring-birth so dim and dewy," and that evoked the genius of Giotto.

182. Lorenzo Ghiberti (1381–1455) created the beautiful bronze gates of the Baptistery of Florence.   Domenico Ghirlandajo ('garland-maker') was a notable Florentine fresco painter of the fifteenth century.

185–86. See ll. 41–48.

198. 'Dree.'   Endure, suffer.   *Cf.* Old English *dreogan.*

201. Bigordi was the family name of Ghirlandajo.   Note the exceptionally grotesque rhymes in this stanza.

202. Sandro Botticelli (1457–1515) was among the most famous of the Florentine painters.

203. Lippino or Filippino Lippi (1460–1505), like his father Fra Lippo Lippi, was a Florentine painter.

204. Fra Angelico (1387–1455) was a holy-hearted Dominican friar and a great painter.   See *Fra Lippo Lippi*, ll. 233–35.

205. Taddeo Gaddi (1300–66) was the godson and assistant of Giotto, and worked on the campanile after his master's death.

206. *Intonaco* refers to the plaster-ground for frescos.

207. Saint Jerome became secretary to Pope Damasus in 382. He translated the Scriptures into the Latin Vulgate.   See *Fra Lippo Lippi*, ll. 73–74.

208. Lorenzo Monaco was a monkish painter belonging to the Angeli.   See *Fra Lippo Lippi*, l. 236.

210. Antonio Pollajolo (1430–98) was a Florentine goldsmith, painter, and sculptor.

214. *Tempera*, or Distemper, uses solid pigments mixed with a solution of water and gum to prevent scaling.

215. Alesso Baldovinetti (1422–99) was a Florentine painter and worker in mosaic.

217. Margheritone Arezzo (1236–1313) was a painter, sculptor and architect.   Browning owned several paintings by these 'lesser' masters.

218. 'Barret.'   A head-covering.

230. Zeno.   Founder of the Stoics.

232. Carlino.   Carlo Dolci (1616–86).

233–40. This stanza explains the humorous reproof in ll. 17–24. The "little tablet" is a beautiful *Last Supper*, lost from the church of San Spirito.

237. Buonarroti.   Michael Angelo (1457–1564).

241–42. San Spirito is a church in Florence, as is also the Ognissanti.   The words mean "Holy Spirit" and "All Saints."

244. *Detur amanti.*   'Bestow it on its lover.'

245. The Koh-i-noor ('Mountain of Light') is a famous Indian diamond belonging since 1850 to the Crown jewels of England.

246. The Jewel of Giamschid.   Perhaps the fabled ruby of Sultan Giamschid.   The Sofi refers to a Persian dynasty.

255. Joseph Wenzel Radetzky (the 'certain dotard') was an Austrian count and field-marshal (1766–1858) in charge of Austrian lands in Italy.

256. Morello.   An Apennine peak near Florence.   See *Andrea del Sarto*, ll. 93–96; 209.

258. *Cf. Casa Guidi Windows*, Book I: sections 14–15.

259. The Witanagemot was the great Anglo-Saxon national assembly, the forerunner of Parliament.

260. Casa Guidi refers to Mrs. Browning's poem, *Casa Guidi Windows.* The Latin phrase means 'which you may have seen before.'

263. The Lorraines were the sixteenth-century Guises.

264. Orgagna (1315–76): Andrea di Cione, a Florentine painter.

265. 'Prologuize.' To begin with a formal preface.

271. The Chimæra was a fabulous animal.

273. Tuscan is the literary language of Italy.

274. '*Issimo*' is the superlative termination.

275. See Chaucer's unfinished *Squire's Tale.*

276. '*Alt* to *altissimo*' means 'high to highest.'

277. 'Beccaccia.' Woodcock.

279. 'Braccia.' Cubits.

"DE GUSTIBUS ––"

Men and Women, 1855. The poet speaks here, first, of the love of English landscapes which characterizes the friend he addresses; and second, of his own delight in Italian home-settings: an Alpine castle, or a sea-side house. The title forms part of the Latin saying "De gustibus non disputandum," — matters of taste are not arguable. This little poem expresses the deep and constant affection which Browning felt for Italy. Italian colour and suggestion saturate a large part of his works.

36–37. Liver-wing means right wing, and in this case, therefore, right arm. Ferdinand II, King of the Two Sicilies, was a Bourbon.

40. Calais was taken by the French in 1588, the last year of Queen Mary's reign. She could not be reconciled to its loss, and declared that the word Calais would be found written on her heart.

HOME THOUGHTS, FROM ABROAD
HOME THOUGHTS, FROM THE SEA

Bells and Pomegranates, VII (*Dramatic Romances and Lyrics*), 1845. *Home Thoughts, from the Sea,* appeared at the same time as *Home Thoughts, from Abroad,* as the third member of a series having the inclusive title afterward restricted to the first. These popular lyrics testify to Browning's deep personal love of England. *Cf.* the following from *Pauline:*

> ...I cherish most
> My love of England — how her name, a word
> Of hers in a strange tongue makes my heart beat.
>
> Then what need of longer exile? Seek
> My England ...

Miss Barrett, in her letter to Browning of October 6, 1845, wrote: "Your spring-song is full of beauty as you know very well — and 'that's the wise thrush,' so characteristic of you (and of the thrush too) that I was sorely tempted to ask you to write 'twice over,' ... and not send the first copy to Mary Hunter, notwithstanding my promise to her." In a letter of October 22, referring to the companion poem, she speaks of "those grand sea sights in the long lines." *Home Thoughts, from the Sea* reflects the poet's sunset view of Cape St. Vincent (off which, on February 14, 1797, a small English fleet defeated the Spanish), from the *Norham Castle*, April 27, 1838, during Browning's first voyage to Italy. Leigh Hunt describes it as "a beautiful lone promontory . . . like something between stone and spirit."

2, 3. In 1596 an English fleet sailed into Cadiz harbour and destroyed the second Spanish Armada. In 1805 (October 21) off Cape Trafalgar, Nelson triumphed over the French and Spanish fleets. See also *Nationality in Drinks*, ll. 29–43.

SAUL

The first nine sections appeared in *Bells and Pomegranates*, VII *(Dramatic Romances and Lyrics)*, 1845. The remainder was written at Rome in 1853–54, and the whole was first published in the second volume of *Men and Women*, 1855. The Biblical background is in I Samuel XVI:14–23. Browning knew and liked Christopher Smart's *Song to David*. Edward Berdoe, in *The Browning Cyclopædia* (pp. 464 ff.), discusses at some length the influence of music in the cure of disease and depression. *Saul* is perhaps the noblest of Browning's religious poems, as it is the most cherished. For Miss Barrett's comments on the first part of *Saul*, see *Letters of Robert Browning and Elizabeth Barrett*, Vol. I, pp. 179, 261, 325, 523, 553, 556. David, alone with his sheep, is reviewing in the poem the "marvels" of the previous day. See ll. 200–06.

1. Abner was Saul's cousin and commander of his army. See I Samuel XIV:50; XXVI:5.

11–19. The "ardours of summer" are skilfully suggested by cumulative touches in ll. 13–14, 16–19. The contrast between the cooling lilies and the stifled day hints at a corresponding spiritual contrast between clear-souled young David and burdened Saul. Browning was thinking of the Palestine "water lily, lotos, which . . . is *blue* altogether."

28–33. Saul's attitude anticipatively symbolizes the Crucifixion. Browning, like Shelley, uses the serpent metaphor with variety and sympathy. See l. 332 and *Paracelsus*, V, ll. 449–50.

34 *sq.* Berdoe suggests that the poet may have known of the series of tunes in Longus's *Daphnis and Chloe* (Smith's translation in the Bohn edition, pp. 303–04, 332–34). David plays first a series of tunes grateful to animals (sheep, quails, crickets, the jerboa or jumping hare); second, a series of "help-tunes" for reapers, mourners, marriages, warriors, priests; and last, a group of songs of high human hope: "the wild joys of living," the joy of contemporary fame, the praise of posterity, God's rewarding future, and the immortal and infinite love of God discernible in the Christ-to-be. In ll. 37–42, says Professor Padelford, "the very movement of a flock of sheep has been caught, and the pervasive twilight tenderness of pastoralism."

65. Male-sapphires are sometimes called star-stones on account of their bright stellar rays.

108. A fine example of onomatopœia.

135–47. The little silk-spinner Pippa has similar fancies.

191–205. These lines are emotionally parenthetical. Hebron: a neighbouring city of refuge set on a hill; Kidron: a stream near Jerusalem.

213–16. See I Samuel, XV.

233–37. Here David, by a great intuition, divines the redemptive purposes of God. The truth of the Incarnation comes upon him prophetically. *Cf.* ll. 257–62 and 287–312.

279–86. *Cf. Rabbi Ben Ezra*, ll. 25–49.

282 sq. *Cf. The Ring and the Book*, X, ll. 1307 *sq.*

295. *Cf.* from *The Ring and the Book*, X, ll. 271–74:

> For I am 'ware it is the seed of act
> God holds appraising in his hollow palm,
> Not act grown great thence on the world below,
> Leafage and branchage, vulgar eyes admire.

300 sq. *Cf. The Ring and the Book*, X, ll. 1434–38.

313 *sq.* Arthur Symons calls these magnificent lines a "choral symphony of earth and all her voices." *Cf.* the Fourth Act of Shelley's *Prometheus Unbound*, and the "spiritual witness new and new" of Caponsacchi in *The Ring and the Book*.

MY STAR

Men and Women, 1855. Set to music by Helen A. Clarke. Browning wrote several beautiful tributes to his wife, including *My Star; One Word More* (the eighteenth section of which expands the present *motif*); *By the Fireside;* the proem to *The Two Poets of Croisic* (which also strikes the note of *My Star*); *Prospice;* and the dedicatory passage in the Prologue to *The Ring and the Book*, beginning "O Lyric Love, half angel and half bird." He was especially fond of applying the 'star' figure to some of his heroines, as to Lady Carlisle in *Strafford*.

4. The Iceland spar prism has the property of polarizing light, and thus of 'darting' many rays of different colours.

10. The bird figure and the flower figure are also favourites with Browning in describing women.

BY THE FIRESIDE

Men and Women, 1855. Although not professedly referring to the poet's wife, this poem does so everywhere by implication, as in ll. 111–20 and 251–59. The poet sits quietly by the fireside with his loved comrade and reviews the story of their comradeship.

28–30. *Cf.* the last lines of "*De Gustibus —*"

92. A pent-house is a sloping roof projecting from a wall.

111. Up to this point the man has thought in silence.

114–15. *Cf.* Mrs. Browning's lyric, *Inclusions*.

151. The reference is to l. 96.

185. Chrysolite. A yellow or green transparent stone of magnesium and iron.

ANY WIFE TO ANY HUSBAND

Men and Women, 1855. A dying wife addresses her much-loved mate, expressing regret and wonder that she is not all in all to him, as he is to her.   When she is gone, he will, she knows, seek others; and although he will come back to her at last in spirit, it will be with something of stain, with need of pardon.   This poem expresses some essential differences between men's and women's ways of loving. *Cf.* Shakespeare's *Twelfth Night*, Act II, 4, ll. 30–33.   *Cf.* also from Arnold Bennett's *Book of Carlotta*, the remark of one woman to another concerning men: "But there, what would you?   We hate them, but we love them."   Observe the Platonic influence in ll. 49–54 and 92–96.

55–60. Contrast the use made of the same figure in *The Ring and the Book*, VII, ll. 1519–27.

67–72. *Cf. James Lee's Wife*, Part IV, ll. 36–40.

73–75. Contrast with ll. 103–08.

85–96. *Cf. James Lee's Wife*, Part IV, ll. 36–40.

103–04. *Cf. James Lee's Wife*, Part IX, ll. 16–20.

126. The thought 'comes full circle.'   *Cf.* the opening note: her fear of his passionate nature's future as against her hope that he may at last understand the spiritual truth of love.

Two in the Campagna

Men and Women, 1855.   As *Love Among the Ruins* has for its background ancient urban Rome, so this poem takes for its setting the ghostly "silence and passion" of the Roman Campagna.   A man speaks here to his beloved, wondering at his inability to see precisely as she sees and to will as she wills.   He is sure of his love for her, and yet he cannot wholly identify himself with that love.   *Cf.* from *Hamlet*, IV, 7, 113–14:

> There lives within the very flame of love
> A kind of wick or snuff that will abate it.

Cf. also from Alice Meynell's *Rhythm of Life*: "Love itself has tidal moments, lapses and flows due to the metrical rule of the interior heart."

These unusually beautiful verses, in which, as Arthur Symons says, "the vague sense of the Roman Campagna is distilled into exquisite words," thus express a somewhat melancholy sense of the inadequacy and incompleteness of love, of the inalienably tragic element in it, which many poets have recognized and lamented.

15. Weft. The threads spanning the web from side to side.

Misconceptions

Men and Women, 1855.   This little love lyric represents something of the spirit of the speaker in *Cristina*, but it is uttered with more humility.   It is the subject of a painting by Byam Shaw, and has been set to music by E. C. Gregory, and also by Georgiana Schuyler. It may be compared with the page's song in *Pippa Passes*.

A Serenade at the Villa

Men and Women, 1855.   A man speaks here of the forbidding unresponsiveness shown in the changeless dark form of the villa where he had serenaded his loved one the night before.   He wonders what spiritual response she may really make: whether she is proud to rely upon his patient loyalty, or whether his song had annoyed her. He poses the problem and leaves it.

ONE WAY OF LOVE
ANOTHER WAY OF LOVE

Men and Women, 1855. In the first poem (set to music by E. C. Gregory), a rejected lover speaks. Although he has not gained 'heaven,' he feels himself to be the better both for his past hope and for the persistent reality of his love.

In the companion poem, a woman speaks in casual yet ironic fashion of the apparent indifference with which her lover now seems to be regarding her, offering him his freedom, and hinting that a future lover may prove more appreciative. Perhaps she may respond to love again, or perhaps her present experience may lead her to scorn would-be lovers. 'June' is a symbol of the speaker herself.

19. '*Eadem semper.*' Always the same.
32. 'June-lightning.' Scorn.

A PRETTY WOMAN

Men and Women, 1855. The portrait of a woman possessing formal or decorative beauty, but without the spiritual quality that makes for pure beauty. She has, therefore, no capacity for love, no understanding of it, and is not to be blamed for failure to respond to it. Let her be what she is, according to the terms of her own nature, an unimprovable pleaser of the eye, merely. Why try to "grace a rose" either by imitating it in precious metals and jewels or by plucking it?

RESPECTABILITY

Men and Women, 1855. An ironic little poem on the world's toleration of love, provided it be a recognized and registered love. Love is free to be love only when stamped with the seal of Society's approval. Professor Hiram Corson thought that the two unconventional lovers of the poem are George Sand and Jules Sandeau, but it is unlikely that the poet wished thus to particularize his thought. *Cf. Youth and Art.*

21. The French Institute.
22. François Guizot the Constitutional Royalist (1787–1874) disliked Charles Montalembert the Ultramontanist (1810–70), yet formally welcomed him on his induction into the Institute.

IN THREE DAYS

Men and Women, 1855. A lover is reminding himself that in three days he is to see his loved one. He muses on the changes that three days, or long years, may bring. At last he resolves to dismiss both 'great fear' and 'small fear' and to count the hours until he shall see her.

IN A YEAR

Men and Women, 1855. A woman speaks here, comparing the

fashion of woman's love with the less constant way of men. The lyric may be usefully compared with *Any Wife to Any Husband*, and with *A Woman's Last Word*.

29–32. *Cf.* the closing lines of *James Lee's Wife*.

WOMEN AND ROSES

Men and Women, 1855. The poet imagines here a faded rose, a full-blown one, and a thornless bud, associating these figuratively with the women of the past, the present and the future. Each group circles its particular rose on his rose tree, unheeding his passion of admiration; and he wonders, as he thinks of the beauty, charm, and high function of women in life, which of these three roses is dearest to his thoughts.

BEFORE
AFTER

Men and Women, 1855. In the former poem a second speaking to his colleague (see the two last lines) discusses the quarrel of two men, in which wronger and wronged are so involved that frankness and forgiveness seem unlikely without a duel. If the wronger will not confess, let him fight as one wrong the more, for his sin, "constant at his side," will sooner or later find him out, whatever his apparent complacence. As for the wronged, let him, as God's champion, trust God. The assonance in ll. 22 and 35 seems technically rather questionable. In the latter poem the winner of the duel speaks. He feels that the death of his old friend and late enemy has settled nothing, save to prove the wickedness of hate and the goodness of forgiveness. *Cf.* with the last intense line Webster's *Duchess of Malfi*, Act IV, 2:

> Cover her face; mine eyes dazzle; she died young;

Shakespeare's *King Lear*, Act V, 3, 243:

> Even so. — Cover their faces.

and Thomas Hardy's *Dynasts*, Part One, Act V, 2:

> Cover my face. There will no good be done
> By drawing their attention off to me.

THE GUARDIAN ANGEL: A PICTURE AT FANO

Men and Women, 1855. This poem, written in modified Rime Royal (*ababcca*), was composed at Ancona in 1848. The picture it describes, called *L'Angelo Custode*, is in the Church of San Agostino at Fano, a town thirty miles to the north of Ancona on the Italian shore of the Adriatic. Its painter, commonly known as Guercino, was Giovanni Francesco Barbieri. He was born at Cento in 1590, and died at Bologna in 1666. His works show his fine sense of light and shade. The picture referred to has an immediate and popular appeal, although it is not among his best works. Browning went to see the picture at Fano, accompanied by his wife, on three occasions. The poem is addressed to Alfred Domett (see Introduction).

who was then in New Zealand, and who is described in *Waring.*

17–18. Compare the dedication of *The Ring and the Book* to Mrs. Browning:

O Lyric Love, half angel and half bird!

Dante uses the phrase "Bird of God" in the fourth canto of the *Purgatorio.*

22–28. At this time Browning suffered a good deal from headaches.

33–35. A poet's declaration of faith.

37. 'Alfred' refers to Domett.

46. A beautifully turned tribute to Mrs. Browning.

54–56. Another direct reference to Alfred Domett. The Wairoa is a river in New Zealand. The suggestion in the last line, as the poet looks beyond Ancona to the sea, seems to be that while the waves separate the two friends, yet in another sense they mysteriously unite them.

MEMORABILIA

Men and Women, 1855. See the Introduction for a discussion of Shelley's influence on Browning. Browning's first contact with Shelley's poetry provoked an immediate enthusiasm which lasted for many years. In this little poem Browning represents himself as meeting with a man who had once known Shelley in the flesh. What would have been Browning's emotion had it been possible for him thus to have seen his first great inspirer! But, to the poet's surprise and disappointment, the individual with whom he is speaking takes a purely casual attitude toward the incident, and appears, on the whole, rather bored by the enthusiastic response to its mention. Accordingly, in order to explain and justify himself a little, the poet speaks in parable of his discovery on a wide moor of a moulted eagle-feather — perhaps Shelley's *Dæmon of the World.* Seeing, however, that his acquaintance still fails to understand the feeling that this chance conversation has induced, the poet foregoes further discussion as unprofitable.

POPULARITY

Men and Women, 1855. As *Memorabilia* pays tribute to Shelley, so does this poem to Keats.

26–30. The blue dye referred to is a colourless glandular secretion in the shell which turns purple when exposed to the air. The Phœnicians discovered it, and it was known also to the Greeks. Ancient Tyre was a principal city of Phœnicia. See Keats's sonnet beginning "Blue! 'Tis the life of heaven." — Astarte of Syria was the Venus of the Greeks and Romans.

42–43. See I Kings VII.

58. These commonplace names are intended to suggest the inferior imitators of the discoverer of "the blue," the mere profiteers that prosper because of his original insight and power.

64. Murex is the genus of molluscs referred to in ll. 26–30.

65. Keats died at Rome, February 23, 1821, young, poor, ill, unhappy, and largely neglected.

Incident of the French Camp

Bells and Pomegranates, III (*Dramatic Lyrics*), 1842, where it appeared as the first poem of two under the title *Camp and Cloister*. The French under Napoleon stormed and took Ratisbon (Regensburg), a Bavarian city on the Danube, April 22, 1809. The incident recorded here, says Mrs. Orr, is true, save that the boy soldier was a man.

11. Jean Lannes, Duc de Montebello (1769–1809) was a distinguished marshal of Napoleon. He received his death-wound at Aspern, soon after taking Ratisbon, and died nine days later.

The Patriot

Men and Women, 1845. The poet intended no reference here to Arnold of Brescia, as some had thought because Brescia was mentioned as the background in the first edition. The imaginary speaker is a sincere patriot who, although only a year ago in high popular favour, has incurred the hatred of the multitude and is now on his way to execution. He recognizes the vanity of popular judgments and commends himself to the sole true judge, God. *Cf. One Word More*, section IX. *Cf.* also Shelley: *Prometheus Unbound*, Act I, ll. 770–71.

30. *Cf. The Ring and the Book*, I, ll. 580–82.

My Last Duchess

Bells and Pomegranates, III (*Dramatic Lyrics*), 1842. The original title was *Italy*. The speaker is a Duke of Ferrara. The monologue illustrates a rather sinister quality that developed concurrently with the culture of the Italian Renaissance, and of which a more exhaustive treatment appears in such works as *The Plough of Shame*, by Mary Bradford Whiting. The Duke, although a fair connoisseur in the technique of painting, etc., can appreciate only the body of art. Of the soul of art — its spiritual and eternal significance — he has no conception. He has married an innocent, lovely young girl for her conspicuous beauty, whom for that very reason it seems fit that he should possess along with his beautiful palace, statuary, and paintings. She is spiritually akin to the heroine of *The Flight of the Duchess*, to Pippa, to Colombe, and to Pompilia. The student will notice how skilfully Browning causes the Duke to reveal not only his own proud, cold, calculating nature, but also, by implications of which he is wholly unaware, the happy, gracious, childlike soul of his young wife.

1. Observe the persistent egotism of the Duke from the first to the last lines of the poem: "*My* last Duchess" and "Cast in bronze for *me*."

3. Fra Pandolf is an imaginary painter.

5, 6. The Duke's question is really a veiled command, as in line 47. "By design." "To have some occasion for telling the story and illustrating part of it." — Kenyon's citation of Browning's letter to the Reverend Sackville A. Berkeley, February 22, 1889.

22. The phrase "too soon made glad" seems to strike the Duke as

too **simply** expressed. He gives it a more elegant turn in the next line.

25. Notice the egotism here also: "My favour at her breast" as against the glory of a sunset.

31–34. Cf. *The Ring and the Book,* V, ll. 140–42.

36. "Which I have not." This is, of course, politely concessive.

46. "Then all smiles stopped together." Many Browning students have been unduly exercised about the meaning of this statement. The late Professor Hiram Corson, of Cornell University, could not induce Browning to indicate whether the Duke had his bride directly assassinated, or whether he gave orders to immure her until she died. Neither of these explanations is really necessary. All that the poet wishes the reader to understand is that the Duke treated his wife with such contempt and cruelty as to cause her death. It is not the business of a poem to convey exact information, but rather to interpret and to inspire.

48. The passage beginning "I repeat" and ending at "object" provides the reason for the Duke's desire to show the envoy of the neighbouring count his picture gallery. The Duke is in treaty for the hand of the count's daughter. He wishes to make no mistake this time, but to marry a woman of wealth and rank, whose dignity will be capable of appreciating his own. These casually uttered lines constitute the message which the Duke would convey to the count. He has detached the envoy from "the company below," chiefly in order to make the opportunity for this private word and partly also to enjoy the grim pleasure of setting forth the causes of his previous wife's failure to be the sort of Duchess he requires. The painting he exhibits gives him more pleasure than the original could have done.

54–56. Neptune taming a sea-horse provides a congenial subject for a man of the Duke's character. Claus of Innsbruck is an imaginary sculptor.

THE BOY AND THE ANGEL

First published in *Hood's Magazine,* August, 1844; afterwards, in expanded form, in *Bells and Pomegranates,* VII (*Dramatic Romances and Lyrics*), 1845. See Miss Barrett's letters to Browning written July 21 and October 27, 1845. *Cf.* for variations on the central theme *Pippa Passes* and *"Imperante Augusto Natus Est—";* Ben Jonson's lyric, *"It is not Growing Like a Tree";* Longfellow's *King Robert of Sicily;* Maeterlinck's drama, *Sister Beatrice.* Notice that in the thirty-nine couplets (one was added in 1868) only twenty rhymes are employed. Miss Barrett suggested several textual revisions of the first edition, virtually all of which were adopted. See Kenyon: *New Poems by Robert Browning and Elizabeth Barrett Browning,* pp. 143–45.

17–18. Contrast ll. 37, 38, which contain the core of the parable.

21-22. Cf. *The Ring and the Book,* VII, l. 1841:

So, let him wait God's instant men call years.

39–40. *Cf. The Ring and the Book,* X, l. 1854:

> Re-introduce the doubt discarded.

51. 'Dight.' Decked or adorned.

INSTANS TYRANNUS

Men and Women, 1855. The poem is based on Horace's *Odes,* III, 3. 'Instans Tyrannus' means 'Menacing Tyrant.' *Cf. The Patriot* and *The Ring and the Book,* I, ll. 577–82, 1072–74.

18. 'Perdue,' lost.

21. 'Cates,' luxurious foods; 'spilth,' overflow. *(Cf. The Ring and the Book,* V, l. 1514.)

66–67. Contrast *Pippa Passes,* I, ll. 190–97.

THE GLOVE

Bells and Pomegranates, VII *(Dramatic Romances and Lyrics),* 1845. The story here contained has frequently been told since its first rendering by St. Croix in *Essais Historiques sur Paris.* Leigh Hunt's *The Glove and the Lions* (1836) after Schiller, is well known. Browning determined to give the tale an entirely different turn, in the interest of soul-discovery. Peter Ronsard (1524–85) was called 'prince of poets' in his day. Miss Barrett wrote Browning (October 27, 1845) that "for your 'Glove' all women should be grateful — and Ronsard, honoured, in this fresh shower of music on his old grave . . . And then, with what a 'curious felicity' you turn the subject 'glove' to another use and strike De Lorge's blow back on him with it . . . And the lady's speech . . . so calm, and proud, yet a little bitter."

1. Francis I (1494–1547) was King of France.

12. By 'Naso' is meant Ovid, or Publius Ovidius Naso.

45. Clement Marot (1496–1544) was a famous French court poet who paraphrased forty-nine of the Psalms.

50. 'That Lion of the Tribe of Judah.'

122. So always Browning himself.

123–56. Single rhymes replace the double ones here, to emphasize the change in tone. *Cf.* the use of the same device in *The Flight of the Duchess.*

189. The Latin 'moral' means 'Encounter the approaching disease,' that is, make sure of the reality of what seeming evil threatens you, and then act accordingly.

190. The theorbo was a light stringed instrument.

THE ITALIAN IN ENGLAND

Bells and Pomegranates, VII *(Dramatic Romances and Lyrics),* 1845. The original title was *Italy in England.* While the poem has no direct historical reference, it finely reflects Browning's ardent desire for Italian liberty. Mrs. Orr notes that "Mr. Browning is proud to remember that Mazzini informed him he had read this poem to certain of his fellow-exiles in England to show how an Englishman could sympathize with them." The speaker is a leading Italian patriot in the rising of 1823, now a refugee in England, who recounts a singular adventure he had had while a fugitive from Austrian pursuers. Elizabeth Barrett thought the poem "noble, serene." See Kenyon: *New Poems of Robert Browning and Elizabeth Barrett Browning*, pp. 150–51.

8. The 'Charles' so often named is Carlo Alberto (1798–1849), the son of Carlo Emmanuel of Savoy Carignano. As a youth he cherished liberal aspirations, even joining the Carbonari. In 1821, as Regent of Turin, he confirmed the new constitution, but the policy of the new King and fear of the Austrians quickly caused him to flee from Turin and abandon the friends of freedom. In 1823 he was a volunteer in the French reactionary offensive against Spain, thus again betraying his earlier principles. When he became King of Sardinia in 1831 he dealt sternly with Mazzini's "Young Italy" and other secret societies. In 1848 he took the leadership of the Italian insurrection against Austrian rule, was defeated at Custozza by Marshal Radetzky, and abdicated after a further crushing defeat by Radetzky at Novara. He died in Portugal four months later.

19. Prince Clemens Wenzel Nepomuk Lothar von Metternich-Winneburg (1773–1859) was a noted Austrian statesman who headed the reactionary element in Europe between 1815 and 1848, when the European uprisings undid him politically. *Cf.* the second Interlude in *Pippa Passes*.

76. '*Tenebrœ*': Darkness. On three days of Holy Week the matins and lauds for the following day are sung, in the Roman service. Fifteen lighted candles are used, one being extinguished after the conclusion of each psalm until but one is left. This one represents Christ as the Light of the world, or as the Light of the Resurrection contrasted with the darkness of the Crucifixion.

THE ENGLISHMAN IN ITALY

Bells and Pomegranates, VII (*Dramatic Romances and Lyrics*), 1845. The original title was *England in Italy*. The scene is, as the sub-title indicates, the beautiful plain of Sorrento, one of the loveliest parts of Italy. The speaker is a friendly English sojourner whom the thousand and one sights and sounds (striking or slight) of this paradise delight with their novel beauty. To cheer and divert Fortù, the trustful little sleepy peasant girl who nestles beside him, he tells, as she tells her beads, the pleasures of his memory, while black Scirocco and the succeeding storm come and pass. "It is," says Symons, "delightfully gay and charming and picturesque, and is the most entirely descriptive poem ever written by Browning." For revisions suggested by Miss Barrett, see Kenyon: *New Poems of Robert Browning and Elizabeth Barrett Browning*, pp. 146–50.

1. Fortù is evidently one of the family with whom the speaker is staying.

3. 'Scirocco' is an intensely hot wind sweeping across from Africa.

24. 'Frails': baskets.

27. Amalfi is a small town beautifully situated on the gulf of Salerno, twenty-two miles southeast of Naples.

30. *sq.* "I do like all this living description," comments Miss Barrett, ". . . which never lived before in poetry, and now will live always."

49. 'Lasagne': A kind of macaroni.

69. 'Sorbs': fruit of the service-tree.

77. *Cf. An Epistle Containing the Strange Medical Experience of Karshish, the Arab Physician,* ll. 291–92.

81. 'Lentisks': mastic-trees.

91–94. *Cf. Childe Roland to the Dark Tower Came,* ll. 163–68; 190–92.

100–01. These three isles of the sirens who tempted Ulysses correspond to those described in the *Odyssey* (XII and XXIII).

110–11. *Cf. Childe Roland to the Dark Tower Came,* ll. 181–84.

123–26. The feast celebrates the naval victory of Lepanto.

133. Vincenzo Bellini (1802–35) was a famous Italian operatic composer; Daniel François Esprit Auber (1782–1871) was a distinguished French composer.

143–46. The Corn Laws were repealed, after long debate, in June, 1846. They placed duties on breadstuffs. Browning greatly disliked them.

IN A GONDOLA

Bells and Pomegranates, III (*Dramatic Lyrics*), 1842. The first stanza was written "on the instant" as a catalogue accompaniment, when Browning heard his friend John Forster describe the "divine Venetian work" called *The Serenade,* painted by Daniel Maclise, and publicly exhibited. After he himself saw the picture he completed the poem, which has no fact-background. "Its method and its magic," says Symons, "are alike its own. We might hear it or fancy it perhaps in one of the Ballades of Chopin, with its entrancing harmonies, its varied and delicate ornamentation, its undertone of passion and sadness, its storms and gusts of wind like lashing notes, and the piercing shiver that thrills through its suave sunshine."

22. *Cf.* ll. 104–09, 229. "The Three" are probably the husband and two of his friends or relatives.

113. The ancient graves of Jews at Lido, near Venice.

127. Giudecca. A wide canal, dividing the island of the same name from the rest of Venice.

186–93. Bartolommeo Schidone (1560–1616) was a painter after Correggio's manner. "Haste-thee-Luke" (Luca-fà-presto) was Luca Giordano of Naples, painter (1632–1705). Castelfranco refers to Giorgio Barbarelli (1478–1511), or Giorgione. He was born at Castelfranco in the Trevisan. Tizian, or Tiziano Vecellio (1477–1576) was a famous Venetian painter surnamed "Il Divino."

225–31. *Cf.* the last line of the Epilogue to *Fifine at the Fair;* and Sonnet LXXI in Dante Gabriel Rossetti's *House of Life.*

WARING

Bells and Pomegranates, III (*Dramatic Lyrics*), 1842. 'Waring' (the original was a King's messenger Browning met in Russia) is

Alfred Domett (1811–87), Browning's close friend, to whom the letter-poem, *The Guardian Angel*, was written. See Kenyon's *Robert Browning and Alfred Domett*. He was a barrister; a traveller in the United States, Canada, Italy, and Switzerland; and himself no mean poet. (See Introduction.) He went out to New Zealand in May, 1842, where he had a successful career, becoming Prime Minister in 1862. In 1871 he returned to England, and took a leading part in the work of the Browning Society. Browning wrote *Waring* upon his friend's departure for New Zealand. It is a glowing appreciation of Domett's appearance, manner, temperament, and attitude toward life, but is not to be literally interpreted in all of its details.

54. *Cf.* the picture of Polyphemus in Vergil's *Æneid*, III, 657:

> Monstrum horrendum, informe, ingens,
> Cui lumen ademtum. . . .

'A horrid monster, deformed and huge, who had been deprived of vision.'

99. See I Samuel IV : 21.

108. 'Vishnu-land' is India, Vishnu being the second person of the Hindu Trinity. 'Avatar' means the incarnation of a god.

111. The Kremlin is the old citadel of Moscow.

112. 'Serpentine' is a mottled greenish rock; 'syenite' is a stone so-called after Syene, Egypt.

122–26. 'The lambwhite maiden' is Iphigenia, whom Diana translated to Taurica when Agamemnon, her father, sought to sacrifice her.

152. Caldara Polidore da Caravaggio (1495–1548) was a notable Italian painter employed by Raphael to paint friezes in the Vatican Browning much admired his *Andromeda*.

155. Henry Purcell (1658–95) was an able English musical composer, *Rosy Bowers* being one of his most popular songs.

168–69. *Cf. The Flight of the Duchess*, l. 512.

190. David Garrick (1717–79) was a famous English actor who played Hamlet, Richard III, and some comedy parts.

193. 'Junius' was the *nom de plume* of the unknown author of the *Letters of Junius*, directed against members of the British Government between 1768 and 1772.

195–96. Thomas Chatterton (1752–70) was a young English poet who invented 'Thomas Rowley' as the mythical priestly author of some fifteenth-century poems presumably discovered but actually written by Chatterton himself.

221. The 'lateen sail' is the triangular sail common to Mediterranean vessels.

The Twins

First published in a sixteen-page volume, *Two Poems by E. B. B. and R. B.*, 1854, to help a charitable enterprise. Included in *Men and Women*, 1855. The source is a little parable in Martin Luther's *Table Talk*. *Cf.* "*Imperante Augusto Natus Est —*"

The Last Ride Together

Men and Women, 1855.   An exalted yet very human love **lyric,** in which the speaker is an unsuccessful lover.   *Cf. Humility* and *One Way of Love.*   As Arthur Symons says, "It has the lyrical 'cry,' and the objectiveness of the drama."   Then, too, it finely develops one of Browning's favourite themes, the paradox of success through failure.

A Grammarian's Funeral: Shortly after the Revival of Learning in Europe

Men and Women, 1855. The speaker is a disciple of a dead scholar of the early Renaissance, addressing his fellow-pupils who share his solemn task in bearing the body at daybreak to symbolic sepulture "on a tall mountain."   The varying, curving measure suggests the movement of the young men as they slowly climb the winding path upward, "singing together."   Their master did not concern himself with time-values, but with the eternal significance of life as only patient and faithful labour in learning can disclose it.   He indomitably resolved "before living" to "learn how to live," since "Man has Forever."   His passion for scholarship at last wrecked his body, but exalted his soul beyond the multitude's understanding.

3. 'Crofts' are enclosed farm-lands; 'thorpes' are tiny villages.

27. *Cf.* Whitman's "*O Captain, my Captain,*" ll. 8, 16, and 24.

41-42. This and the other passages in parentheses are directions to the bearers.

45-46. The elusive results of past experience, relatively little of which can be recorded.

55-72. *Cf. Cleon,* ll. 214-20; 278-83.

86-88. 'Calculus': The disease called the stone. 'Tussis': A bronchial cough.   *Cf. Cleon,* ll. 313-17.

95. 'Hydroptic' here means thirsty.

113-24. Browning teaches this doctrine also in *Old Pictures in Florence, Andrea del Sarto, Abt Vogler,* etc.

129-31. Greek particles involving critical points of syntax.

"Childe Roland to the Dark Tower Came"

Men and Women, 1855.   Browning wrote *Childe Roland* at Paris, January 3, 1852, in a single day.   Its cryptic, apparently allegorical character has provoked various interpretations, some of them ingeniously detailed and, perhaps, complacently precise, although Browning always insisted that the poem is not intentionally allegorical, but a purely dramatic romance.   Too many admirers of Browning have treated his more subtle poems as though they were intellectual puzzles challenging clever solution.   To adopt this attitude is to wrong the poet, for "poetry is like shot silk, with many glancing colours."   *Childe Roland* is based on 'mad' Edgar's song in *King Lear,* Act III, 4, 171-73:

> Child Rowland to the dark tower came;
> His word was still, — Fie, foh, and fum,
> I smell the blood of a British man.

The title 'Child' was given a young knight who had not yet won his spurs. The progress of the speaker here through difficult and even dire obstacles toward the 'Dark Tower' that marks his knighthood's crisis-test is described with extraordinarily vivid realism, although the whole story and situation are romantically conceived and intended. A suggestion of this great imaginative adventure, half-fantasy, half-parable, is to be found in the kindred suffering and courage suggested in the last lines of *Prospice*. The story is the world-old story of the struggle of true men toward higher truth — the tragedy of human life consisting in such men's increasing awareness of their own imperfection as seekers and finders of truth. Happiness, as Stevenson declares, is but man's "wayside camping; his soul is in the journey. He was born for the struggle, and only tastes his life in effort and on the condition that he is opposed." It is the story of Bunyan's Christian, of Shakespeare's Hamlet, of Shelley's Alastor, of Hauptmann's Heinrich, of Conrad's Heyst and Lingard. "Though he slay me, yet will I trust in him." It is the sublimation of the best in the characters of Paracelsus and Sordello.

For attempts at specific interpretation, see Nettleship's *Robert Browning: Essays and Thoughts;* John Esten Cooke's paper, *Mr. Browning's Great Puzzle,* in the *Critic* for April 24, 1886; J. Kirkman's paper in *The Browning Society's Papers,* Part III, p. 21; etc.

For corresponding effects in the beauty of horror, as regards description and artistic treatment of sinister landscapes, see Shelley's *Prometheus Unbound,* Act I, ll. 170–79 and *The Sensitive Plant,* ll. 220–91 (Browning may have been especially aware of ll. 220–43); the opening stanzas of Meredith's *Woods of Westermain;* Coleridge's *Christabel;* Madison Cawein's *Waste Land.* See also Chesterton's *Robert Browning,* pp. 158–59.

15. Mrs. Orr states that the picturesque materials used in the poem include "a tower which Mr. Browning once saw in the Carrara Mountains; a painting which caught his eye later in Paris; and the figure of a horse in the tapestry in his own drawing-room — welded together in the remembrance of the line from *King Lear* which forms the heading of the poem." Griffin and Minchin, however, insist that in "the horror which pervades *King Lear* . . . lies the true inspiration of the poem."

45-48. *Cf.* ll. 187–89.

58. 'Cockle': a weed. 'Spurge': There are several varieties of this plant. Browning probably has in mind the sun-spurge, or wart-weed.

61-75. These lines would describe closely enough some of the torn, tortured areas on the Western Front during the Great War.

160. Apollyon. *Cf. Revelation* IX : 2.

175-76. *Cf.* Walter de la Mare's *The Listeners. Cf.* also, from John Buchan's story, *Mr. Standfast:* "But that dark mountain mass changed my outlook. I began to have a queer instinct that that was the place, that something might be concealed there, something pretty damnable."

181-84. *Cf. The Englishman in Italy,* ll. 110–11.

189. In Chapter XXII of Hardy's *A Pair of Blue Eyes,* the sun becomes "a splotch of vermilion red upon a leaden ground — a red face looking on with a drunken leer."

190 *sq. Cf. The Englishman in Italy*, ll. 91–94; *The Ring and the Book*, VI, ll. 1135–37; X, ll. 621–29.

How it Strikes a Contemporary

Men and Women, 1855.   Among the several poems in which Browning suggests his theory of poetry this monologue stands out vividly for its insistence upon the poet's Terentian curiosity in 'everything that is of human interest.'   The speaker here is a sociable Spaniard from Valladolid who describes to his friend the strange manner of the only poet he has ever known, a manner inducing variously humorous surprise, uneasy suspicion, and even something of awed wonder.   The vulgar notion, based on his scrutinizing manner, is that he was a spy in the pay of the reigning monarch, but the speaker repudiates that theory, realizing that somehow this man had been serving a greater King.

11. 'Scenting the world.'   The poet's function in a phrase.

13–32. These lines reflect Browning's own habits.

40. *Cf.* Shelley's remark (in his *Defence of Poetry*) that "poets are the unacknowledged legislators of mankind."

90. The Corregidor was the local magistrate. *Cf. corregir*, to correct.

115. The Prado is the 'main promenade' of Madrid.

An Epistle, Containing the Strange Medical Experience of Karshish, the Arab Physician

Men and Women, 1855.   See John XI : 1–44.   See also, for other artistic treatments of the story of Lazarus, the poems of Stephen Phillips and Gerald Massey, Maeterlinck's *Mary Magdalene*, and Tennyson's reference in *In Memoriam*, XXXI–XXXII.   The normal professionalism of Karshish as against his finally outbreaking humanity is a sort of sheath or envelope for the kernel of the poem: the new and abnormal spiritual awareness of Lazarus as against his former earth-bound condition, — "the spiritual life around the earthly life."   The fine unity of this double-motived tale, its understanding sympathy for both Karshish and Lazarus, and the skilful verisimilitude of its telling give it large worth and power.

6, 11. *Cf. Fra Lippo Lippi*, ll. 184–88.

17. The name 'snake-stone' suggests any substance regarded as a remedy for snake-bites.

28, 146–47, 222–24. Under Titus Flavius Sabinus Vespasianus (9–79) Jerusalem was destroyed by his son Titus.   Vespasian was Roman Emperor from 70 to 79, and had himself campaigned against the Jews.

45 *sq.* Dr. H. C. McCook, a specialist on the subject, has commented at length upon this reference.   See *Poet-Lore*, Vol. I, p. 518.   The spider in question is perhaps the Zebra spider, of the Saltigrade species.

103. Browning frequently uses the word 'fume' in this meaning of mental vapour.   *Cf. The Ring and the Book*, II, l. 435.

146–53. Note the implied antithesis between the first 'prodigious' and the second.   See also l. 251.

167. See l. 254.

177. Greek fire (an anachronism here) was apparently a compound based on naphtha. The poet probably has in mind some form of ancient liquid fire.

178–90. *Cf.* this analysis of the psychology of Lazarus as corresponding in some respects with elements in Hamlet's character.

209–12. *Cf. The Ring and the Book*, X, ll. 434–35.

281. This borage is supposed to have cheering or exhilarating properties. — Aleppo is a Syrian town.

304–12. *Cf.* for a similarly postponed expression of long restrained emotion, the last line of *Giuseppe Caponsacchi*, in *The Ring and the Book*, VI. *Cf.* also for spiritual aspiration the conclusion of *Saul*. Contrast the closing lines of *Cleon*.

PICTOR IGNOTUS

Bells and Pomegranates, VII (*Dramatic Romances and Lyrics*), 1845. This unknown mediæval monastic painter, although he would have enjoyed and worthily used the power of worldly popularity and could, perhaps, actually have achieved it by painting more humanly (like Raphael, for example), sensitively shrank from doing so when he remembered that there are other reactions to art than the ardencies of those spiritually helped by it: there is the world of coldly appraising criticism, of trafficking merchants. Rather than have to do with these, he will quietly remain within his cloistered sanctuary and paint for God. *Cf. Popularity.* See Kenyon: *New Poems by Robert Browning and Elizabeth Barrett Browning*, pp. 151–53.

19–20. "A most exquisite image, and perfect in the expression of it, I think." — Miss Barrett.

32. According to Vasari, the Borgo Allegri, Florence, was so named because of popular joy when a Madonna painted by Cimabue was borne along it in procession.

41. The voice of his own peculiar genius.

60–61. The speaker regrets a little the monotony of even his cherished task. Contrast the frank irony of *Fra Lippo Lippi*, ll. 347–52.

FRA LIPPO LIPPI

Men and Women, 1855. Fra Filippo di Tommaso Lippi, son of Tommaso Lippi, a butcher, was born in Florence in 1412 (possibly 1406). At two years of age he was left an orphan. Mona Lapaccia, his father's sister, then cared for him, and in 1420 placed him with the neighbouring Carmelite friars of the Carmine in Florence. He stayed with the monks for twelve years, and studied there the chapel paintings of Tommasaccio or Masaccio. Although he left the monastery in 1432, he was not at that time permitted to renounce the vows he took in 1421. Nevertheless, he led a rather roving and romantic life (see Vasari). Cosimo de' Medici was his patron. In 1452 he became chaplain to the Convent of San Giovannino in Florence, and in 1457 rector of San Quirico at Legnaia. Despite his large earnings, he was frequently pressed for money, what he had being freely spent on the pleasures of life. Vasari gives a detailed account of his union with Lucrezia Buti, whom he is said to have abducted from the Convent of Santa Margherita, in Prato, in 1456, while she was his model. This union was regularized by Pope Pius II in 1461. She became the mother of Filippino Lippi (1460–1505). who studied under Sandro Botticelli (1447–1515). Botticelli's influence and that of Filippino's father appear in the son's works. Fra Lippo's frescos in the Choir of the Duomo at Prato represent the stories of John the Baptist and of Saint Stephen. His Madonnas are in the galleries of Florence, Paris, and Berlin. His style is naturalistic, but not unpleasantly so, having a naïve and warmly human quality. He died at Spoleto, where he was painting scenes in the life of the Virgin Mary, October 8, 1469. See E. C. Strutt: *Fra Lippo Lippi;* B. Supino: *Fra Filippo Lippi;* Emilio Castelar: *Fra Filippo Lippi;* A. J. Anderson: *The Romance of Fra Lippo Lippi;* Margaret V. Farrington: *Fra Lippo Lippi;* and Walter Savage Landor: *Fra Filippo Lippi and Pope Eugenius the Fourth (Imaginary Conversations).*

The student will note the complementary relation between *Fra Lippo Lippi* and *Andrea del Sarto,* as employing symbolically vernal and autumnal backgrounds, suggesting corresponding differences in the two painters' personal characters, their artistic manners, and their relations to the Renaissance.

1 *sq.* Lippo is remonstrating with the Florentine civic guard, who require an explanation of his nocturnal frolic.

7. 'The Carmine.' See account given above.

15–18. Cosimo of the Medici (1389–1464) was a great Florentine statesman and art patron, styled "Father of his Country." The painter intentionally delays disclosing the name of his patron, in order to enjoy the effect upon the officers.

21–22. Here Lippo directly addresses the captain of the civic guard, as again in l. 26.

23. 'Pilchards' are a common Mediterranean fish.

28. The florin (so styled because of its floral design) was a gold Florentine coin.

46. The pre-Lenten days were and are kept as Carnival.

53 *sq.* The "whiffs of song" in this poem are known as *stornelli,* and contain three lines. The name of the flower or other article chosen for the first line of each *stornello* controls the sound of the last words in the two other lines. Browning gives his *stornelli* only two lines, but follows the folk-spirit of these little improvisations.

67. The reference is to the Church of San Lorenzo at Florence, where are the tombs of the Medici and Michael Angelo's sculptured *Day* and *Night, Morning* and *Evening,* etc.

73. Jerome. See note on *Old Pictures in Florence,* l. 207. Saint Jerome lived in the desert for some years as a penance for his youthful follies.

88. For the reference to Mona Lapaccia, see account given above. 'Trussed' means held firmly.

93 *sq.* Cf. *The Ring and the Book,* VI, ll. 261–71.

121. The Eight were a Magistracy of that number established by the Florentines in 1376.

130. The anti-honary is the Roman Service-Book for following the choir, compiled by Gregory the Great.

131. The music-notes were square or oblong.

139-40. The Carmelite Order was established in the twelfth century. The Camaldolese monks belong to the Convent of Camaldoli, their order having been founded by Saint Romualdo in 1027. The Preaching Friars are the Dominicans, so named after Saint Dominic.

149-62. Cf. *The Ring and the Book*, II, ll. 83–84; X, ll. 786- 89.

170. Lippo's romantic interest in the Prior's 'niece' appears also in ll. 196, 209, 370, and 387.

183 *sq.* Lippo enjoys describing the Prior's embarrassment in the attempt to define 'soul.' Cf. *An Epistle*, etc., l. 6. Note how Lippo himself later discloses the way to 'soul.'

188 *sq.* Here Fra Lippo sets forth his defence of realism in art as against the romantic methods of the monastic painters, such as Fra Angelico.

189. See note on *Old Pictures in Florence*, l. 15.

196. See Matthew XIV : 6–11.

205-08. Cf. *Rabbi Ben Ezra*, ll. 67–72.

235-36. Fra Angelico, Giovanni da Fiesole (1387–1455) held to the old mediæval ideas of painting 'soul' as preached by the Prior. Lorenzo Monaco belonged to the same school.

276. Tommaso Guidi, or Masaccio (1401–28), with his pupil Fra Lippo, led the reaction against the romantic school. Browning makes the predecessor the successor, as he then, with reasonable authority, believed was actually the case.

280-311. The core of Lippo's defence of naturalism in art.

313-15. The *Credo* of the artist.

323. Some of Fra Lippo's finest frescos are in the Duomo at Prato. Saint Laurence was martyred in Valerian's reign, 258, by being broiled to death on a gridiron.

339. Chianti wine is so called after the place of its origin.

346. Saint Ambrose's Church in Florence. The picture he goes on to describe is called *The Coronation of the Virgin* and is now in the Accademia delle Velle Arti, Florence.

349. Assonance for the sake of irony. Cf. *The Ring and the Book*, I, l. 241; III, l. 131. See also *Pictor Ignotus*, ll. 57–61.

354. John the Baptist. See ll. 374–75.

357-58. See Job I : 1.

377. 'This one executed the work.'

ANDREA DEL SARTO: CALLED "THE FAULTLESS PAINTER"

Men and Women, 1855. Andrea 'del Sarto,' son of a Florentine tailor, was born in the parish of Santa Maria Novella in 1486. His true name was Andrea d'Angelo di Francesca. At the age of seven he was apprenticed to a goldsmith, and afterward to a painter named Gian Barilo. His third master was Piero di Cosimo, under whom he studied technique for several years. The flawless accuracy of his works in the Church of the Santissima Annunziata (the Church of the Order of the Servi) soon won for him the title of "Andrea senza Errori" or "Il Pittore senza Errori." His wife, Lucrezia di Baccii, del Fede, was born in 1490 and was first married to Carlo di Domenico Recanati, a prosperous cap-maker. After the latter's death del

Sarto married her, December 26, 1512. Vasari describes her as "a most beautiful girl . . . who, though born of a poor and vicious father, carried about her as much pride and haughtiness as beauty and fascination. She delighted in trapping the hearts of men, and among others, ensnared the unlucky Andrea, whose immoderate love for her soon caused him to neglect the studies demanded by his art, and in great measure to discontinue the assistance which he had given to his parents. . . . But he destroyed his own peace by this act [his marriage], seeing that he soon became jealous, and found that he had besides fallen into the hands of an artful woman, who made him do as she pleased in all things." These words are quoted from the first edition of Vasari's *Lives*, which Browning follows, but a later version and succeeding chronicles (Biadi's biography, etc.) tone down this account. Andrea painted her again and again as Madonna and in other similitudes. For example, in the Scalzi frescos, representing the life of John the Baptist, she is the figure of Faith; she is Madonna in the *Madonna di San Francesco*, in the Servi *Nativity*, and in the *Madonna del Sacco;* and she is Magdalen in the *Disputà*. Although Andrea learned something of her true character through hard experience, he tried to excuse her neglect and her 'despiteful' attitude toward his pupils, one of whom was Vasari. "But though he lived in the midst of all that torment, he counted it a high pleasure." In 1518 Francis I of France invited del Sarto to come to Fontainebleau, where he was encouraged to work freely and was liberally rewarded. Lucrezia, however, insisted on his early return. The king assented on condition that he should soon revisit the Court, and placed a sum of money with him as royal agent in the purchase of works of art. Andrea weakly succumbed to temptation and embezzled this money in order to build for himself a house on the Via Gino Capponi. He endured the siege of 1529, but died of the plague on January 22, 1531, his wife and servants deserting him in his last illness. He was buried in the Church of the Servi. Lucrezia survived him some forty years.

Vasari describes del Sarto as having "a certain timidity of mind, a sort of diffidence and want of force in his nature, which rendered it impossible that those evidences of ardour and animation which are proper to the more exalted character, should ever appear in him." Had he had "elevation" he might have become "a truly divine painter," but Vasari concedes to him perfection in his drawing, draperies, colouring, and sense of proportion. In Browning's poem this listless self-distrust tones in and deepens with the night and autumn of the background. There is in the Sala di Giove in the Pitti Palace, Florence, a picture by del Sarto representing the painter and his wife. John Kenyon, a cousin of Mrs. Browning, had asked Browning to secure for him a copy of this painting, and the poet, unable to satisfy the request, wrote the poem instead as an interpretation of the picture. See the play, *André del Sarto*, by Alfred de Musset. See also Hermann Grimm's *Life of Michael Angelo*, Vol. II, pp. 51 *sq.*

10. Note how the 'to-morrow' *motif* is cumulatively built up. See ll. 18, 20, 234, 259–60.

15. Fiesole is a small hilly suburb about three miles northeast of Florence.

27. ". . . those perfect ears." It was precisely the formal perfection of Lucrezia's physical beauty that attracted Andrea, just as he sought formal perfection in his art. See also ll. 63, 98–99, 122–23, 175–76.

33. Cf. ll. 203–04, 222–23.

34. Note Lucrezia's indifference and ignorance. She knows little or nothing of even the elementary truths of the painter's art, despite her wifehood and environment. Cf. ll. 54–55, 74–75.

43. A symbol of Andrea's own situation. Cf. ll. 169–70.

93. Morello is a high Apennine peak north of Florence. Cf. l. 209.

97–98. A man's reach as against a mountain's. With the mountain, grasp and reach are one. With a man, growth and constant aspiration alone make for true success. "I say that man was made to grow, not stop." (See A Death in the Desert, ll. 424–31.) Cf. ll. 84, 109, 116 of the present poem. Cf. also The Ring and the Book, I, ll. 711–19.

105. Raphael Sanzio (1483–1520) was called 'the Urbinate,' having been born in Urbino.

106. The parenthetical line seems to deprecate a possible mercenary gleam in Lucrezia's eyes. A mere copy would have slight value, an original much. George Vasari (1512–74) was a painter of Arezzo, who wrote the Lives of the Most Eminent Painters, Sculptors and Architects.

120. Lucrezia has probably made some gesture of impatience.

130. Michael Agnolo Buonarroti (1475–1564), great as painter, sculptor, and architect.

149–50. Francis I (1494–1547) was King of France and a constant patron of the arts. Fontainebleau was the richest of his palaces.

185. Andrea resolves to tell Lucrezia a cherished secret, which she half hears and half ignores. See ll. 199–200, 232.

220. 'Cousin' is a weakly accepted euphemism for lover. See ll. 29–32, 239, 267.

241. The 'scudo' was then worth nearly a dollar.

261. See Revelation XXI : 15–17.

263. Leonardo da Vinci (1452–1519), great master of several arts. Andrea's unrealizable ambition to be added as a fourth to that supreme trio of the Renaissance flames into expression for a bare moment.

THE BISHOP ORDERS HIS TOMB AT SAINT PRAXED'S CHURCH

First published in Hood's Magazine, March, 1845, under the title, The Tomb at St. Praxed's (Rome, 15—); afterward in Bells and Pomegranates, VII (Dramatic Romances and Lyrics), 1845. The old richly adorned parish church of Saint Praxed, or Praxedes, in Rome is so called after the virgin daughter of Pudens, a Roman senator under Antoninus Pius. Her sister Pudentiana was also canonized. These two charitable women abounded in good works. For a further account of them see Mrs. Jameson's Sacred and Legendary Art.

The Bishop who speaks here is a type of the worldly, sensuous ecclesiastic of the Renaissance, given over to luxury and self-indulgence. *Cf.* the Duke in *My Last Duchess*. The Bishop is facing death, yet his chief thought is of the imposing grandeur of his projected tomb, mingled with some fear that he may be cheated of it. In Volume IV, Chapter 20, of his *Modern Painters*, Ruskin remarks generally that "Robert Browning is unerring in every sentence he writes of the Middle Ages; always vital, right and profound; so that in the matter of art . . . there is hardly a principle connected with the mediæval temper, that he has not struck upon in those seemingly careless and too rugged rhymes of his." And Ruskin knows specifically "no other piece of modern English, prose or poetry, in which there is so much told, as in these lines, of the Renaissance spirit, — its worldliness, inconsistency, pride, hypocrisy, ignorance of itself, love of art, of luxury, and of good Latin. It is nearly all that I have said of the central Renaissance in thirty pages of the *Stones of Venice*, put into as many lines, Browning's also being the antecedent work." See Kenyon: *New Poems of Robert Browning and Elizabeth Barrett Browning*, pp. 145–46.

1. A professional remark, ironically out of key with the general tone of the speaker. See Ecclesiastes I : 2. See also ll. 51–52, 101.

3. 'Nephews' is a euphemism for 'sons.' *Cf. Fra Lippo Lippi*, l. 196; *The Ring and the Book*, XI, ll. 1088, 1097.

5. Old Gandolf, the Bishop's predecessor and rival, in love as in their profession, who has forestalled him in death by taking the best remaining niche for his own tomb.

21. The epistle-side is to the right as one faces the altar, the left being the gospel-side.

25. Basalt is a hard trap rock dark in colour.

26. The tabernacle is a protecting canopy.

31. Gandolf's onion-stone, which the Bishop belittles, is a greenish marble called 'cipollino' (from 'cipolla,' onion) because the strata crack and split.

34 *sq.* The dying man confesses that he has actually stolen and secreted *lapis lazuli* (a rich blue stone) from among the treasures of his own church, to enhance the glory of his tomb.

41. 'Olive-frail': a basket used for holding olives.

46. Frascati, some twelve miles southeast of Rome, is a society resort, with ancient ruins and modern villas.

49. The great Roman Jesuit church.

51. See Job VII : 6.

54. 'Antique-black' stands for 'Nero antico,' an attractive black stone.

56 *sq.* Note the curious jumble of Christian and pagan symbols. The tripod was the three-footed throne of the priestesses of Apollo who served the Delphic oracle; the thyrsus was a decorated staff used in the Bacchic revels.

66. Travertine is a hard smooth limestone.

69. The jasper is probably fine blood-stone.

77. By Tully is meant Marcus Tullius Cicero (106 B.C.–43 B.C.), whose lucid Latinity has always served as a model of style.

79. Ulpian (Domitius Ulpianus: 170–228) was a noted Roman jurist of Phœnician descent.

82. A reference to the Eucharist.

95. The dying man's thoughts wander confusedly.

99. '*Elucescebat*' is a post-classic form, the classic verb 'to be illustrious' being *elucere*.

101. See Job XIV : 1.

108. 'Visor' means mask; and 'Term' is part of a statue seeming to spring from a square pillar.

116. 'Gritstone' is a kind of coarse sandstone.

CLEON

Men and Women, 1855. The motto is from Acts XVII : 28: "As certain also of your own poets have said, 'For we are also his offspring.'" Berdoe cites Cleanthes the Stoic and especially Aratus in his *Phænomena*. Cleon is imagined as another and aged Greek poet who is replying here to a letter from his friend the Tyrant Protus (also unhistorical), accompanied by magnificent gifts. He sets forth in dignified but disillusioned fashion his views on the meanings of life and death. He writes of a pagan religion already decadent in the dawn of Christianity (to which he refers with sceptical scorn), and finds no consolations in prospect and but few in retrospect. As Professor Edward Dowden has said, "the poem is . . . an Ecclesiastes of pagan religion," and Professor William J. Alexander: "If neither Protus, the successful man of action who possesses power and the other substantial aims of life, nor Cleon, the contemplative spirit, king in the creative realm of the thinker and artist, has found satisfaction here for the aspirations of the soul, the solution of the problem must be sought elsewhere." In this poem, then, Browning not only unfolds the universal human desire for an immortality of growth in insight and in joy, but presents, by implication, a vigorous argument for the truth of the idea.

1. The "sprinkled isles" are, no doubt, the Sporades.

51. The image of Apollo on the lighthouse, or phare (from the island of Pharos, opposite Alexandria, site of the great lighthouse of the Ptolemies).

53. The Pœcile is the portico at Athens, covered with painted scenes of war.

60. The 'moods' or modes are the scales.

68. *Cf.* l. 142.

114. *Cf. A Death in the Desert*, ll. 424–31; *Luria*, Act V ("How inexhaustibly the spirit grows!"); *The Ring and the Book*, X, ll. 1429–38.

140–41. Terpander was a Lesbian musician and poet of the seventh century, called "the father of Greek music." Phidias was a great Athenian sculptor living between 500 and 430 B.C. Pericles, who ruled Athens from 444 to 429 B.C., was his intimate friend.

174–80. *Cf.* Shelley's sonnet *Ozymandias*.

181–86. Contrast *Abt Vogler*, ll. 65–96.

211. "Cleon," says Mrs. Orr, "constantly uses the word soul as antithesis to body: but he uses it . . . as expressing the sentient life,

not the spiritual; and this perhaps explains the anomaly of his believing that it is independent of the lower physical powers, and yet
not destined to survive them."

214–20. See also ll. 278–83. *Cf. A Grammarian's Funeral*, ll.
55–72.

304–05. Sappho was the great Lesbian lyrist who lived and wrote
about 600 B.C. — Æschylus (525–456 B.C.) was the greatest of the
Greek tragedians.

313–17. *Cf. A Grammarian's Funeral*, ll. 85–88.

323–35. The core of Cleon's rationalized doubt and despair.

336–53. Contrast the closing lines of *An Epistle.*

340. Paul of Tarsus (the home also of the poet Aratus) died about
67 A.D. He made many missionary visits to the Gentiles of Asia
Minor, Greece, etc. Cultivated Cleon gently reproves Protus for
troubling himself about the teachings of "a mere barbarian Jew,"
and is not even clear whether Paul and Christus may not be one.
At any rate, he concludes, no sane man could accept their doctrines.
Cf. "Imperante Augusto Natus Est — ," ll. 157–60.

RUDEL TO THE LADY OF TRIPOLI

Bells and Pomegranates, III (*Dramatic Lyrics*), 1842. It was
originally the first poem under the title *Queen Worship, Cristina*
being the other. Geoffrey de Rudel was a Provençal troubadour of
the twelfth century. His two successive patrons were Agoult, lord
of Soult, and Count Geoffrey, brother of Richard I. In 1162 he set
out for the Holy Land with his friend, Bertrand d'Alamanon, hoping to see the Countess of Tripoli, whose fame had inspired many of
his songs. Illness overtook him and he reached Tripoli only in time
to be welcomed by the Countess and to die in her arms. See Mrs.
Jameson's *Loves of the Poets.* In this poem Browning conceives of
Rudel as entrusting to a pilgrim a message to his as yet unseen beloved. As is the sun to the mimic sunflower, always turning toward
its master and moulder, so is Love to Rudel, but not, apparently,
to the Mount with "its large calm front of snow," by which symbol
is meant the great lady of his worship.

ONE WORD MORE

This poem, as Browning explains, was "originally appended to the
collection of Poems called *Men and Women*, the greater portion of
which has now been, more correctly, distributed under the other
titles of this edition." See note on *My Star* for a list of the poems
Browning wrote in praise of his wife. The present poem is intended
as a dedication of *Men and Women* to E. B. B., and is the only poem
carrying the poet's subscribed initials, being one of the few in which
he speaks 'in his true person.' It is sometimes said that it is in a
sense a response to Mrs. Browning's *Sonnets from the Portuguese,*
but this relationship, while recognizable, is hardly deliberate. Several years separate the two poems. It was early in 1847, a few
months after their marriage, when Mrs. Browning stole into her
husband's study and placed the manuscript of the *Sonnets* (composed before the marriage) in his pocket. His enthusiasm for them

would brook no sort of opposition to their publication, and, after a preliminary private printing, they appeared in 1850 for the first time under the well-known title which Mrs. Browning's poem *Catarina to Camoens* had led Browning to suggest. It is sufficient to say that *One Word More* is a deeply personal and tender tribute of love and gratitude from a man to a woman, a husband to a wife, a poet to a poet.

5–31. Rafael or Raffaello Sanzio (or Santi) (1483–1520) was one of the most famous of the Italian Renaissance painters. His early masters were his father, Giovanni Santi, and Pietro Vannucci (Perugino). Among his masterpieces are The Coronation of the Virgin (Vatican), *Madonna di Foligno* (Vatican), Sposalizio (Milan), Entombment of Christ (Borghese, Rome), La Fornarina (Barberini, Rome), The Resurrection (Vatican), Saint George and the Dragon (Louvre), Saint Michael (Louvre), Madonna degli Ansidei (National, London), *Madonna del Granduca* (Pitti, Florence), Saint John (Louvre), *Madonna di San Sisto* (Dresden), Madonna della Sedia (Pitti, Florence), *La Belle Jardinière* (Louvre), Madonna del Baldacchino (Pitti, Florence), Madonna della Casa d' Alba (Hermitage, Petrograd). It is historically true that Raphael wrote three sonnets and a part of a fourth to Margherita, the young woman he loved, often called La Fornarina. Guido Reni (1575–1642) bought in Rome a book containing a hundred of Raphael's original designs, which 'treasure-book' Reni left to Signorini, but the 'century of sonnets' seems apocryphal. The paintings directly referred to by Browning are italicized in the list given above.

32–57. The poet now cites Dante Alighieri (1265–1321) as another example of a great artist who sought to honour his beloved by using an art alien to him. Dante loved Beatrice Portinari, whom he immortalized in his *Vita Nuova* and his *Divina Commedia*, and he wished on the first anniversary of her death to "paint an angel" — for he was a good draughtsman — as a memorial to her (see *La Vita Nuova*, XXXV). Cf. Landor's *Imaginary Conversations: Dante and Beatrice*. 'Bice' is a more familiar form of 'Beatrice.'

36–37. See the *Inferno*, XXXII and XXXIII.

58 *sq.* Cf. Wordsworth: *Elegiac Stanzas Suggested by a Picture of Peele Castle*, ll. 13–16.

72. The artist's sorrow comes from his consciousness of limitations: the imperfections of life, the incompleteness of love, the inadequacy of artifice fully to meet the needs of art.

73–108. The experience of Moses, as narrated in Exodus XVI–XIX, Numbers XII and XX (see also Psalms LXXVIII : 10–20), is now employed as a reënforcing illustration of the poet's thought and theme. — "Jethro's daughter" was Zipporah, Moses' wife (see Exodus II : 16–21; III : 1; IV : 18). *Cf. The Patriot*.

117–28. Since Browning cannot praise his wife by means of an alien art, he will instead "make a strange art of an art familiar," as he does in *One Word More*, writing for "the first time and the last time" in rhymeless five-foot trochaics.

135–38. The heroes of six of the *Men and Women* poems are named.

144 *sq.* Recently in Florence they had watched the new moon together; now in London they see her attenuated, in her last quarter.

150. Samminiato is the Church of San Miniato, rising high on an eastern elevation above Florence.

160. A reference to the story of Endymion and Diana. See Keats's *Endymion*.

163. Zoroaster founded the Perso-Iranian racial religion which lasted some ten centuries, and compiled the *Zend-Avesta*. He often pondered on skyey aspects.

164. Galileo (1564–1642) was a great Italian astronomer. He discovered the moon's libration in 1637.

165. The references are to Homer's *Hymn to Diana* (*Iliad* XXI) and to Keats's *Endymion*.

172–79. See Exodus XXIV : 1–11.

187–97. *Cf. My Star.*

BEN KARSHOOK'S WISDOM

Written in Rome, April 27, 1854. First appeared in the annual, *The Keepsake*, 1856. The poet did not include it in any edition of his works, although he mentions it erroneously in the earlier editions of *One Word More* as belonging to *Men and Women*. 'Karshook' is Hebrew for 'thistle.' Browning later conceived a dislike for these lines, referring to them as "the snarling verses I remember to have written, but forget for whom."

17–20. See I Kings VII : 13–22, 41.

JAMES LEE'S WIFE

The first six stanzas of the sixth part appeared in 1836, as *Lines*, signed 'Z,' in Fox's *Monthly Repository*. The poem as a whole was published in *Dramatis Personæ*, 1864, under the title *James Lee*, but in 1868 (*Poetical Works*) the present title was used, the sub-titles were modified, and revisions and additions were made. The poem develops the series of moods experienced by James Lee's wife (who speaks or muses throughout) as she reflects on the spiritual failure that her marriage has become. "The development of disillusion, the melancholy progress of change," writes Arthur Symons, "is finely indicated in the successive stages of this lyric sequence, from the first clear strain of believing love (shaken already by a faint tremor of fear), through gradual alienation and inevitable severance, to the final resolved parting." The woman, although physically not beautiful, has a mind and a spirit of delicate poetic quality, if rather too plaintively introspective. E. C. Gregory has set the poem to music, and Part I has been set also by Mrs. H. H. A. Beech.

Part I. With the unhappy happiness of this anticipative welcome of the returning husband by the waiting wife may be compared the truer but more timid joy of the woman in *A Woman's Last Word*. It is now the end of summer.

Part II. Autumn has come. Their fire is made of odd pieces of wreckage, a fact in which the wife sees possible symbolism. She thinks ironically of the envy with which storm-drenched sailors must regard that lighted casement, and wonders whether other pairs in like perplexity have lived here before her coming.

Part III. In a letter to Miss Blagden, written August 18, 1865,

Browning describes the hamlet of Sainte-Marie near Pornic, as seen from the window at which he sits. "Such a soft sea, and such a mournful wind!" That window, as Mrs. Orr tells us, was the *Door-way* in *James Lee's Wife*. "The sea, the field, and the fig-tree were visible from it." Again the wife feels her heart shrivel with the impending cold of Winter, but summons her courage and challenges Winter to estrange the two whom Summer has blessed.

Part IV. The presence of the husband is implied, if in any member of the series, in this one only. The two apparently are walking along the beach. The wife, reviewing their relationship, wonders how her love, constant though clear-sighted, which was once earnestly besought by him, now seems to him a wearying fault. The word 'Love' of line 16 (as in the first line of Part I) does not refer to the man, but to the spiritual reality whose worth she knows and the persistence of which in their two lives she longs for.

36-40. *Cf. Any Wife to Any Husband*, ll. 67-72, 85-96.

Part V. Here, on the cliff, alone, the wife observes the withered turf, the rock worn by sea buffetings. On one a cricket suddenly alights, on the other a butterfly. Turf and rock alike are transformed by the beauty of their guests. So Love transforms the hearts of men.

15. Browning particularly loved the cricket, as many passages in his poems testify.

16. 'Bard' and 'chanfron' are parts of a warhorse's armour.

19-30. *Cf. My Star.*

Part VI. She is now reading a book of poems as she sits in the shadow of the cliff, and rather resents the young poet's arms'-length interpretation of the meaning of the wind's sighing (Browning wrote these lines on the wind at twenty-three). For herself, life has taught and is teaching her the meaning of the moan of the wind. It is the ministry, however unwelcome, of change. Much of Browning's theory of life is compactly expressed in the last three stanzas of this part.

Part VII. Again she renews her confidence in the principle of Love, as self-justifying, self-sustaining. It does not require as indispensable condition the assurance of worth in its object, but feels and acts unselfishly, looking above for its gain.

Part VIII. The second and third sections of this Part (save the last two lines) were added in 1868. The wife has been sketching a little peasant girl's hand, and afterward drawing the outlines of the cast of a woman's hand modelled by Leonardo da Vinci. She contrasts the two, fancying a faintly moulded ring on the finger of the perfect hand placed there by the master as a symbol of his worship; and feeling the relative crudeness of the fleshly hand. Upon reflection she admonishes herself, learning the lessons that in life as in art imperfection is necessary to growth, and that to serve humanity is to serve Beauty also.

Part IX. She is now leaving James Lee, setting him free, for Love's own sake, since she no longer symbolizes Love to him. She loves him and will always love him, for which very reason she accepts the separation that his changed attitude imposes upon her, and will seek to lead a useful and unembittered though lonely life, hoping (yet not admitting the hope) that time may reveal to him his spiritual need of her.

3. Professor Corson suggests that these words refer to her art-work.
16-20. *Cf. Any Wife to Any Husband*, ll. 103-14.

ABT VOGLER, AFTER HE HAS BEEN EXTEMPORIZING UPON THE MUSICAL INSTRUMENT OF HIS INVENTION.

Dramatis Personæ, 1864. Georg Joseph Vogler (1749-1814) was born at Würzburg, Germany, June 15, and became a great organist and a composer and critic of music. He studied counterpoint under Abbé Martini at Bologna for a short time, and harmony under Abbé Vallotti at Padua. In 1773 he was admitted to the priesthood at Rome and was given many honours at the Vatican. Two years later he established a school of music at Mannheim, and was soon made *kapellmeister* there. In 1779 he went to Munich, and in 1786 was made *kapellmeister* to the King of Sweden at Stockholm, where he opened another school. In 1790 he gave a very successful series of organ-recitals in London. In 1807 the Grand Duke of Hesse-Darmstadt made him his *kapellmeister*. At Darmstadt he organized a third school, attended by Weber, Gänsbacher, and Meyerbeer. Besides composing a number of operas and fugues, he advocated several reforms in organ building, musical fingering, etc., and invented the orchestrion, described by Sir G. Grove as a portable organ having four key-boards of five octaves each, and a pedal-board of thirty-six keys, with swell complete, all contained in a cube of nine feet. *Castor and Pollux* was one of the most popular of his operas. His *Missa Pastoricia* is still performed at Christmas in Vienna. Abbé, or Abt, Vogler soliloquizes in the poem, after he has been extemporizing upon the instrument described above.

3. Solomon was traditionally supposed to be possessed of a magic seal bearing the name of God, which gave him power over supernatural beings.

7. *Cf. The Ring and the Book*, VI, ll. 280-89; *The Names*, ll. 5-8.
19. 'Rampired' means having ramparts. *Cf. Hervé Riel*, l. 92.
23. Saint Peter's dome has been illuminated on such high days as Easter Sunday.
34. A 'protoplast' is the original model, the criterion of succeeding copies.
41 *sq.* Abt Vogler feels that the art of music requires and receives more of the Divine inspiration and coöperation than other arts, because it is less dependent on objective environment and less able to introspect its sources and appraise its results. It is "the finger of God" behind all the laws of art, for out of combinations of tones there sometimes emerges a miraculous beauty beyond our subtlest understanding.
57-64. For kindred references to the "palace of music" *cf.* Amphion's raising of the walls of Thebes; and see Tennyson's *Gareth and Lynette*, ll. 270-74; Keats's *Lamia*, Book II, ll. 119-24; Mrs. Browning's *A Vision of Poets* and Coleridge's *Kubla Khan*. The composer now sorrows at the vacancy that has succeeded his glorious

extemporization, and at his inability to reproduce the lost sounds perfectly. *Cf. James Lee's Wife*, Part VI, ll. 60–65.

65 *sq.* Abt Vogler comforts himself with the assurance of the mighty power and eternal love of the "ineffable Name." God will reproduce all of good that man produces, will perfect all man's imperfections, will affirm in eternity "the conception of an hour." Philosophy and poetry are finely wedded in these lines, — the thought of Hegel, Boehme and Spinoza with the manly music of Browning. *Cf. Cleon*, ll. 181 *sq.*

91–96. The "common chord" consists of the fundamental tone, with its major or minor third, and perfect fifth. C major is the natural scale without sharps or flats, hence symbolic of everyday experience. See Helen J. Ormerod's contributions (2 : 221 and 229) to *The Browning Society's Papers*, X.

Rabbi Ben Ezra

Dramatis Personæ, 1864. According to Dr. M. Friedländer, the family name was Ibn Ezra. Abraham Ibn Ezra (the Rabbi) was the son of Meir Ibn Ezra. Abraham was born in Toledo, in 1092 or 1093, and died in 1167 or 1168. Although born in poverty, he made the most of every opportunity to read and study, becoming famed eventually as seer, traveller, commentator, physician, poet, and astronomer. His master work was his complete series of commentaries on the Books of the Old Testament. He also wrote treatises on astronomy, Hebrew grammar, and the *Talmud*. His travels took him to Italy (where he lived, chiefly in Rome and Lucca, for several years), Egypt, Arabia, Persia, Greece, France, England, and other countries. One of his friends and teachers was Rabbi Japhet Hallevi, of whom he became the son-in-law. See Furst's *Bibliotheca Judaica* (Leipzig), Friedländer's several expository volumes on Ibn Ezra (London: Trübner), and Berdoe's *Browning's Message to his Time*. In his *Browning Cyclopædia* Berdoe gives a number of notes made by A. J. Campbell relating the Rabbi of the poem to the actual Rabbi Ibn Ezra. Browning was so closely familiar with rabbinical lore, however, that the speaker in the poem (like the Pope in *The Ring and the Book*) is really a composite mouthpiece for the transmission of ideas revised and revitalized by the poet himself. "What the *Psalm of Life* is to the people who do not think," says Arthur Symons, "*Rabbi Ben Ezra* might and should be to those who do: a light through the darkness, a lantern of guidance and a beacon of hope, to the wanderers lost and weary in the *selva selvaggia*." It is a noble assurance of the worth of life, the necessity of death, the truth of immortality. Corson summarizes the argument. Georgiana Schuyler has set the first part of the poem to music.

1 *sq.* The Rabbi is speaking to a young student or disciple. He urges his hearer to realize the unity and continuity of the scheme of life, in which age ("the best to be") will make it possible to give their due meanings to youth and manhood. *Cf. Saul*, ll. 161–64.

16. *Cf.* Tennyson: *In Memoriam*, lyric XCV.

25–36. *Cf. Easter Day*, XXXIII, ll. 12–19; Emerson: *The Sphinx*, ll. 73–104.

37–42. There is much of Browning in these tonic words. *Cf.* *Saul*, ll. 294–96.

45. *Cf. Colombe's Birthday*, Act III, ll. 55–58.

61–72. *Cf. Fra Lippo Lippi*, ll. 205–14.

84. 'Indue' means to don, or put on.

150–92. See Isaiah XXIX : 16; LXIV : 8; Jeremiah XVIII : 1–6. See also Omar Khayyám: *Rubáiyát* (Fitzgerald's translation), stanzas 82–90.

159. *Cf. La Saisiaz*, ll. 223–24.

CALIBAN UPON SETEBOS; OR, NATURAL THEOLOGY IN THE ISLAND. *Dramatis Personæ*, 1864. Caliban, the besotted savage of Shakespeare's *Tempest*, is brooding on the difficult problem of the nature of his god Setebos. It is a warm summer day on the island, when "talk is safer than in winter time," and Caliban is lying in the cool mud at the mouth of a cave idly soliloquizing. His conception of Setebos, based necessarily on his own crude memories, is that of a power-god, a sense-god merely, untouched by love or mercy. The poet ironically suggests, both in the key-passage from the fiftieth Psalm and in the content of the poem, that there is a certain relation between Caliban's perplexed argument and the facile anthropomorphism of many human beings. The poem is a plea, therefore, for the enlargement of our ignoble God-concepts, since the noblest thought of God is utterly inadequate to express Him. "Canst thou by searching find out God?" "Your religiousness," says George Burman Foster, "is not that you have a God; it is your God-conceiving capacity . . . The main thing is the kind of spiritual worth that the deity or deities stand for." Even Caliban (who is psychologically less a mere single savage than a composite symbol of crude thinking) finds himself profoundly dissatisfied with the kind of god he deduces from his experience and environment, and dimly dreams of a god beyond Setebos, as superior to the latter as Prospero, for instance, is superior to Caliban. Setebos was the devil-god of the uncouth primitives of Patagonia, discovered by Magellan in 1520. Their god is described by Richard Eden in his *History of Travaile*, 1577, who relies on Antonio Pigafetta's account of Magellan's voyages. *Cf.* the Eskimos' devil-god, Tor-nar-suk. See also, for references to remote and savage peoples, Hakluyt's *Voyages;* Silvester Jourdan: *A Discovery of the Barmudas, otherwise called the Ile of Divels: by Sir Thomas Gates, Sir George Sommers, and Captaine Newport, with divers others,* 1610; Marco Polo and the so-called Sir John Mandeville. Shakespeare was probably familiar with Jourdan's account and with some narrative concerning Magellan's discoveries. Browning makes Caliban speak in the third person in harmony with his place in the evolutionary scheme. Other poems in which Browning deals with religious problems and longings are mentioned in the Introduction. See J. Cotter Morison's study of the present poem in *The Browning Society's Papers*, Part V; and Josiah Royce's paper on *Browning's Theism* in *The Boston Browning Society's Papers*, 1886–97. See also Renan's drama, *Caliban, Suite de la Tempête.*

1–23. Caliban describes here his physical background and the occasion for his plunge into theology.

16. Caliban's dam was the witch Sycorax, who taught him of the godship of Setebos. See *The Tempest*, Act I, ll. 257–93, 329–31, 338–39, 370–72.

19. In summer, since Caliban is then comfortable enough physically, Setebos, he argues, must somehow be farther off and less likely to overhear. In winter, "the cold o' the moon" (where Setebos dwells) perhaps induces the cold of the island. See l. 25.

26–30. Setebos made the moon and the sun; the clouds, winds, etc.; the island and the surrounding sea; but not the stars. Caliban excepts the stars, apparently, because of their far and lonely mystery, their strange self-sufficiency, and later (l. 138) associates them with the Quiet. In line 30 Caliban's certainty that on earth there is nothing but his isle and the snaky sea parallels our too often limited planetary conceptions of the universe.

31–43. Setebos created the world, etc., because he desired diversion from his environment of aching cold. Caliban illustrates this idea by reference to the fresh-water fish which seeks a change in warm sea-water, "not her life," yet cannot long endure such change. *Cf. Colombe's Birthday*, Act III, ll. 241–44; Ibsen's *Lady from the Sea*, Act III, ll. 54–61; Ibsen's *Brand*, Act I, l. 121.

75–97. If Caliban were able to "make a live bird out of clay," and put it under his orders, he would gladly do so. If physical ill befell it and it prayed him for succour, he might or might not heed its prayer. Such must be the attitude of Setebos toward Caliban himself. With l. 86 *cf.* Psalms II : 4; LIX : 8.

98–108. *Cf.* the Calvinistic doctrine of predestination. Another argument from experience.

109–26. Any creature of Setebos that should venture to glorify its own acts would justly incur His wrath and punishment, for, even if His creatures seem sometimes worthier than their creator, He alone possesses power.

127–41, 170–71, 241–55. In these lines Caliban darkly develops his thought of the Quiet, who is mysteriously 'over' Setebos. In *The Tempest* (Act I, 2, ll. 370–72) he recognizes that there are realities superior to Setebos. To Browning, as to Shelley, Love is superior to Force and Necessity. See Royce's discussion (*Browning's Theism*, mentioned above) of the God of Love, the God beyond God, as opposed to the God of power; see also Shelley's similar antithesis between Prometheus and Jupiter, in *Prometheus Unbound*, and *cf.* the following passages: "I conclude that there is an existence, a something higher than soul — better, higher and more perfect than deity. Earnestly I pray to find . . . this Highest Soul, this greater than deity, this better than God." (Richard Jefferies: *The Story of My Heart*.) "When we have broken our god of tradition, and ceased from our god of rhetoric, then may God fire the heart with his presence." (Ralph Waldo Emerson: *The Over-Soul*.) *Cf.* also the line from Emerson's *Brahma:* "The strong gods pine for my abode." In his *Outline of History* (Vol. I, p. 127), H. G. Wells thus accounts for the superstitious awe with which Neolithic Man regarded the stars: "The sun by day and presently the stars by night helped to guide his migrations; he began to find after many ages that the stars are steadier guides than the sun. He would begin to note particular stars and star groups, and to distinguish any individual thing, was, for primitive man, to believe it individualized and personal. He would begin to think of the chief stars as persons, very shining and dignified and trustworthy persons looking at him like bright eyes in the night."

170–78. Caliban's theology differs from that of Sycorax. She thought that the Quiet was the Creator of all things, but Caliban regards this as unfair to the character of the Quiet. "Who made them weak meant weakness He might vex," hence Setebos bears the onus of creation. Caliban differs again with Sycorax in ll. 250–57 touching a future life.

179–240. Because Setebos apparently does what He does at random, to satisfy whims or grudges (just as he, Caliban, does or would do), there is no hope of pleasing or deceiving Him always; yet one must keep a propitiatory attitude.

241–49. The only possible hope is that Setebos may decide to make another world, and so cease to plague this one; or (and here Caliban achieves his highest thought) He may develop into something better and become merged in the Quiet, for do not grubs grow butterflies? Perhaps, failing this (ll. 281–83) the Quiet may "catch and conquer Setebos" or He may fall into a deathly lethargy.

263–83. Meanwhile, the important thing is to placate and propitiate Setebos. *Cf.* Ibsen: *Peer Gynt*, Act IV, 2.

284–95. The little epilogue shows Caliban thoroughly alarmed at the sudden coming of a tropical thunderstorm (powerfully suggested), which he attributes to the officious babbling of a treacherous raven "that has told Him all." Caliban cringingly deprecates the anger of Setebos.

Confessions

Dramatis Personæ, 1864. The dying man half-triumphantly, half-deprecatingly, tells his mournful priest of the one great event in his life, a true love experience. Clandestine as it was, it has redeemed him from selfishness and makes it impossible for him now to "view the world as a vale of tears."

35. *Cf. In a Balcony*, ll. 180–83.

May and Death

First published in *The Keepsake*, 1857 (London: David Bogue). Reprinted in revised form in *Dramatis Personæ*, 1864. The 'Charles' of this slight but intimate elegy is James (or 'Jim'), one of Browning's three Silverthorne cousins, James, John, and George, who were neighbours of his at Camberwell. Browning was especially fond of James, who was the only friend present at his wedding in 1846. James died in May, 1852.

1–8. *Cf.* Tennyson's sensitive allusions in *In Memoriam* to the recurrences of Spring after Hallam's death. *Cf.* also Shelley: *Adonais*, stanzas XVI and XVIII.

13–20. The plant is the Spotted Persicaria (*Polygonum Persicaria*). The central purplish tintings on its leaves have given rise to the legend that this common plant was growing beneath the Saviour's Cross during the Crucifixion, and received falling drops of blood from his wounds.

PROSPICE

Dramatis Personæ, 1864. The title means 'Look Forward!' The poem was written during the autumn after Mrs. Browning's death, and expresses the writer's faith and hope in persona' immortality. Browning's adherence to this faith was persistent to the end, as many of his poems and letters testify. In 1876 he said in a letter to a friend ". . . Dante wrote what I will transcribe from my wife's Testament wherein I recorded it fourteen years ago, 'Thus I believe, thus I affirm, thus I am certain it is, that from this life I shall pass to another, there where that lady lives of whom my soul was enamoured.'" In *La Saisiaz* (ll. 207–16) he faces the problem of immortality thus:

> . . . Why should I want courage here?
> I will ask and have an answer, — with no favour, with no fear, —
> From myself. How much, how little, do I inwardly believe
> True that controverted doctrine? Is it fact to which I cleave,
> Is it fancy I but cherish, when I take upon my lips
> Phrase the solemn Tuscan fashioned, and declare the soul's eclipse
> Not the soul's extinction? take his "I believe and I declare —
> Certain am I — from this life I pass into a better, there,
> Where that lady lives of whom enamoured was my soul" — where this
> Other lady, my companion dear and true, she also is?

Again he wrote, to another correspondent: "Why, *amico mio*, you know as well as I that death is life, just as our daily, our momentarily, dying body is none the less alive and ever recruiting new forces of existence. Without death, which is our crape-like churchyardy word for change, for growth, there could be no prolongation of that which we call life. . . . Never say of me that I am dead." The American Shakespearean critic, Dr. Henry Howard Furness, wrote to the poet through Mr. Edmund Gosse: "Tell him how deeply, how fervently, I bless him for writing *Prospice*." The poem has been set to music by Sir C. Villiers Stanford.

17–20. *Cf.* the closing lines of *Childe Roland to the Dark Tower Came*.

EURYDICE TO ORPHEUS

First published (in prose form!) in the Royal Academy Catalogue for 1864, to accompany a picture by Browning's friend, Sir Frederick (afterwards Lord) Leighton (1830–96), famous as a painter of portraits and historical scenes. Leighton drew Browning's portrait, March 28, 1859 (see frontispiece to Mrs. Orr's biography) and designed Mrs. Browning's monument in Florence. In Greek mythology, Eurydice, wife of Orpheus (son of Apollo), having died through the bite of a serpent, her husband descended into Hades and through his lyre-playing induced Pluto to restore her to life. Pluto made the condition that she should walk behind Orpheus, who was not to turn and regard her until they were again in the upper world. This condition Orpheus violated, and so again lost Eurydice. The painting

and the poem both suggest that Eurydice, overcome by her yearning for his look, over-persuaded him. *Cf.* the price paid in *Prospice*
for reunion with the price paid here for an eternal memory. See also
Gluck's opera, *Orfeo ed Euridice,* played in Paris as *Orphée et Euridice.* original Italian libretto by Calsabigi, translated into French by
Moline.

YOUTH AND ART

Dramatis Personœ, 1864. The theme is "life unfulfilled" through a
prudential turning away from love. *Cf.* Ibsen: *When We Dead
Awaken,* Act V: "*Professor Rubek* (*as though looking back into himself*): 'And yet — Irene —.' *Irene* (*completing his thought*): 'Yet we
two let slip all that life and its beauty.'" *Cf.* also *The Statue and the
Bust* and *Bifurcation* for the sin of "the unlit lamp and the ungirt
loin." The speaker here is 'Kate Brown,' whose half-humorous,
half-wistful tone covers a real and abiding regret.

8. John Gibson (1790–1866) was a notable English sculptor,
trained at Rome by Canova and Thorwaldsen, and personally known
to Browning.

12. Giulia Grisi (1811–69) was a famous Italian operatic soprano.

58. *Bals-parés* are fancy-dress balls.

A LIKENESS

Dramatis Personœ, 1864. "It would be difficult," says Arthur
Symons, "to find a more vivid bit of *genre* painting than the three-
panelled picture in this single frame."

11–32. A realistic (and reminiscent) picture of bachelor quarters.

35, 36. *Cf. The Ring and the Book,* I, ll. 464, 706:

> Fancy with fact is just one fact the more.

> Is fiction which makes fact alive, fact too?

55, 56. *Cf. The Inn Album,* ll. 645–54. — *Festina lente!* Make
haste slowly!

APPARENT FAILURE

Dramatis Personœ, 1864. Browning wrote this poem in the hope
of saving from demolition the little Doric Morgue he had visited in
1856, during his visit to Paris to see the baptism of Prince Louis
Napoleon, son of Emperor Napoleon III, born March 16, 1856. The
poet's meliorism sees the best even in this worst. *Cf.* Whitman's
To Those Who Have Failed.

7, 8. The Congress of Paris, composed of delegates from several
European powers, met in Paris in 1856 to discuss Italian unity.
Prince Alexander Mikhailovitch Gortchakoff (1798–1883) was an
able Russian statesman, then Minister of Foreign Affairs. Count
Camillo Benso di Cavour (1810–61), the great unifier of Italy, re-
presented Sardinia at the Congress of Paris. Count Karl Ferdinand
von Buol-Schauenstein (1797–1865), was Austrian Premier and
Foreign Minister from 1852 to 1859.

12. The Fountain of Vaucluse is the source of the small river Sorgue.   Petrarch once lived in this village near Avignon.

HOUSE
   Pacchiarotto, with Other Poems, 1876.   See Wordsworth's *Scorn not the Sonnet*, ll. 2, 3; see also *At the "Mermaid."*

HERVÉ RIEL
   Written at Le Croisic, Brittany, September 30, 1867.   Published in the *Cornhill Magazine*, March, 1871, after many revisions.   Reprinted in *Pacchiarotto, with Other Poems*, 1876.   The *Cornhill* paid a hundred guineas for the poem, which sum Browning gave to the Paris Relief Fund, to help the sufferers from the siege.   (See letter to George Murray Smith, February 4, 1871.)   This stirring ballad has been translated into French.   See *The Two Poets of Croisic* for a picture of the Breton fishers' village, the home of Hervé Riel.   The important naval battle of La Hogue, May 19, 1692, was fought to further the plan of Louis XIV to restore James II to the throne of England.   The united fleets of England and Holland, under Admiral Russell, crushed the French fleet, under Admiral Tourville, but several of the French ships were saved from capture through the peasant pilot Hervé Riel, who skilfully guided them through the dangerous shallows of the river Rance "to Solidor past Grève."
   1. La Hogue is a fort near the northeast point of the Cape of the same name, on the coast of Normandy.   The battle could be seen from the fort.
   5. Saint Malo is a strongly fortified seaport on an island at the mouth of the Rance.
   8. Damfreville was in charge of the squadron that escaped.
   30. Plymouth is a great British naval station, with immense docks.
   43. Comte de Anne Hilarion de Cotentin de Tourville (1642–1701), Admiral of France, although victorious in the naval battles of Palermo (1677) and Cape Saint Vincent (1693), was defeated at La Hogue.
   44–46. Croisickese and Malouins are people of Croisic and Saint-Malo, respectively.
   49. 'Grève' refers to the sands spreading about Mont Saint-Michel. — 'Disembogues' means 'empties.'
   61. Solidor is an old fourteenth-century fort on the mainland.
   89. 'The bay' of Saint-Michel.
   92. 'Rampired' means 'ramparted.'   *Cf. Abt Vogler*, l. 19.
   114–25. The poet departs here from his fact-background.   Hervé Riel asked for a permanent release, the French Admiralty report reading: "Ce brave homme ne demanda pour récompense d'un service aussi signalé, qu'un congé absolu pour rejoindre sa femme, qu'il nommait la Belle Aurore."   Although Browning acknowledged to Dr. Furnivall that he had overlooked this point, the reward Riel asked for in the poem heightens the dramatic value of the story.
   129. 'A head': a figure-head.

PHEIDIPPIDES

Dramatic Idyls, First Series, 1879. Before the Battle of Marathon (see note on *Echetlos*) the Persians had landed on the coast of Attica, by the plain of Marathon. When the Athenians heard of this, tney sent Pheidippides, a trained runner, to Sparta (nearly 140 miles distant) to ask for aid. At this time the Spartans were holding their festival, *Carneia*, which prevented them from engaging in warfare until its end, nor would they march until the moon was at the full. On his return Pheidippides encounters the goat-god Pan, who promises to bring success to Athens. The youth fights at Marathon, but dies of joy on reaching the Acropolis twenty-six miles away, as the runner bearing news of the great victory. See Herodotus: *History*, Book VI, 94–106; Pausanias: *Description of Greece*, I, 28; VIII, 54. The Greek motto to the poem means 'Rejoice! we conquer!' — the words carried to Athens by Pheidippides from the battle-field.

1–104. These lines constitute the message uttered in monologue by Pheidippides to the Archons of Athens on his return from Sparta. The remaining lines are the poet's comment.

2. 'Daimons' were guardian spirits.

4–5. Zeus (Jupiter), Athene (Minerva), and Artemis (Diana) are referred to.

8. Pan was the god of the herds, herdsmen, fields, and hunters. He had the horns and hoofs of the goat.

9. There were nine Archons, or rulers, of Athens. The 'tettix' (grasshopper) wrought in gold was worn as an ornament.

12. Sparta was the capital of Laconia.

18. Darius in 493 B.C. required the Greek communities to bring earth and water to the Persians as a sign of submission.

19. Eretria was an important city of Euboea, an Ægean island.

32. Phoibos, or Phœbus, was Apollo; Artemis, Diana.

47. 'Fulsome' means satisfying, liberal.

52. Parnes are mountains north of Attica. Herodotus places the meeting near Mount Parthenium, above Tegea.

62. 'Erebos': the dark lower world of shades.

81–84. The word Μαραθόν means 'fennel-field.' *Cf.* ll. 98, 109.

89. For note on Miltiades, see comment on *Echetlos*.

HALBERT AND HOB

Dramatic Idyls, First Series, 1879. The source is an illustration used by Aristotle in his *Nicomachean Ethics*, Book VII, chapter VI, section 5.

65, 66. That Browning was especially interested in *King Lear* [as in *Othello*] seems evident from this reference to the tragedy (see *King Lear*, Act III, 6, ll. 74 *sq.*), from his use of the line from Edgar's song in *Childe Roland*, and from his argument *contra* Emerson that Shakespeare does not always avoid the revolting in his plays, Browning citing the blinding of Gloucester in *Lear*, Act III, vii. The poet was long the president of the new Shakespeare Society. See his sonnet, *The Names*. With line 66 *cf.* from *Luria*, Act V:

All men become good creatures: but so slow!

ECHETLOS

Dramatic Idyls, Second Series, 1880. The title-word means 'holder or wielder of the ploughshare.' Like *Pheidippides*, the story refers to the Battle of Marathon, fought in September, 490 B.C., between the Athenians and Platæans under Miltiades, and the Persians under Datis and Artaphernes. Although the Persians outnumbered the Greeks ten to one, the Greeks achieved a great and decisive victory. According to the legend, the figure with the ploughshare wrought terrible havoc among the Persians, but when, after the battle, the Greeks asked the oracles his name, the only reply was: "Let him be called Echetlos!" See Pausanias's *Description of Greece*, Book I, chapter 32.

15. Polemarchs in Athens were those supervising military matters. Kallimachos was Polemarch at this time.

18. The Sakæ were Scythians under Persian domination.

28–30. After his victory at Marathon, Miltiades warred on the island of Paros to satisfy a personal grudge, was fined fifty talents for so doing, and died (489 B.C.) in prison. Themistocles was charged with treason, lived in exile, and died in Magnesia, Persia, about 460.

"WANTING IS — WHAT?"

This little lyric serves as a prologue to the group entitled *Jocoseria*, 1883. Life is not life until animated and directed by the spirit of love. See Berdoe and Corson for specifically religious interpretations.

DONALD

Jocoseria, 1883. Browning is frequently concerned with the spirit of good sportsmanship (*cf. The Ring and the Book*, VI, ll. 1360–64; X, ll. 721–23; *How They Brought the Good News from Ghent to Aix; The Glove; Tray; The Lady and the Painter*), perhaps nowhere more so than in this transcript of a true story he once heard told by a man who had had it from 'Donald' himself. Browning wrote the tale more than forty years after this hearing. The story as related by Sir Walter Scott appears in the annual called *The Keepsake* for 1832 (pp. 283–86), most of Scott's narrative being reproduced in G. W. Cooke's *Guide-Book to the Works of Browning*. It is summarized in the Browning Society's *Notes and Queries*, 209, p. 328.

"NEVER THE TIME AND THE PLACE"

Jocoseria, 1883. A love-song filled with recollection of the happy Past, with dissatisfaction at the vacant Present, and with faith in the renewing Future.

HUMILITY

Asolando, 1889. *Cf. Misconceptions, One Way of Love*, and *Colombe's Birthday*, Act V, ll. 298–301.

POETICS

Asolando, 1889. Browning is fond of using the flower-figure and the moon-metaphor in writing of women.

8. *Cf.* the tercets appended to *Ferishtah's Fancies*, IV.

Summum Bonum

Asolando, 1889. Love is Browning's 'highest good,' as his poems
frequently attest.

4. *Cf. The Ring and the Book*, III, ll. 982, 1342.

Which

Asolando, 1889. *Cf. Adam, Lilith and Eve*.

8, 9. Note the correspondences in ll. 17, 18, and 23.

13–18. The Marquise prefers the ideal indicated in such lyrics as
Lovelace's *To Lucasta, on Going to the Wars*.

19–24. *Cf. A Blot in the 'Scutcheon*, Act II, ll. 300–10.

'Imperante Augusto Natus Est —"

Asolando, 1889. Caius Octavius, later known as Caius Julius
Cæsar Octavianus (63 B.C.–14 A.D.), great-nephew of Julius Cæsar
(102 B.C.–44 B.C.) and Emperor of Rome, was given the title of
Augustus in 27 B.C. by the Roman Senate. Although Julius Cæsar
was made imperator (commander of the army) in perpetuity and
dictator and although he became ruler *de facto*, Caius Octavius was
the first recognized Emperor. His epithet 'Augustus' means 'con-
secrated by augury' and implies a divine character. The first Emperor was a firm ruler, a thoughtful student of public affairs, a unifier
of the Roman state, and so able a re-shaper of physical Rome that he
was justified in declaring that he had found the city brick and left
it marble. The speaker in the poem is a Roman senator who addresses his friend Publius (not historical) while the two are await-
ing their turn at the baths. He tells Publius how the poet Varius
yesterday had hailed Cæsar as a god, and how he (the speaker) had
encountered some time afterward an outcast beggar craving alms on
the steps of the Temple of Jupiter. This beggar turned out to be
the Emperor himself, who was said to have the habit of thus propi-
pitiating annually "Fate's envy." The speaker adds his reflective
comment.

8–16. Lucius Varius Rufus was a Roman epic and tragic poet.
Quintilian compared his tragedy *Thyestes* with the Greek tragedies.
His *Panegyric* on Augustus is lost, but Quintus Horatius Flaccus
(l. 11) quotes from it in his first *Epistle*. Caius Cilnius Mæcenas
was a great patron of literature, adviser of the Emperor and friend
of the poets mentioned above and of Vergil. He traced his ancestry
to the Etruscan Kings.

17. The Roman coin quadrans was the price of a bath at the
Thermæ.

72–74. Publius Vergilius Maro (70 B.C.–19 B.C.), the great Roman
epic and idyllic poet, was a close friend of Horace and Mæcenas, and
enjoyed the favour of Augustus. Varius is best known as having
edited the *Æneid* after Vergil's death. These three lines reinforce
the main theme unfolded in ll. 131–35 and 152–60.

104. Suburra was an unsavoury street in Rome.

109–13. Quæstors were magistrates who prosecuted those guilty
of capital crimes, or officers having duties chiefly financial. Ædiles
were magistrates who exercised police functions and supervised

public buildings, games, and baths. Censores were superior magistrates who administered the quinquennial census, etc. 'Pol!' is an
oath meaning 'By Pollux!' The quarter-as was a small coin.

126–38. *Cf. The Twins* and *The Boy and the Angel*.

157–60. Part of the quoted passage constitutes the title of the
poem. "This particular prophecy of the Tiburtine sibyl to Augustus," says Mrs. Jameson in her *Legends of the Madonna* (p. 197),
"rests on some very antique traditions, pagan as well as Christian.
It is supposed to have suggested the *Pollio* of Vergil, which suggested
the *Messiah* of Pope." See also the *Lexicon* of Suidas. Brettano's
Sibyllina Oracula (Paris: 1599) gives on pp. 458–61 the substance of
the several sibylline prophecies concerning Christ. See also the
paintings on this subject by Baldassare Peruzzi, Garofalo and Titian.

163. A 'strigil' is a flesh-brush.

DEVELOPMENT

Asolando, 1889. The poem is reflectively autobiographical. *Cf.*
Masefield's *Biography*.

11. See the poem, *Tray*.

30. Alexander Pope (1688–1744) published his translation of the
Iliad in 1720, and of the *Odyssey* in 1725. The latter translation
was not wholly Pope's.

43. Philipp Karl Buttmann (1764–1829) was a German grammarian, author of *Ausführliche Griechische Sprachlehre, Lexilogus oder
Beiträge zur Griechischen Worterklärung*, etc.

46. Christian Gottlob Heyne (1729–1812) was a German philolo-
gist who edited Vergil, Pindar, and the *Iliad*.

57. The seven cities are Chios (Scio), Smyrna, Colophon, Rhodes,
Salamis (in Cyprus), Athens, and Argos.

59, 60. *The Battle of the Frogs and Mice* (*Batrachomyomachia*) is a
poem attributed to Homer. The *Margites* is another humorous
work no longer supposed to be his.

64. Friedrich August Wolf (1759–1824), Professor of Philology at
Halle, argued in *Prologomena in Homerum* (1795) that the *Iliad* and
Odyssey are not 'Homeric' as being the works of one man, but are
really compilations of the hymns of various rhapsodists conveyed
through a long oral tradition.

73–78. *Cf. The Ring and the Book*, I, ll. 464, 705.

99. See Shakespeare's *Tempest*, Act III, 3, 3.

106. The *Nicomachean Ethics* is a great work of Aristotle's.

113. The Stagirite is Aristotle (384–22 B.C.) so called because
born at Stagira, in Chalcidice

EPILOGUE TO ASOLANDO

Asolando, 1889. This is the last of Browning's published poems,
Asolando appearing in London on December 12, 1889, when the poet
died in Venice. The *Pall Mall Gazette* of February 1, 1890, contains
this reference to the third stanza: "One evening, just before his death
illness, the poet was reading this from a proof to his daughter-in-law
and sister. He said: 'It almost looks like bragging to say this, and

as if I ought to cancel it; but it's the simple truth; and as it's true it shall stand.' All Browning was there — 'as it's true it shall stand.'" *Cf.* Tennyson's farewell poem, *Crossing the Bar;* and Emerson's *Terminus*.

16–20. *Cf.* the closing lines of *Pauline* and of *Prospice.*

BIBLIOGRAPHY

THE following list of books may serve the student as a useful working bibliography. He should consult Dr. Frederick J. Furnivall's *Bibliography of Robert Browning from 1833 to 1881*, published by the Browning Society, of London; and he may also examine the Bibliography compiled by John P. Anderson, of the British Museum, and appended to Sharp's *Life of Browning*. Many magazine articles on Browning or on specific works of his are catalogued in Poole's *Index to Periodical Literature* and *The Reader's Guide to Periodical Literature*.

The editions of the poet's works mentioned below are recommended both for their format and for their reliability. No attempt is made to mention editions or critical treatments of individual poems or groups of poems.

LIVES AND RECORDS

Mrs. Sutherland Orr: *Life and Letters of Robert Browning*. Revised and in Part Rewritten by Frederic G. Kenyon. Houghton Mifflin.

W. Hall Griffin and H. C. Minchin: *The Life of Robert Browning*. Macmillan.

Edward Dowden: *Robert Browning*. London: Dent. New York: Dutton.

William G. Kingsland: *Robert Browning: Chief Poet of the Age*. Boston: Poet Lore Publishing Co.

William Sharp: *Life of Robert Browning*. London: Walter Scott.

G. K. Chesterton: *Robert Browning*. Macmillan.

Edmund Gosse: *Robert Browning: Personalia*. Houghton Mifflin.

Frederic G. Kenyon: *Robert Browning and Alfred Domett*. London: Smith, Elder. New York: Dutton.

*The Letters of Robert Browning and Elizabeth Barrett, 1845–
1846.* Two vols. Harpers.

Letters from Robert Browning to Various Correspondents.
Edited by Thomas J. Wise. Two vols. London.

Same. Second Series. Two vols. London.

Letters of Robert Browning to Isa Blagden. Waco, Texas:
Baylor University Press.

The Letters of Elizabeth Barrett Browning. Edited by Frederic G. Kenyon. Macmillan.

GUIDE-BOOKS

Leslie N. Broughton and Benjamin F. Stelter: *A Concord-
ance to the Poems of Robert Browning.* G. E. Stechert & Co.

George Willis Cooke: *A Guide-Book to the Poetic and Dramatic Works of Robert Browning.* Houghton Mifflin.

Edward Berdoe: *The Browning Cyclopædia.* London:
Allen & Unwin. New York: Macmillan.

A Primer of Browning. London: George Routledge & Sons.
New York: Dutton.

Mrs. Sutherland Orr: *A Handbook to the Works of Robert
Browning.* London: G. Bell & Sons.

M. A. Molyneaux: *Phrase Book from the Poetic and Dramatic
Works of Robert Browning.*

Esther Phœbe Defries: *A Browning Primer.* London: Sonnenschein. New York: Macmillan.

CRITICISM AND EXPOSITION

The Browning Society's Papers. Three vols. London.

*Browning Studies. Select Papers from the Browning Society's
Papers.* Edited by Edward Berdoe.

Boston Browning Society Papers, 1886–97.

Arthur Symons: *An Introduction to the Study of Browning.*
London: Dent. New York: Dutton.

William John Alexander: *An Introduction to the Poetry of
Robert Browning.* Ginn.

Hiram Corson: *An Introduction to the Study of Robert Browning's Poetry.* Heath.

Edward Berdoe: *Browning's Message to his Time: His Religion, Philosophy and Science.* London Sonnenschein. New York: Macmillan.

James Fotheringham: *Studies of the Mind and Art of Robert Browning.* London: Horace Marshall & Son. New York: Scribners.

Henry Jones: *Browning as a Philosophical and Religious Teacher.* Glasgow: James Maclehose. New York: Macmillan.

John T. Nettleship: *Robert Browning: Essays and Thoughts.* London: John Lane. New York: Scribners.

Frances M. Sim: *Robert Browning, the Poet and the Man.* Two vols. London: T. Fisher Unwin.

Stopford A. Brooke: *The Poetry of Robert Browning.* Crowell.

Frederic May Holland: *Stories from Robert Browning.* London: G. Bell & Sons.

Thomas Rain: *Browning for Beginners.* London: Sonnenschein.

Thomas R. Lounsbury: *The Early Literary Career of Robert Browning.* Scribners.

William F. Revell: *Browning's Criticism of Life.* London: Sonnenschein. New York: Macmillan.

Frederic A. Pottle: *Shelley and Browning: A Myth and Some Facts.* Chicago: Pembroke Press.

Edward Dowden: *Studies in Literature.* London: Kegan Paul, Trench & Co.

Hugh Walker: *The Greater Victorian Poets.* London: Sonnenschein.

R. H. Hutton: *Literary Essays.* Macmillan.

Edmund C. Stedman: *Victorian Poets.* Houghton Mifflin.

William Charles Macready: *Reminiscences and Selections from His Diary and Letters.*

Walter Bagehot: *Literary Studies*, Vol. II. London: Longmans.

George Willis Cooke: *Poets and Problems: Tennyson, Ruskin, Browning.*

BIBLIOGRAPHY

BIBLIOGRAPHY

George Edward Woodberry: *Makers of Literature*. Scribners.

Vida D. Scudder: *The Life of the Spirit in the Modern English Poets*. Houghton Mifflin.

EDITIONS

The Poetical Works of Robert Browning. Seventeen vols. London: Smith, Elder. Vols. I–XVI, 1889; Vol. XVII, 1894.

The Poetical Works of Robert Browning. Two vols. London: Smith, Elder. 1896.

Poems of Robert Browning, from the Author's Revised Text of 1889. His own Selections. London: Smith, Elder. New York: (with Notes by Charlotte Porter and Helen A. Clarke) Crowell.

The Poetic and Dramatic Works of Robert Browning. Riverside Edition. Six vols. Houghton Mifflin.

The Complete Poetic and Dramatic Works of Robert Browning. Cambridge Edition. Edited by Horace E. Scudder. Houghton Mifflin.

The Poetical Works of Robert Browning. Nine vols. Macmillan.

Same. Globe Edition. Two vols.

The Complete Poetical Works of Robert Browning. Edited by Charlotte Porter and Helen A. Clarke. Camberwell edition. Twelve vols. Crowell.

New Poems by Robert Browning and Elizabeth Barrett Browning. Edited by Frederic G. Kenyon. Macmillan.

INDEX OF FIRST LINES